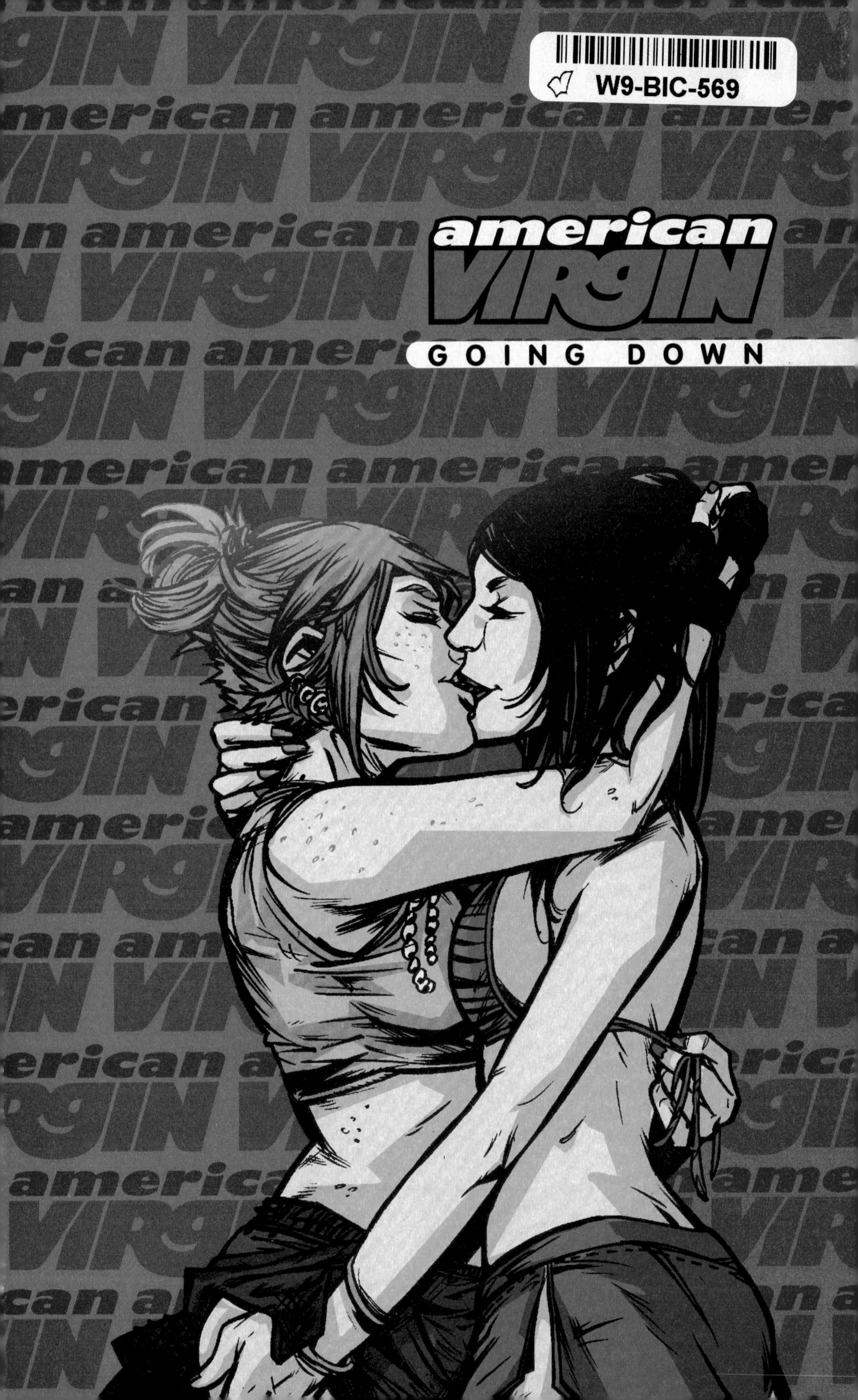
american
VIRGIN
GOING DOWN

american **VIRGIN** GOING DOWN

STEVEN T. SEAGLE WRITER BECKY CLOONAN PENCILLER

BECKY CLOONAN (CHAPTER 1) RYAN KELLY (CHAPTERS 2-5) INKERS

BRIAN MILLER COLORIST JARED K. FLETCHER LETTERER

JOSHUA MIDDLETON ORIGINAL COVER ARTIST

AMERICAN VIRGIN CREATED BY STEVEN T. SEAGLE AND BECKY CLOONAN

Karen Berger Senior VP-Executive Editor   Shelly Bond Editor-original series   Angela Rufino Assistant Editor-original series
Bob Harras Editor-collected edition   Robbin Brosterman Senior Art Director   Paul Levitz President & Publisher
Georg Brewer VP-Design & DC Direct Creative   Richard Bruning Senior VP-Creative Director   Patrick Caldon Executive VP-Finance & Operations
Chris Caramalis VP-Finance   John Cunningham VP-Marketing   Terri Cunningham VP-Managing Editor   Alison Gill VP-Manufacturing
Hank Kanalz VP-General Manager, WildStorm   Jim Lee Editorial Director-WildStorm   Paula Lowitt Senior VP-Business & Legal Affairs
MaryEllen McLaughlin VP-Advertising & Custom Publishing   John Nee VP-Business Development   Gregory Noveck Senior VP-Creative Affairs
Sue Pohja VP-Book Trade Sales   Cheryl Rubin Senior VP-Brand Management   Jeff Trojan VP-Business Development, DC Direct   Bob Wayne VP-Sales

Cover illustration by Joshua Middleton. Logo design by Steve Cook. Publication design by Amelia Grohman.

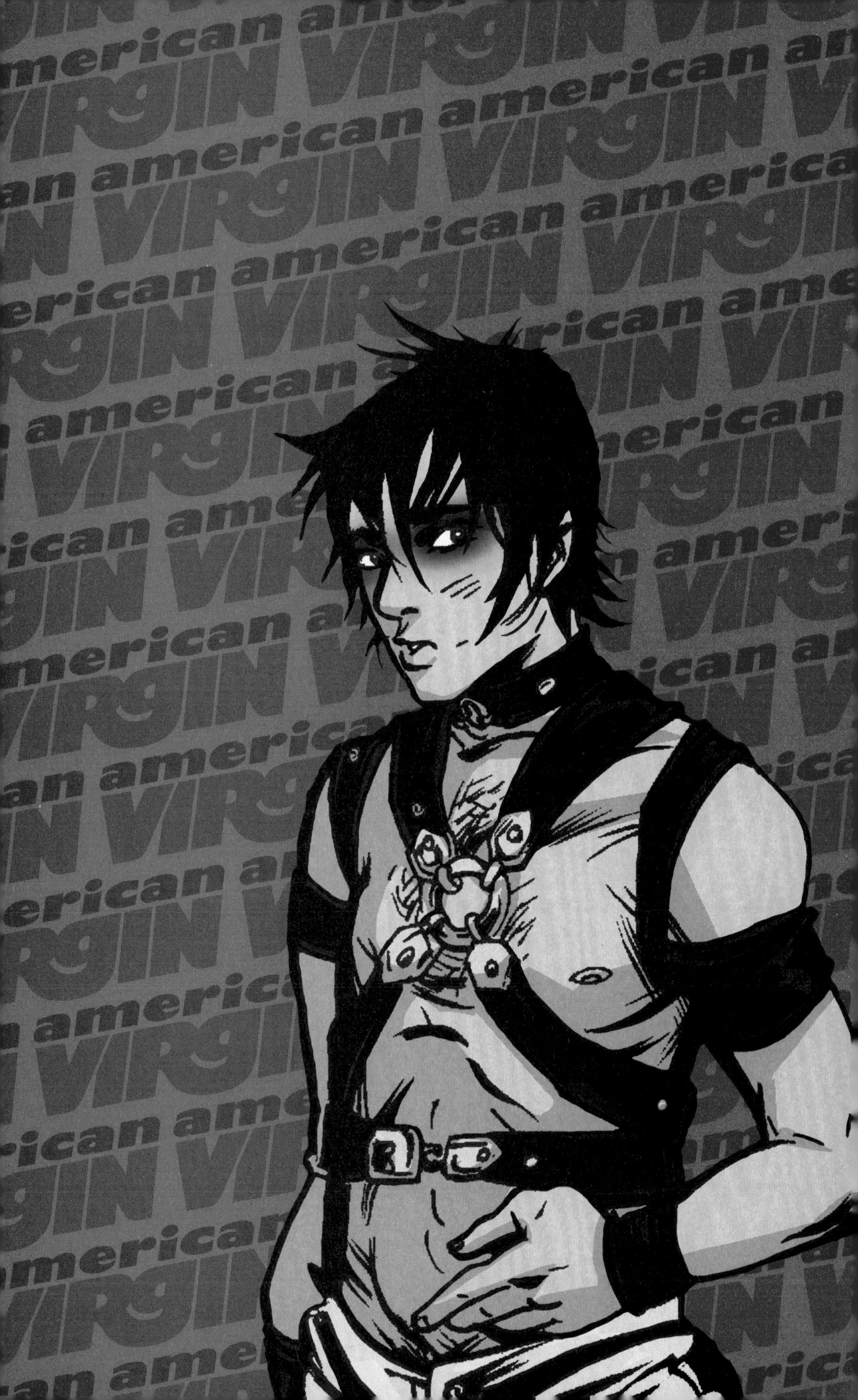
american
VIRGIN

PREVIOUSLY IN AMERICAN VIRGIN...

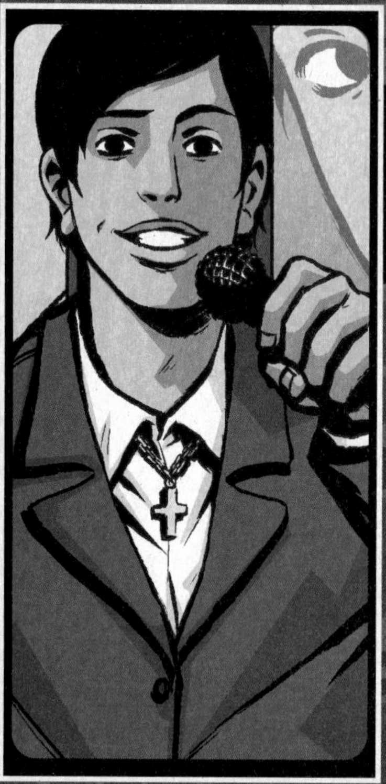

Christian youth minister and virginity advocate ADAM CHAMBERLAIN led a dream life: natural charisma, a best-selling book, a national speaking tour — he had it all.

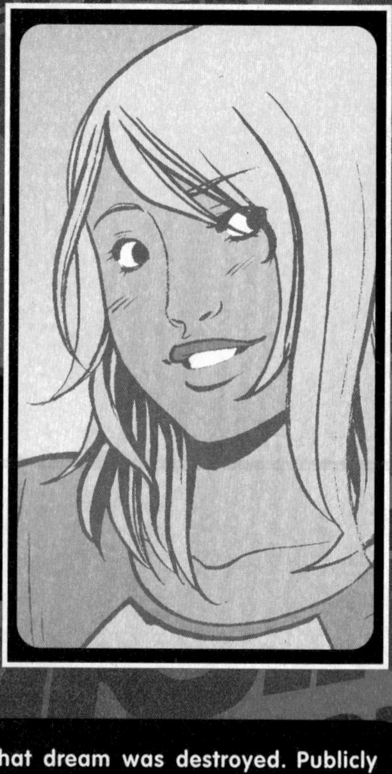

But his most cherished possession was his beautiful fiancée CASSIE. They had planned to wed upon her return from Peace Corps work in Africa. The pinnacle of their union was to be their gift of virginity to one another.

In one horrible instant, that dream was destroyed. Publicly beheaded by the terrorist cartel Batu Balan, Cassie was no longer in Adam's life, even though God had "told him" she was the only woman he would ever be with sexually.

Against the wishes of his dominating mother, MAMIE...

...and limp noodle stepfather, EARL, Adam traveled to Africa...

...in the company of his black sheep half-sister CYNDI — who was only too happy to run from problems of her own.

PREVIOUSLY IN AMERICAN VIRGIN...

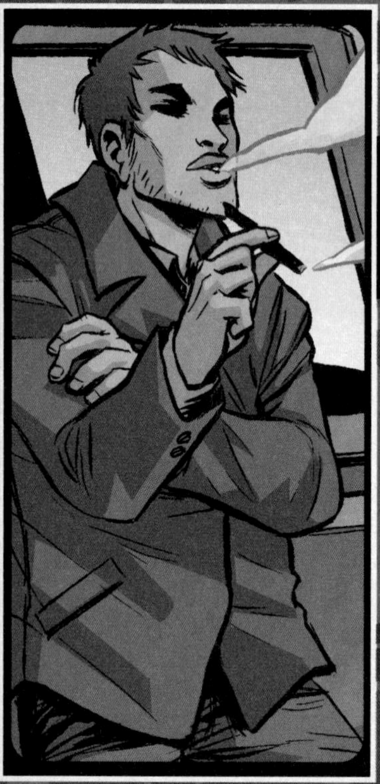

Enlisting the aid of the enigmatic mercenary MEL, Adam tracked down the man who held Cassie in place as she met her end.

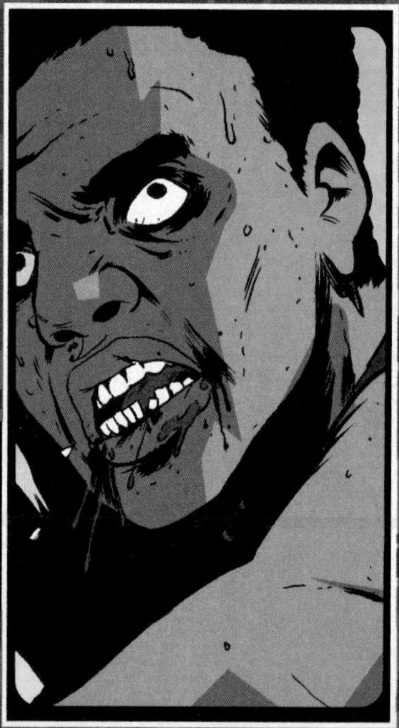

Willing to watch this cold-blooded killer take his own life, Adam has begun to stray from his Chosen Path.

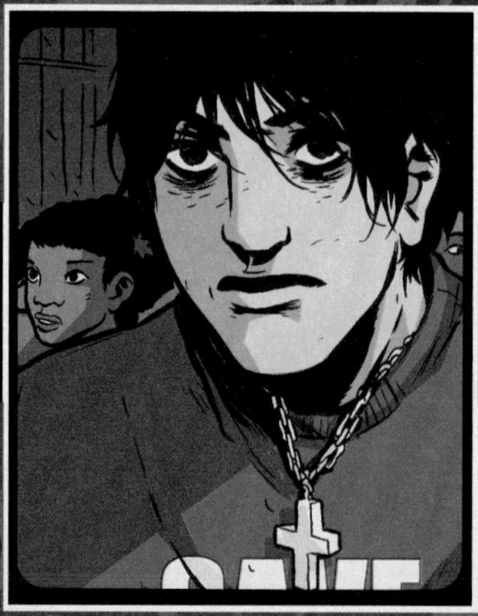

How much further is he willing to go in order to calm the desire for vengeance he feels welling in his broken heart?!

CHAPTER ONE

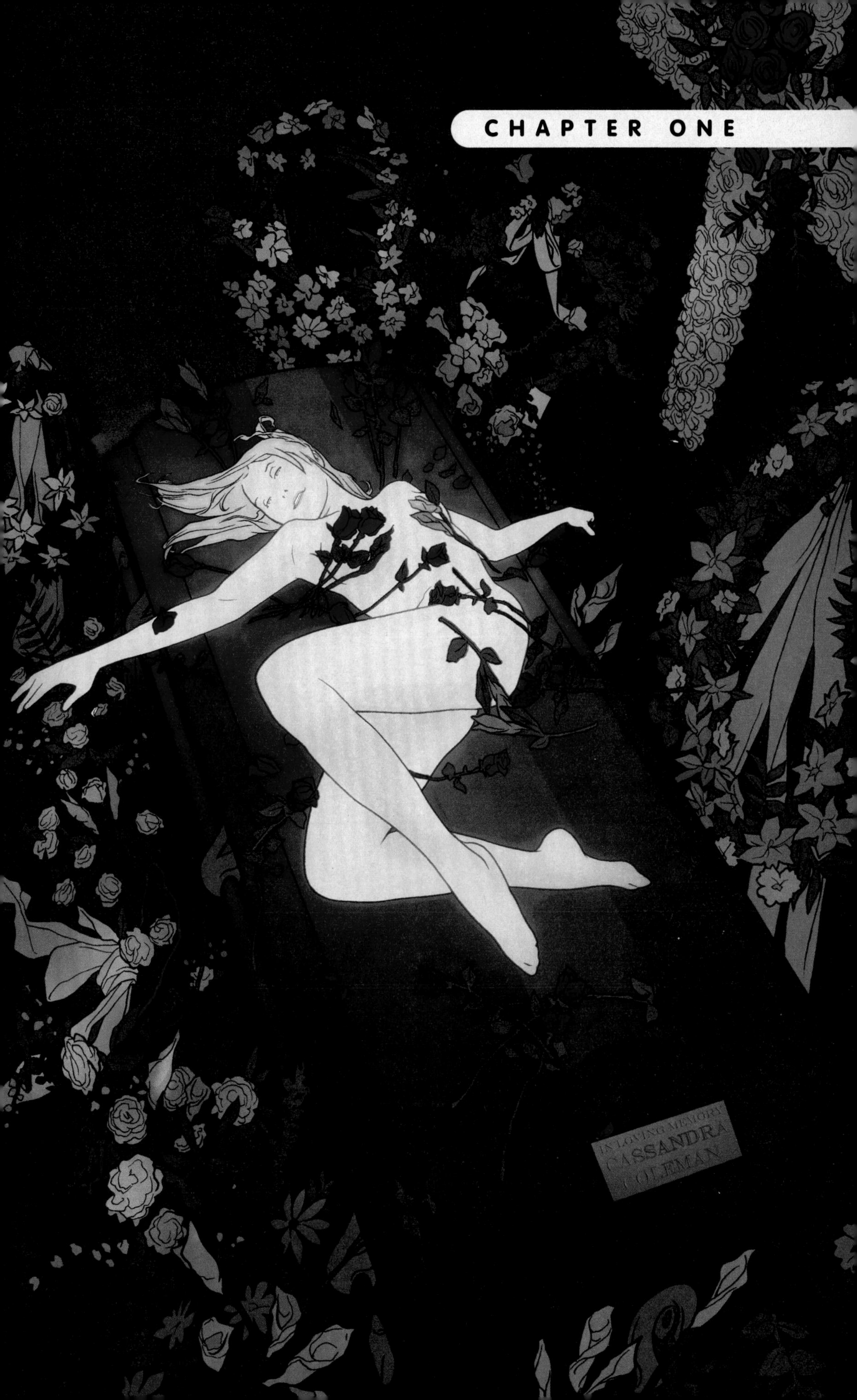
IN LOVING MEMORY
CASSANDRA
COLEMAN

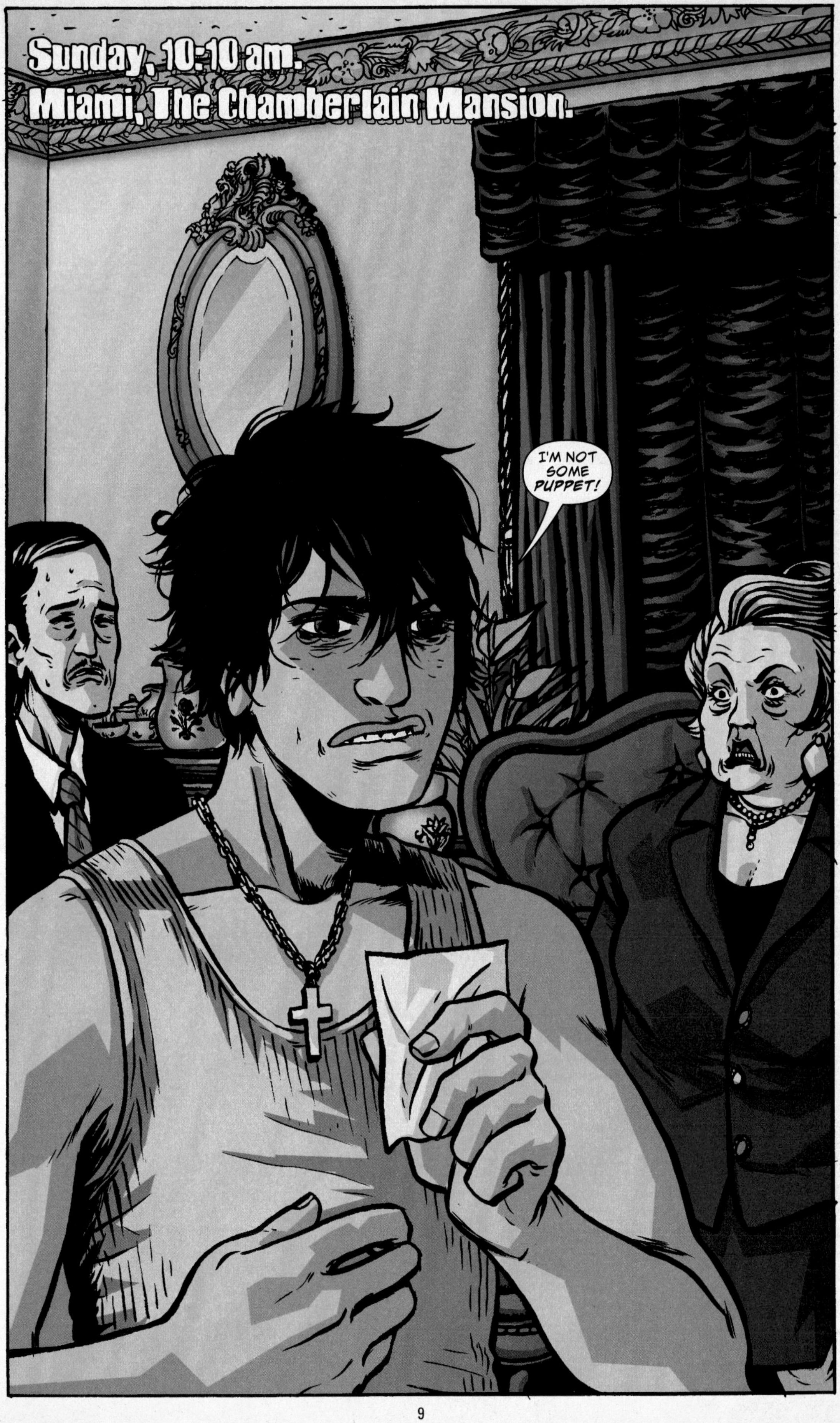
Sunday, 10:10 am.
Miami, The Chamberlain Mansion.
I'M NOT SOME PUPPET!

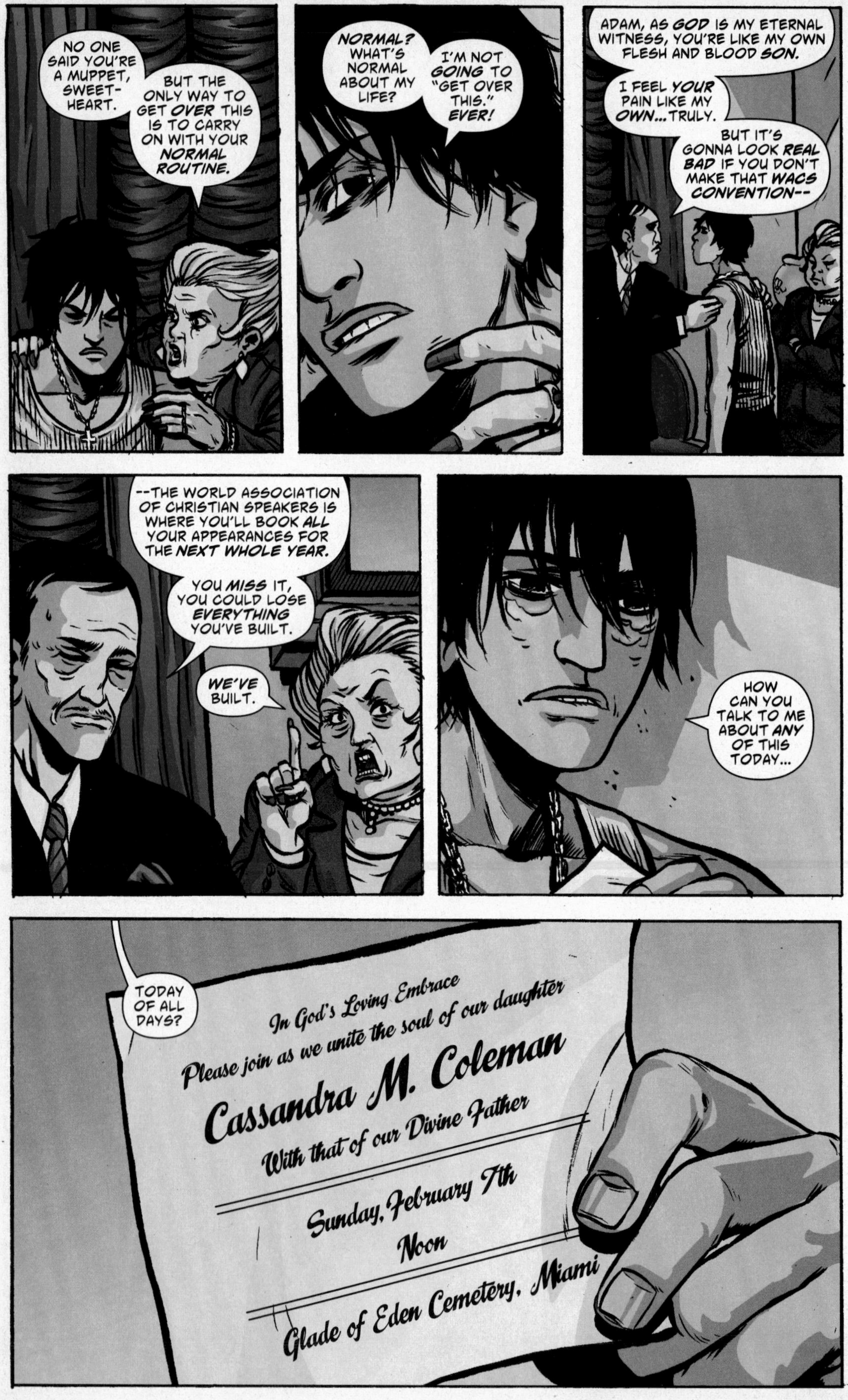
NO ONE SAID YOU'RE A MUPPET, SWEET-HEART.
BUT THE ONLY WAY TO GET OVER THIS IS TO CARRY ON WITH YOUR NORMAL ROUTINE.
NORMAL? WHAT'S NORMAL ABOUT MY LIFE?
I'M NOT GOING TO "GET OVER THIS." EVER!
ADAM, AS GOD IS MY ETERNAL WITNESS, YOU'RE LIKE MY OWN FLESH AND BLOOD SON.
I FEEL YOUR PAIN LIKE MY OWN... TRULY.
BUT IT'S GONNA LOOK REAL BAD IF YOU DON'T MAKE THAT WACS CONVENTION--
--THE WORLD ASSOCIATION OF CHRISTIAN SPEAKERS IS WHERE YOU'LL BOOK ALL YOUR APPEARANCES FOR THE NEXT WHOLE YEAR.
YOU MISS IT, YOU COULD LOSE EVERYTHING YOU'VE BUILT.
WE'VE BUILT.
HOW CAN YOU TALK TO ME ABOUT ANY OF THIS TODAY...
TODAY OF ALL DAYS?
In God's Loving Embrace
Please join as we unite the soul of our daughter
Cassandra M. Coleman
With that of our Divine Father
Sunday, February 7th
Noon
Glade of Eden Cemetery, Miami

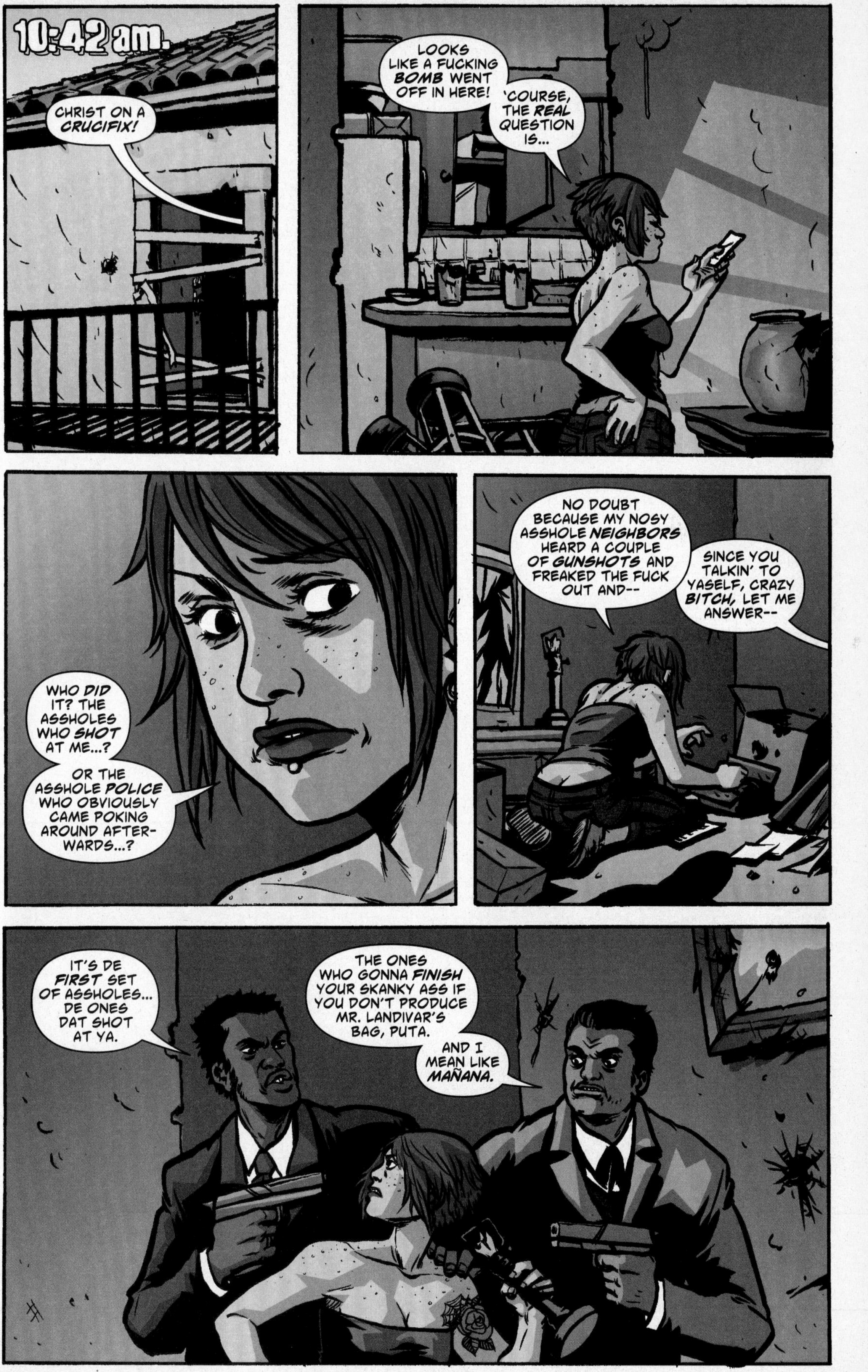
10:42 am.
CHRIST ON A CRUCIFIX!
LOOKS LIKE A FUCKING BOMB WENT OFF IN HERE!
'COURSE, THE REAL QUESTION IS...
WHO DID IT? THE ASSHOLES WHO SHOT AT ME...?
OR THE ASSHOLE POLICE WHO OBVIOUSLY CAME POKING AROUND AFTER-WARDS...?
NO DOUBT BECAUSE MY NOSY ASSHOLE NEIGHBORS HEARD A COUPLE OF GUNSHOTS AND FREAKED THE FUCK OUT AND--
SINCE YOU TALKIN' TO YASELF, CRAZY BITCH, LET ME ANSWER--
IT'S DE FIRST SET OF ASSHOLES... DE ONES DAT SHOT AT YA.
THE ONES WHO GONNA FINISH YOUR SKANKY ASS IF YOU DON'T PRODUCE MR. LANDIVAR'S BAG, PUTA.
AND I MEAN LIKE MAÑANA.

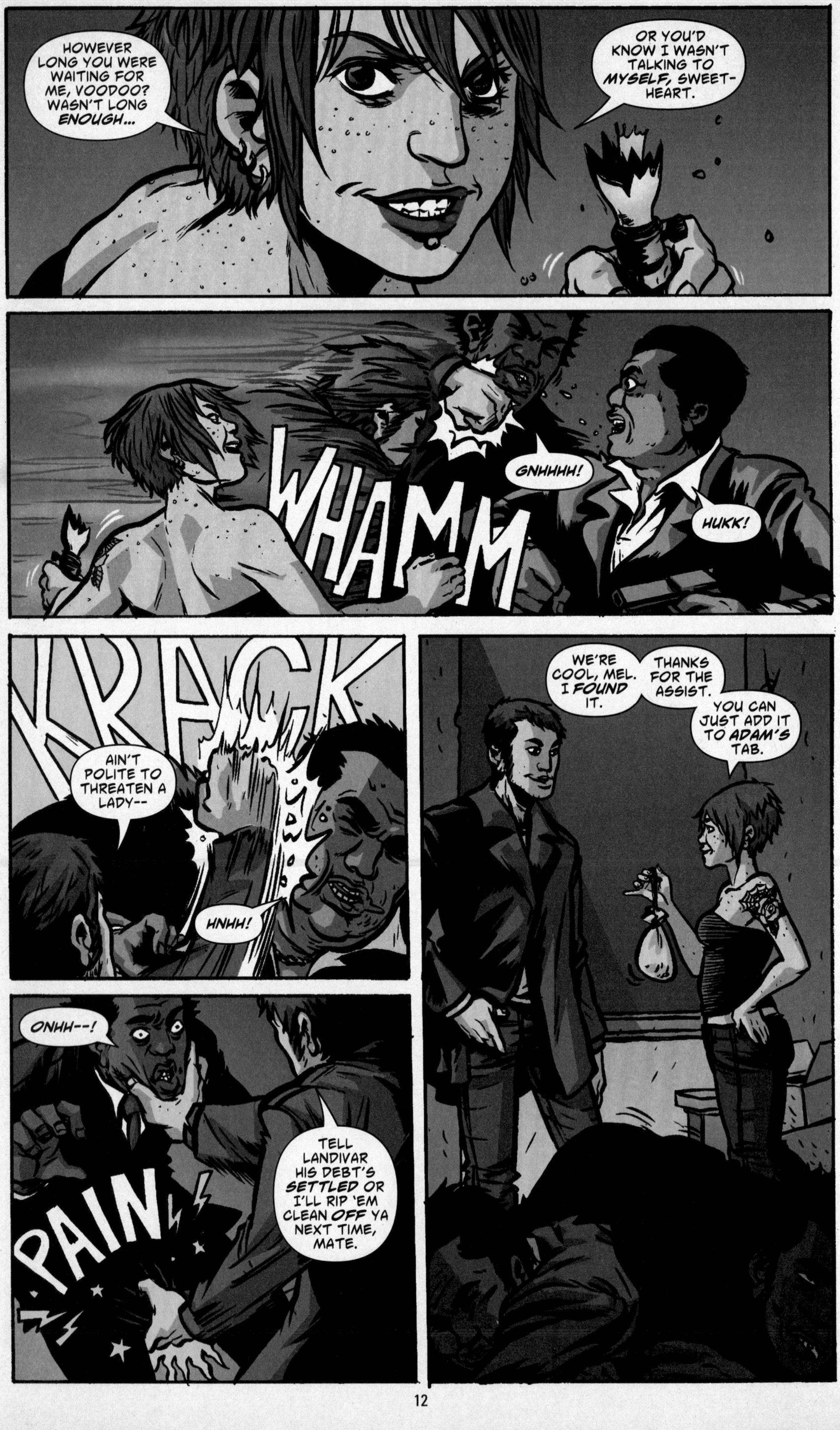
HOWEVER LONG YOU WERE WAITING FOR ME, VOODOO? WASN'T LONG ENOUGH...
OR YOU'D KNOW I WASN'T TALKING TO MYSELF, SWEET-HEART.
WHAMM
GNHHHH!
HUKK!
KRACK
AIN'T POLITE TO THREATEN A LADY--
HNHH!
ONHH--!
TELL LANDIVAR HIS DEBT'S SETTLED OR I'LL RIP 'EM CLEAN OFF YA NEXT TIME, MATE.
PAIN
WE'RE COOL, MEL. I FOUND IT.
THANKS FOR THE ASSIST.
YOU CAN JUST ADD IT TO ADAM'S TAB.

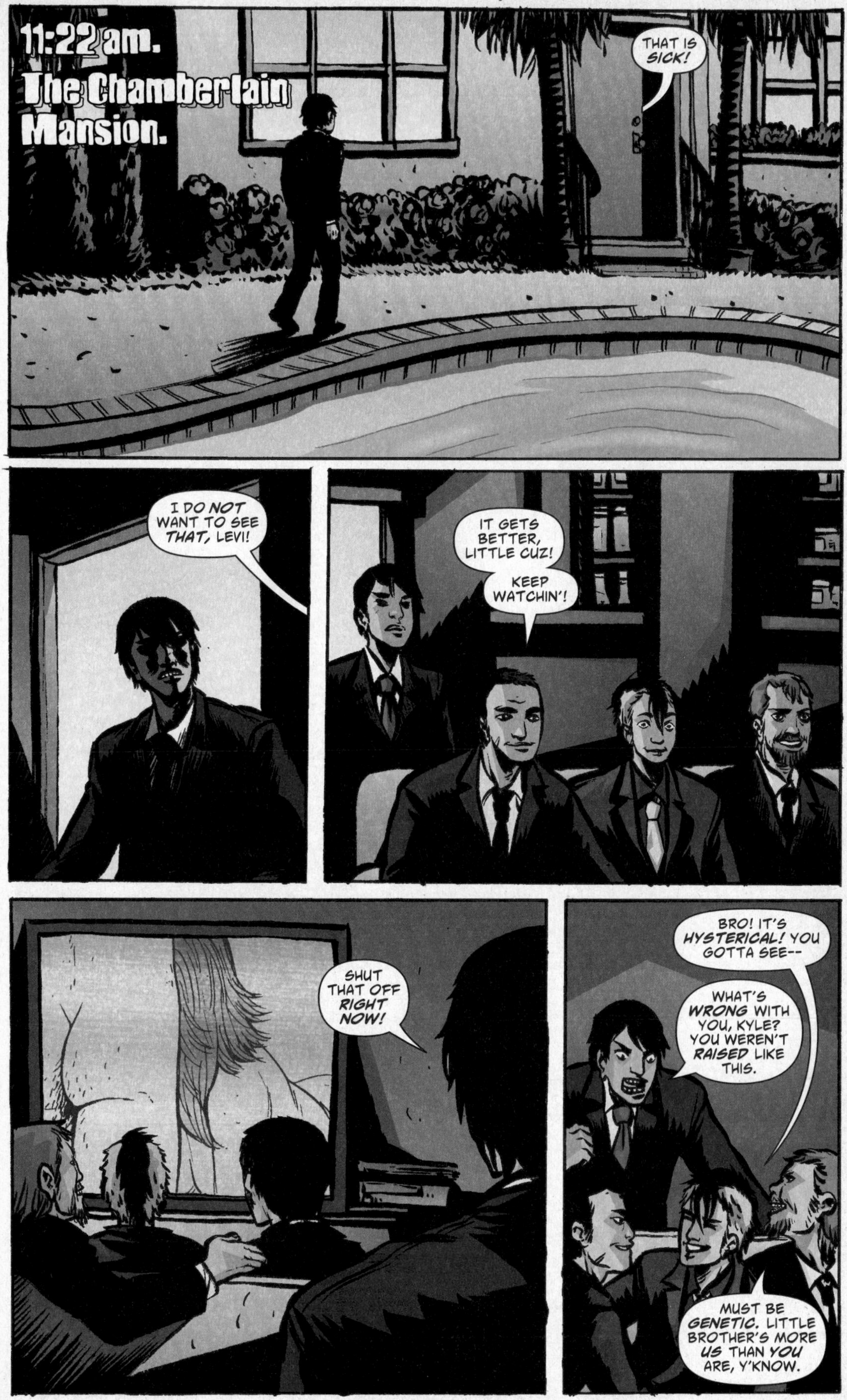
11:22 am.
The Chamberlain Mansion.
THAT IS SICK!
I DO NOT WANT TO SEE THAT, LEVI!
IT GETS BETTER, LITTLE CUZ!
KEEP WATCHIN'!
SHUT THAT OFF RIGHT NOW!
BRO! IT'S HYSTERICAL! YOU GOTTA SEE--
WHAT'S WRONG WITH YOU, KYLE? YOU WEREN'T RAISED LIKE THIS.
MUST BE GENETIC. LITTLE BROTHER'S MORE US THAN YOU ARE, Y'KNOW.

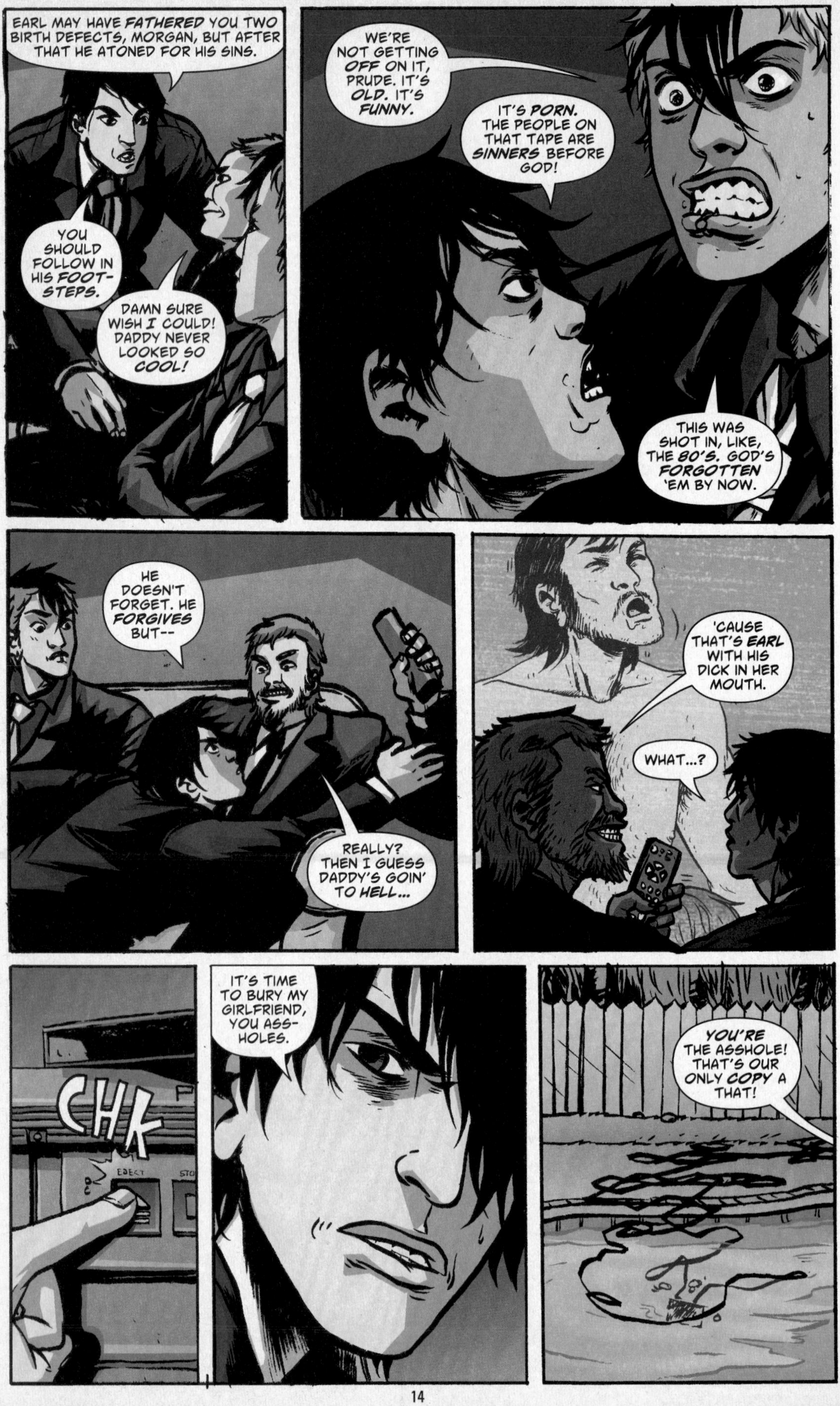
EARL MAY HAVE FATHERED YOU TWO BIRTH DEFECTS, MORGAN, BUT AFTER THAT HE ATONED FOR HIS SINS.
YOU SHOULD FOLLOW IN HIS FOOT-STEPS.
DAMN SURE WISH I COULD! DADDY NEVER LOOKED SO COOL!
WE'RE NOT GETTING OFF ON IT, PRUDE. IT'S OLD. IT'S FUNNY.
IT'S PORN. THE PEOPLE ON THAT TAPE ARE SINNERS BEFORE GOD!
THIS WAS SHOT IN, LIKE, THE 80'S. GOD'S FORGOTTEN 'EM BY NOW.
HE DOESN'T FORGET. HE FORGIVES BUT--
REALLY? THEN I GUESS DADDY'S GOIN' TO HELL...
'CAUSE THAT'S EARL WITH HIS DICK IN HER MOUTH.
WHAT...?
CHK
EJECT
IT'S TIME TO BURY MY GIRLFRIEND, YOU ASS-HOLES.
YOU'RE THE ASSHOLE! THAT'S OUR ONLY COPY A THAT!

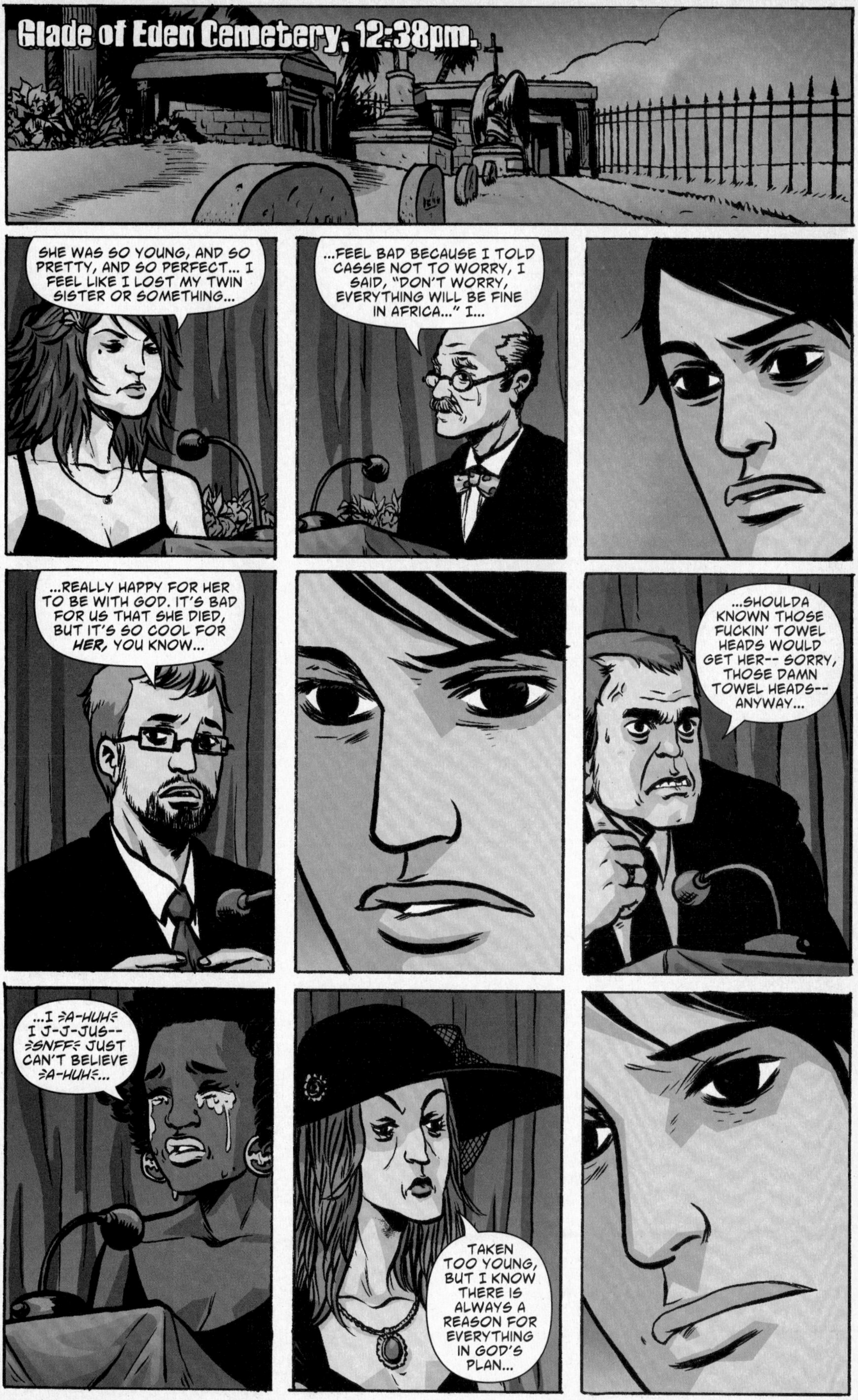
Glade of Eden Cemetery, 12:38pm.
SHE WAS SO YOUNG, AND SO PRETTY, AND SO PERFECT... I FEEL LIKE I LOST MY TWIN SISTER OR SOMETHING...
...FEEL BAD BECAUSE I TOLD CASSIE NOT TO WORRY, I SAID, "DON'T WORRY, EVERYTHING WILL BE FINE IN AFRICA..." I...
...REALLY HAPPY FOR HER TO BE WITH GOD. IT'S BAD FOR US THAT SHE DIED, BUT IT'S SO COOL FOR *HER,* YOU KNOW...
...SHOULDA KNOWN THOSE FUCKIN' TOWEL HEADS WOULD GET HER-- SORRY, THOSE DAMN TOWEL HEADS-- ANYWAY...
...I *A-HUH* I J-J-JUS-- *SNFF* JUST CAN'T BELIEVE *A-HUH*...
TAKEN TOO YOUNG, BUT I KNOW THERE IS ALWAYS A REASON FOR EVERYTHING IN GOD'S PLAN...

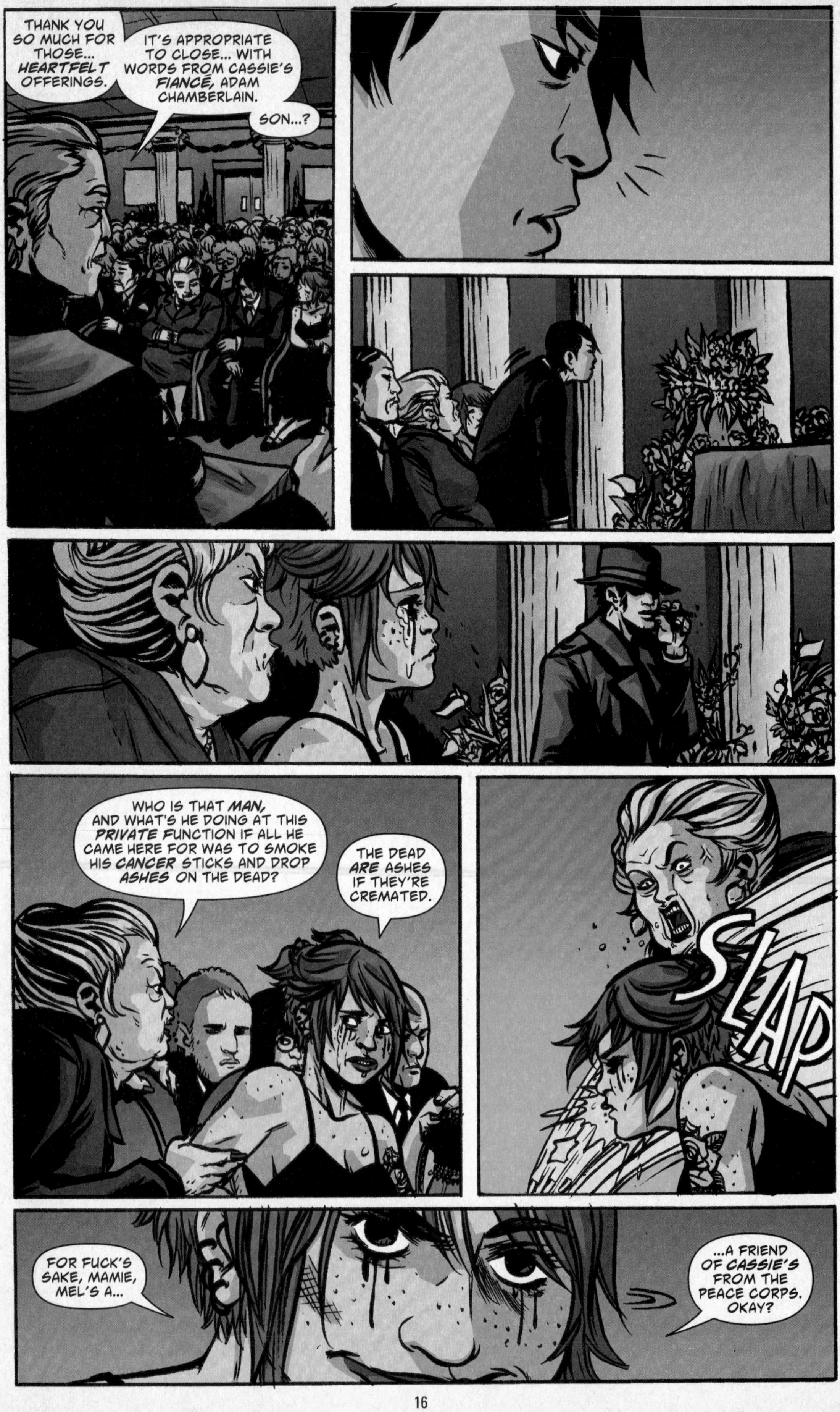
THANK YOU SO MUCH FOR THOSE... HEARTFELT OFFERINGS.
IT'S APPROPRIATE TO CLOSE... WITH WORDS FROM CASSIE'S FIANCÉ, ADAM CHAMBERLAIN.
SON...?
WHO IS THAT MAN, AND WHAT'S HE DOING AT THIS PRIVATE FUNCTION IF ALL HE CAME HERE FOR WAS TO SMOKE HIS CANCER STICKS AND DROP ASHES ON THE DEAD?
THE DEAD ARE ASHES IF THEY'RE CREMATED.
SLAP
FOR FUCK'S SAKE, MAMIE, MEL'S A...
...A FRIEND OF CASSIE'S FROM THE PEACE CORPS. OKAY?

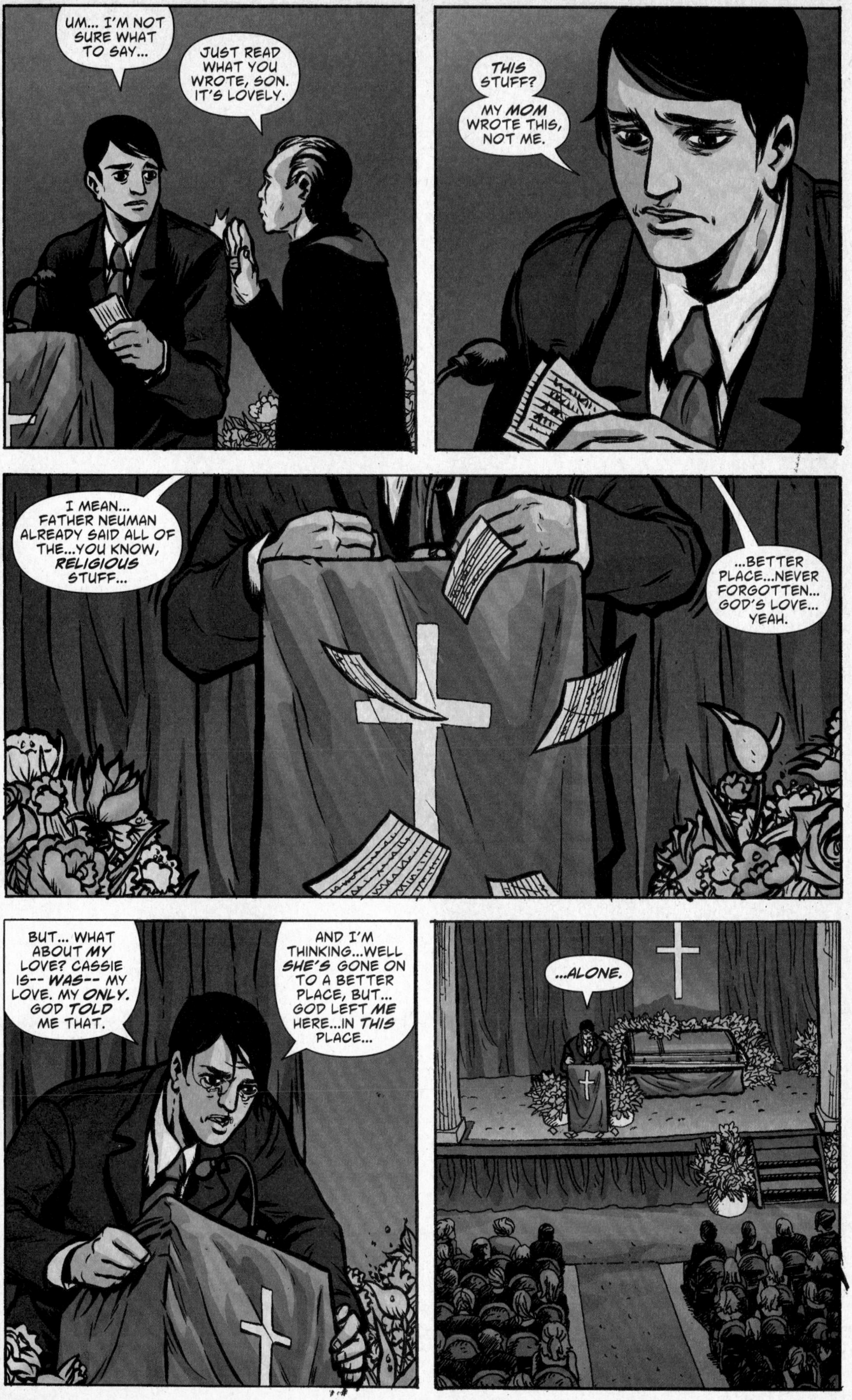
UM... I'M NOT SURE WHAT TO SAY...
JUST READ WHAT YOU WROTE, SON. IT'S LOVELY.
THIS STUFF?
MY MOM WROTE THIS, NOT ME.
I MEAN... FATHER NEUMAN ALREADY SAID ALL OF THE...YOU KNOW, RELIGIOUS STUFF...
...BETTER PLACE...NEVER FORGOTTEN... GOD'S LOVE... YEAH.
BUT... WHAT ABOUT MY LOVE? CASSIE IS-- WAS-- MY LOVE. MY ONLY. GOD TOLD ME THAT.
AND I'M THINKING...WELL SHE'S GONE ON TO A BETTER PLACE, BUT... GOD LEFT ME HERE...IN THIS PLACE...
...ALONE.

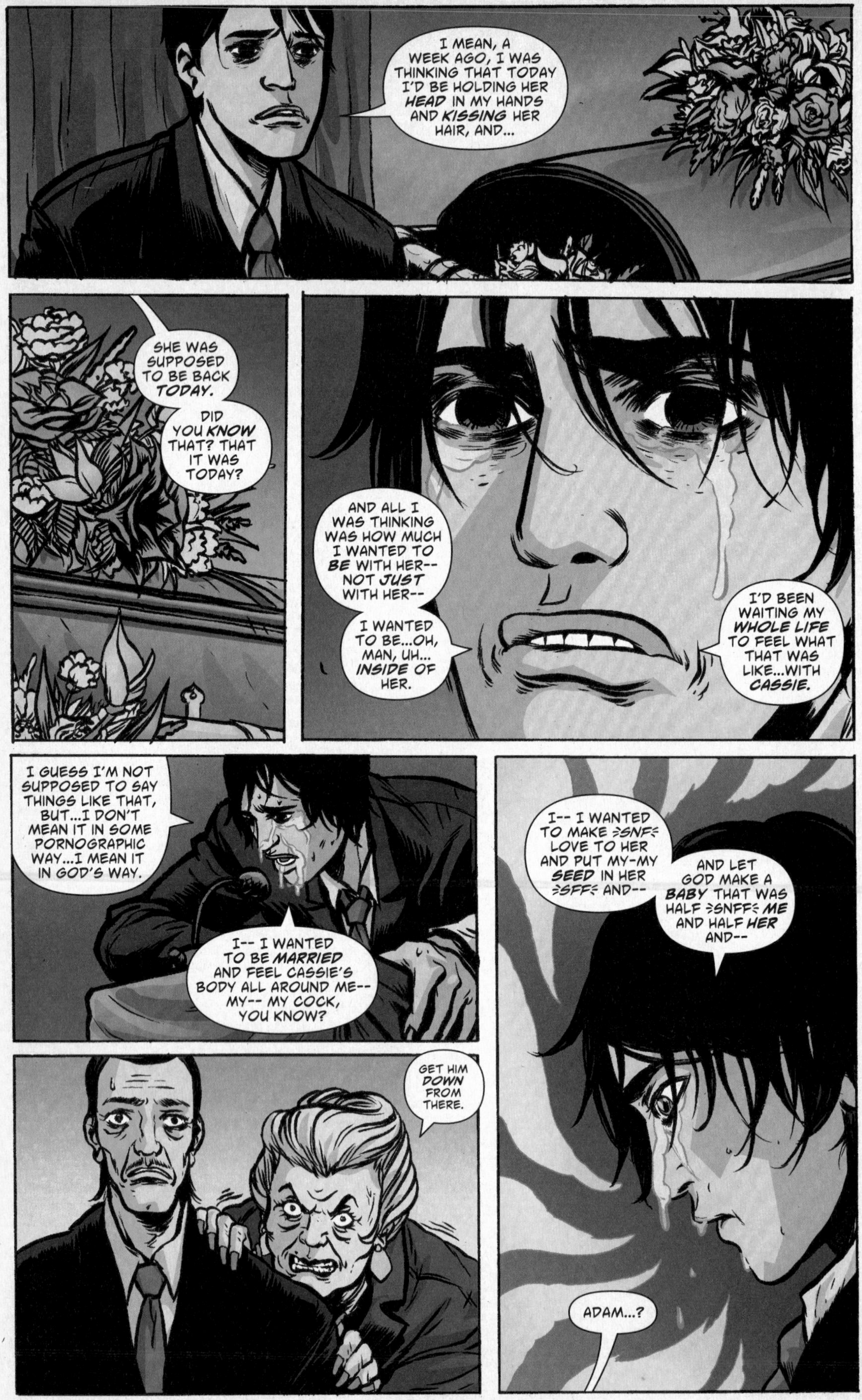
I MEAN, A WEEK AGO, I WAS THINKING THAT TODAY I'D BE HOLDING HER HEAD IN MY HANDS AND KISSING HER HAIR, AND...
SHE WAS SUPPOSED TO BE BACK TODAY.
DID YOU KNOW THAT? THAT IT WAS TODAY?
AND ALL I WAS THINKING WAS HOW MUCH I WANTED TO BE WITH HER-- NOT JUST WITH HER--
I WANTED TO BE...OH, MAN, UH... INSIDE OF HER.
I'D BEEN WAITING MY WHOLE LIFE TO FEEL WHAT THAT WAS LIKE...WITH CASSIE.
I GUESS I'M NOT SUPPOSED TO SAY THINGS LIKE THAT, BUT...I DON'T MEAN IT IN SOME PORNOGRAPHIC WAY...I MEAN IT IN GOD'S WAY.
I-- I WANTED TO BE MARRIED AND FEEL CASSIE'S BODY ALL AROUND ME-- MY-- MY COCK, YOU KNOW?
I-- I WANTED TO MAKE ≶SNF≶ LOVE TO HER AND PUT MY-MY SEED IN HER ≶SFF≶ AND--
AND LET GOD MAKE A BABY THAT WAS HALF ≶SNFF≶ ME AND HALF HER AND--
GET HIM DOWN FROM THERE.
ADAM...?

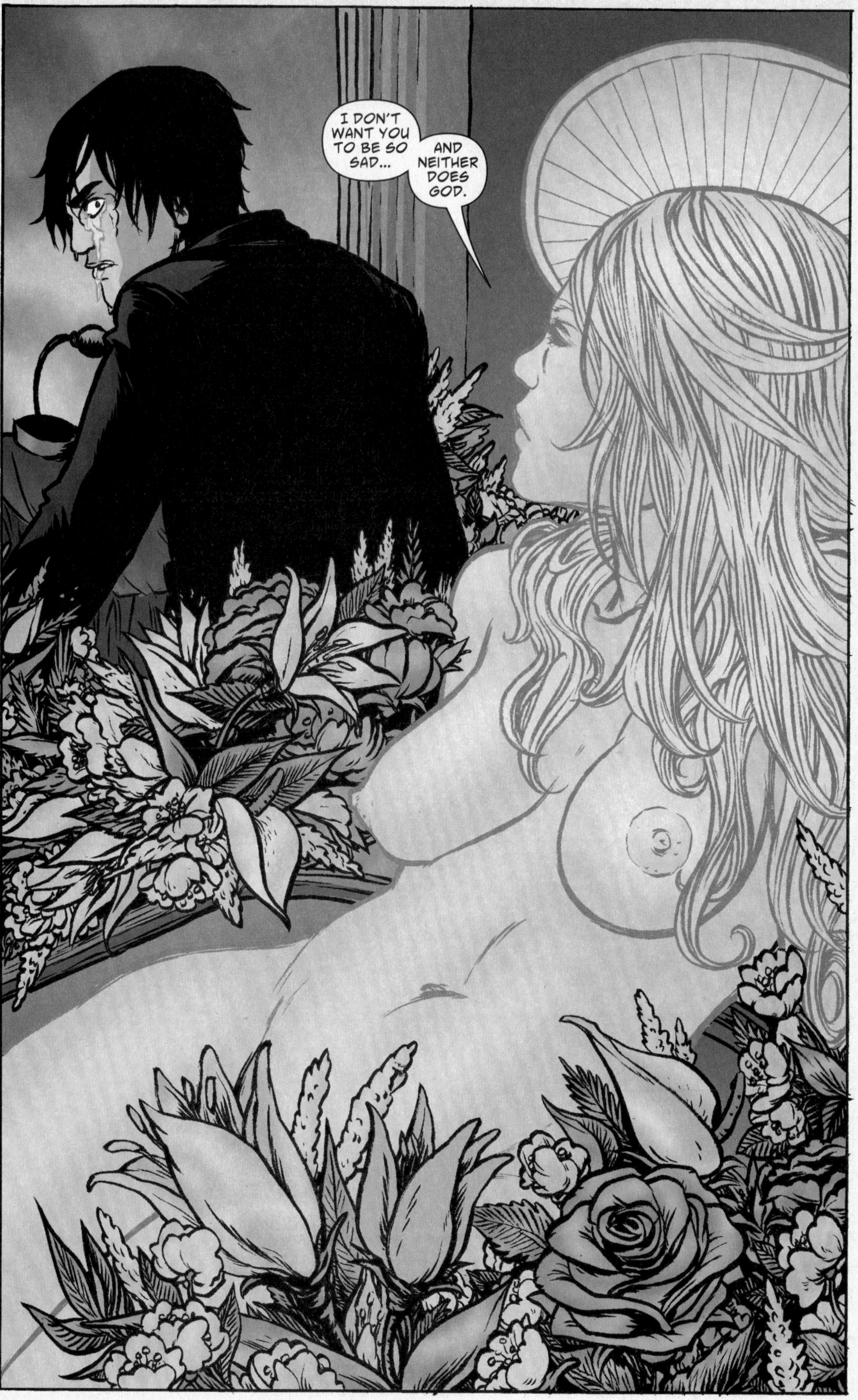
I DON'T WANT YOU TO BE SO SAD...
AND NEITHER DOES GOD.

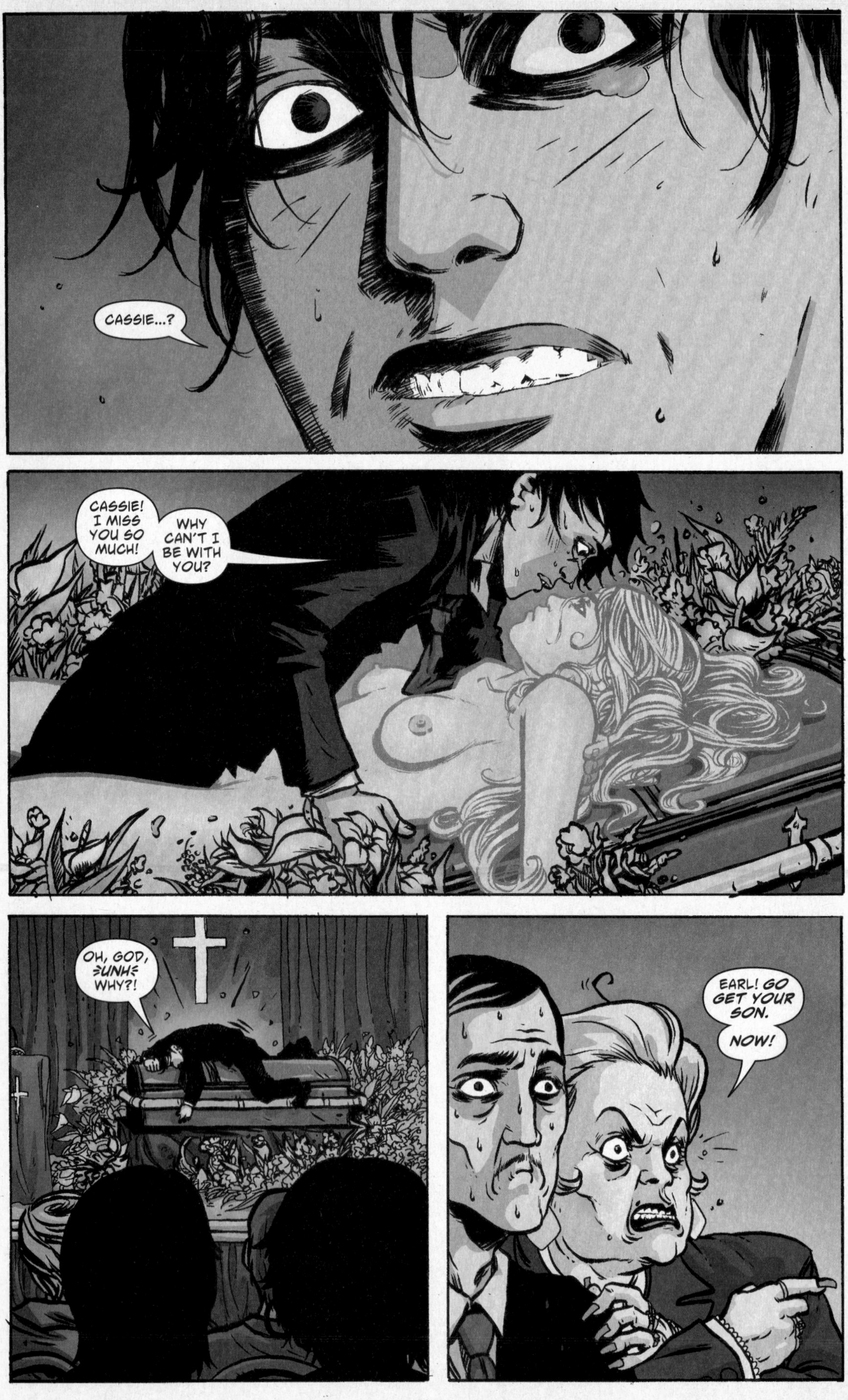
CASSIE...?
CASSIE! I MISS YOU SO MUCH!
WHY CAN'T I BE WITH YOU?
OH, GOD, UNH WHY?!
EARL! GO GET YOUR SON.
NOW!

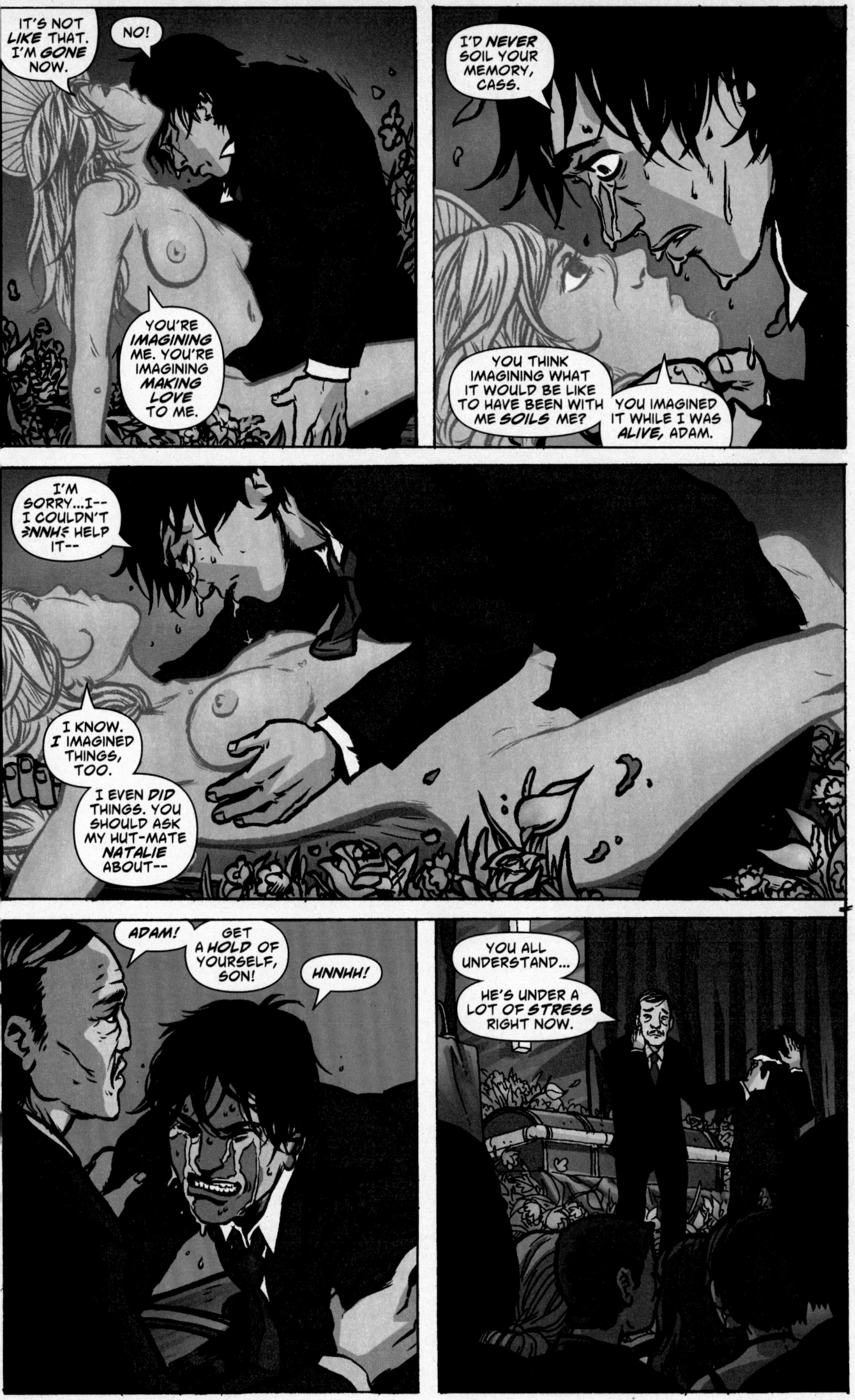

IT'S NOT LIKE THAT. I'M GONE NOW.
NO!
YOU'RE IMAGINING ME. YOU'RE IMAGINING MAKING LOVE TO ME.
I'D NEVER SOIL YOUR MEMORY, CASS.
YOU THINK IMAGINING WHAT IT WOULD BE LIKE TO HAVE BEEN WITH ME SOILS ME?
YOU IMAGINED IT WHILE I WAS ALIVE, ADAM.
I'M SORRY...I-- I COULDN'T <NNH> HELP IT--
I KNOW. I IMAGINED THINGS, TOO.
I EVEN DID THINGS. YOU SHOULD ASK MY HUT-MATE NATALIE ABOUT--
ADAM!
GET A HOLD OF YOURSELF, SON!
HNNHH!
YOU ALL UNDERSTAND...
HE'S UNDER A LOT OF STRESS RIGHT NOW.

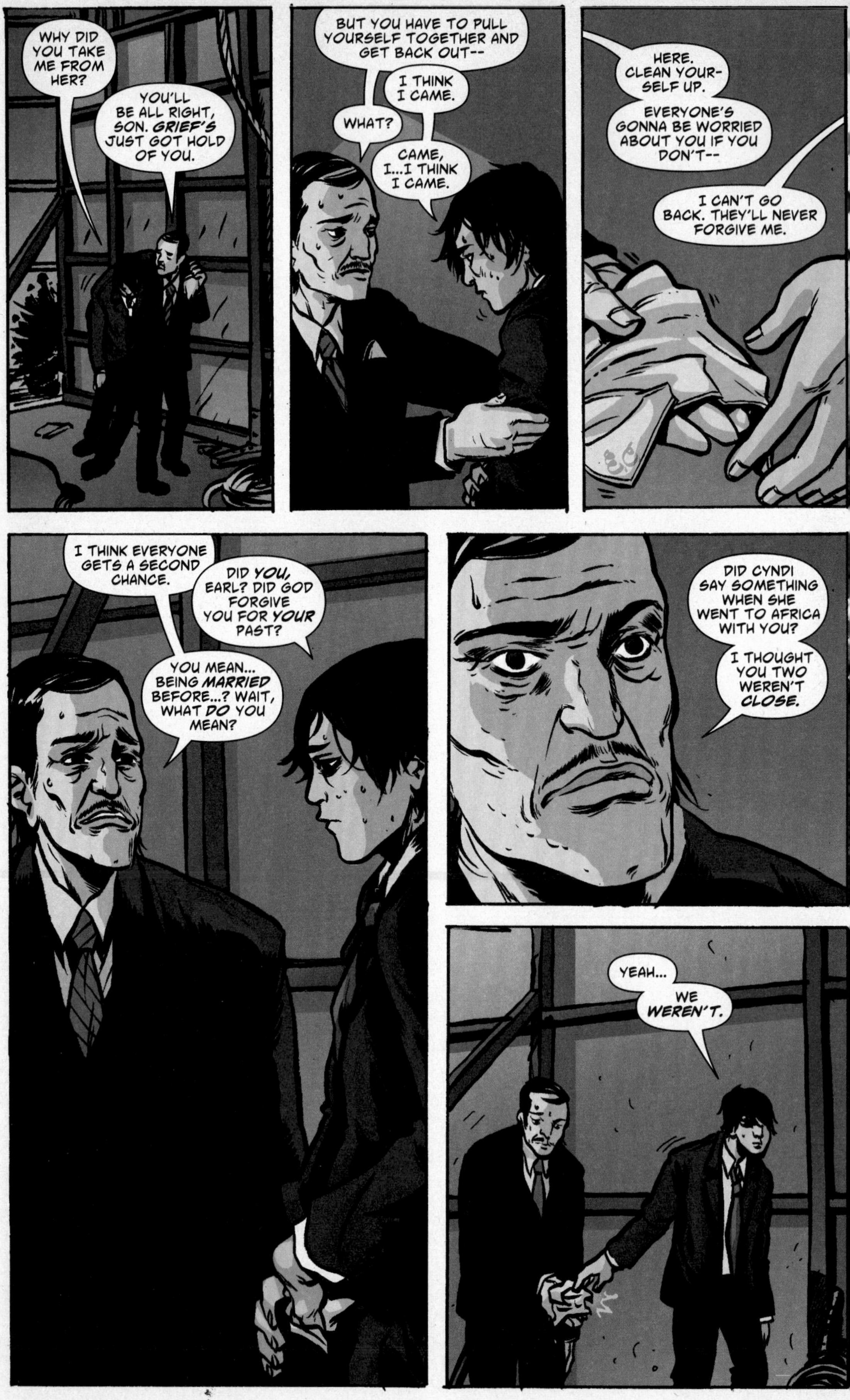
WHY DID YOU TAKE ME FROM HER?
YOU'LL BE ALL RIGHT, SON. GRIEF'S JUST GOT HOLD OF YOU.
BUT YOU HAVE TO PULL YOURSELF TOGETHER AND GET BACK OUT--
I THINK I CAME.
WHAT?
CAME, I...I THINK I CAME.
HERE. CLEAN YOURSELF UP.
EVERYONE'S GONNA BE WORRIED ABOUT YOU IF YOU DON'T--
I CAN'T GO BACK. THEY'LL NEVER FORGIVE ME.
I THINK EVERYONE GETS A SECOND CHANCE.
DID YOU, EARL? DID GOD FORGIVE YOU FOR YOUR PAST?
YOU MEAN... BEING MARRIED BEFORE...? WAIT, WHAT DO YOU MEAN?
DID CYNDI SAY SOMETHING WHEN SHE WENT TO AFRICA WITH YOU?
I THOUGHT YOU TWO WEREN'T CLOSE.
YEAH...
WE WEREN'T.

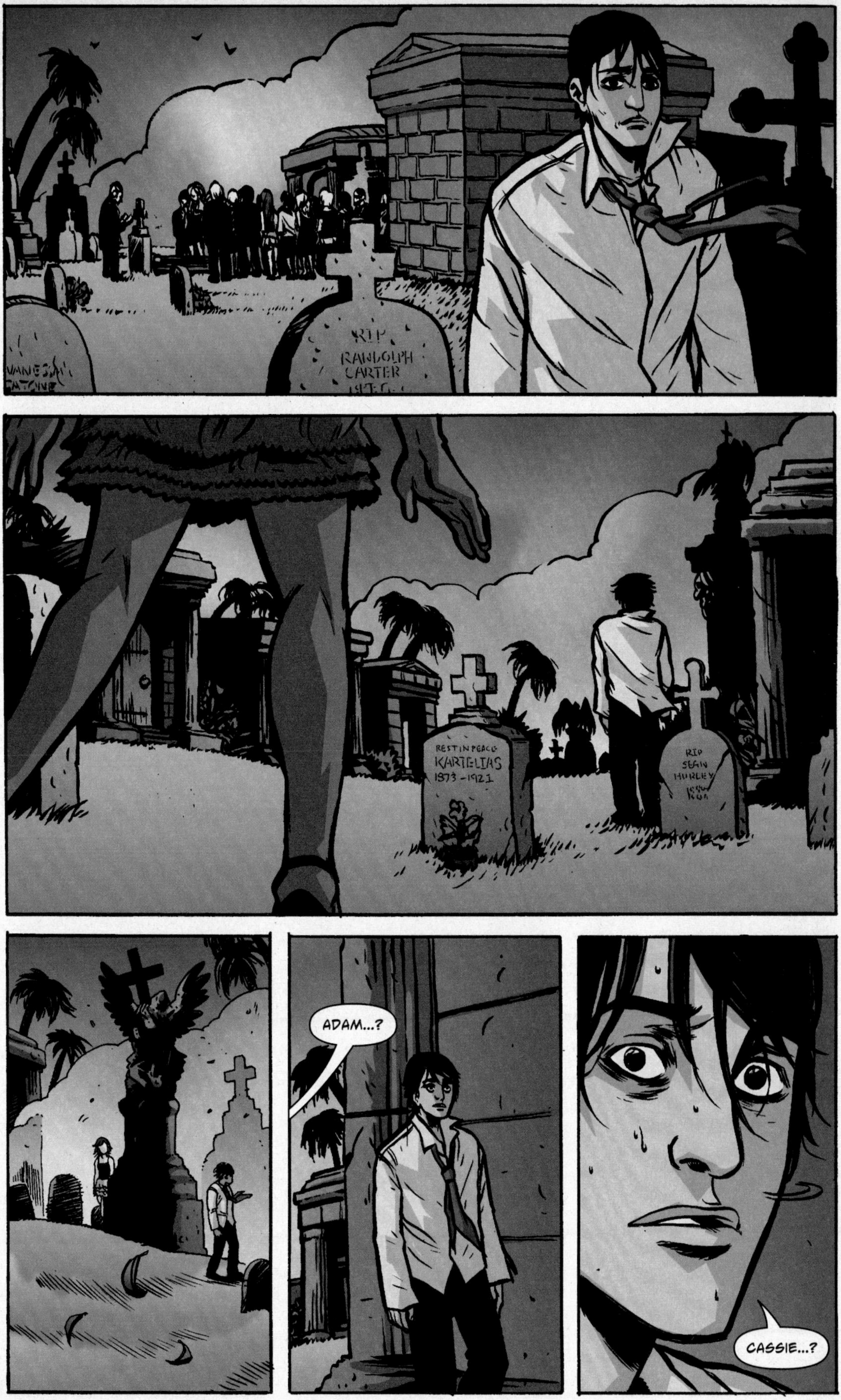
RIP
RANDOLPH
CARTER
REST IN PEACE
KARTELIAS
1873-1921
RIP
SEAN
HURLEY
ADAM...?
CASSIE...?

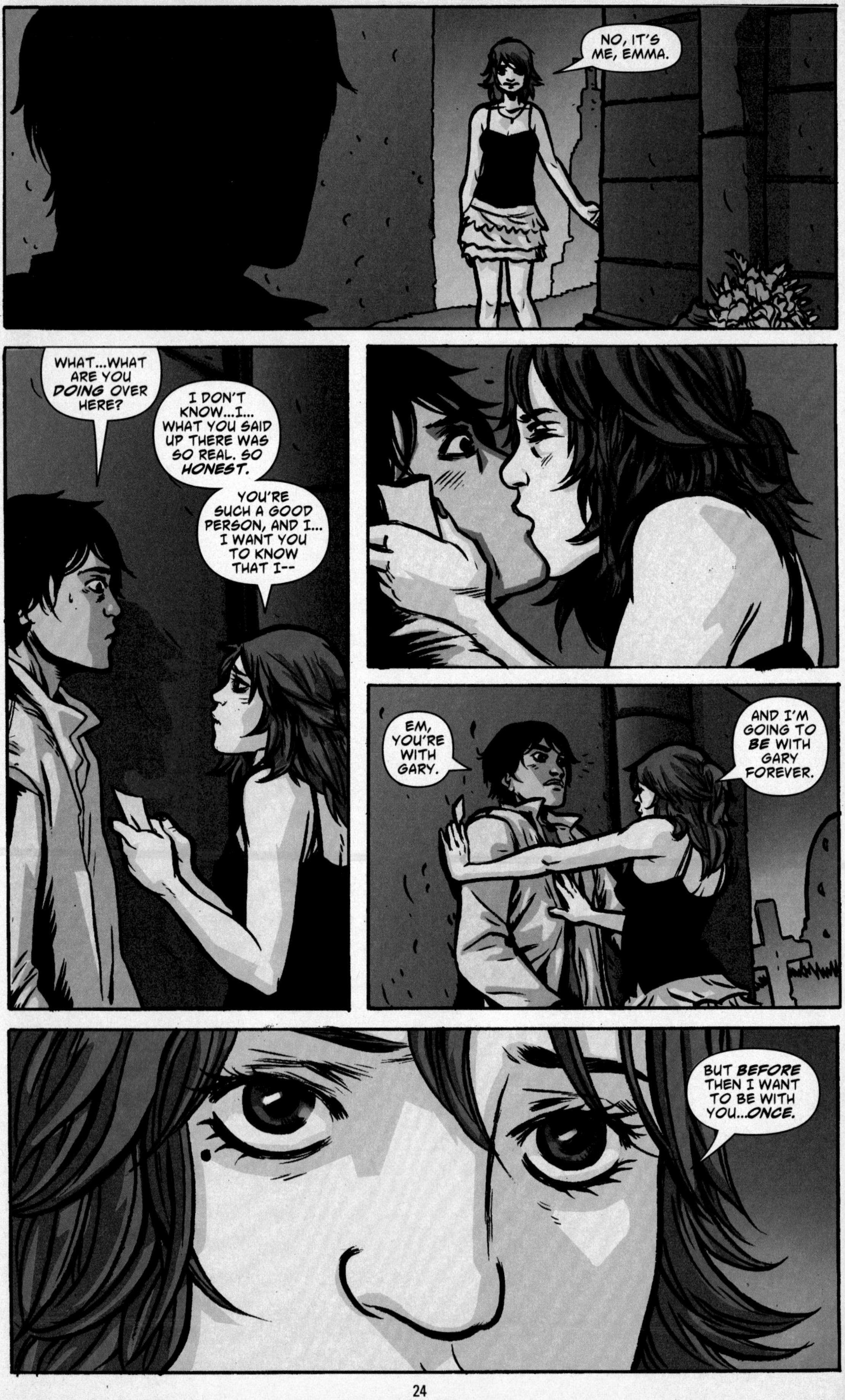
NO, IT'S ME, EMMA.
WHAT...WHAT ARE YOU DOING OVER HERE?
I DON'T KNOW...I... WHAT YOU SAID UP THERE WAS SO REAL. SO HONEST.
YOU'RE SUCH A GOOD PERSON, AND I... I WANT YOU TO KNOW THAT I--
EM, YOU'RE WITH GARY.
AND I'M GOING TO BE WITH GARY FOREVER.
BUT BEFORE THEN I WANT TO BE WITH YOU...ONCE.

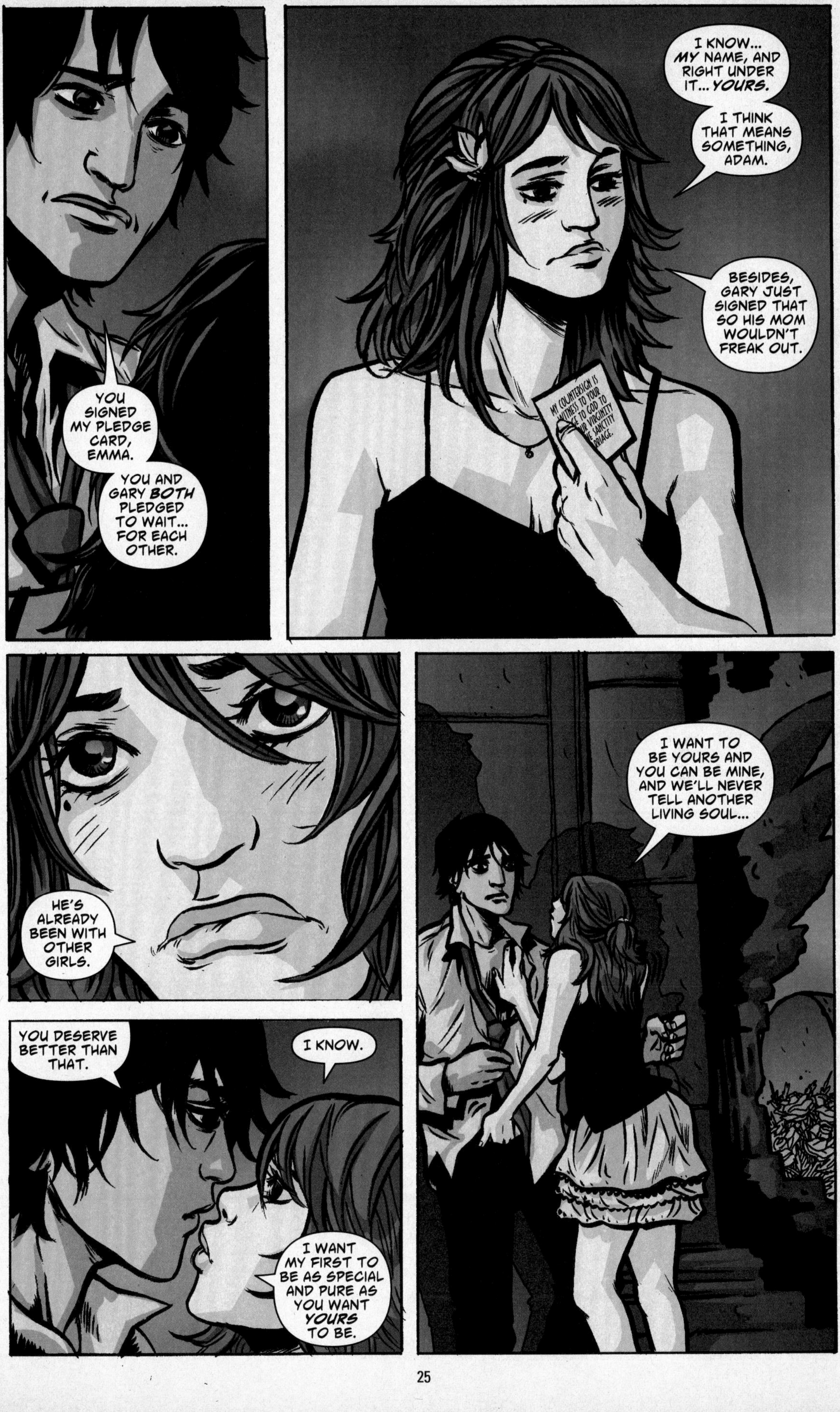
YOU SIGNED MY PLEDGE CARD, EMMA.
YOU AND GARY *BOTH* PLEDGED TO WAIT... FOR EACH OTHER.
I KNOW... *MY* NAME, AND RIGHT UNDER IT... *YOURS.*
I THINK THAT MEANS SOMETHING, ADAM.
BESIDES, GARY JUST SIGNED THAT SO HIS MOM WOULDN'T FREAK OUT.
HE'S ALREADY BEEN WITH OTHER GIRLS.
YOU DESERVE BETTER THAN THAT.
I KNOW.
I WANT MY FIRST TO BE AS SPECIAL AND PURE AS YOU WANT *YOURS* TO BE.
I WANT TO BE YOURS AND YOU CAN BE MINE, AND WE'LL NEVER TELL ANOTHER LIVING SOUL...

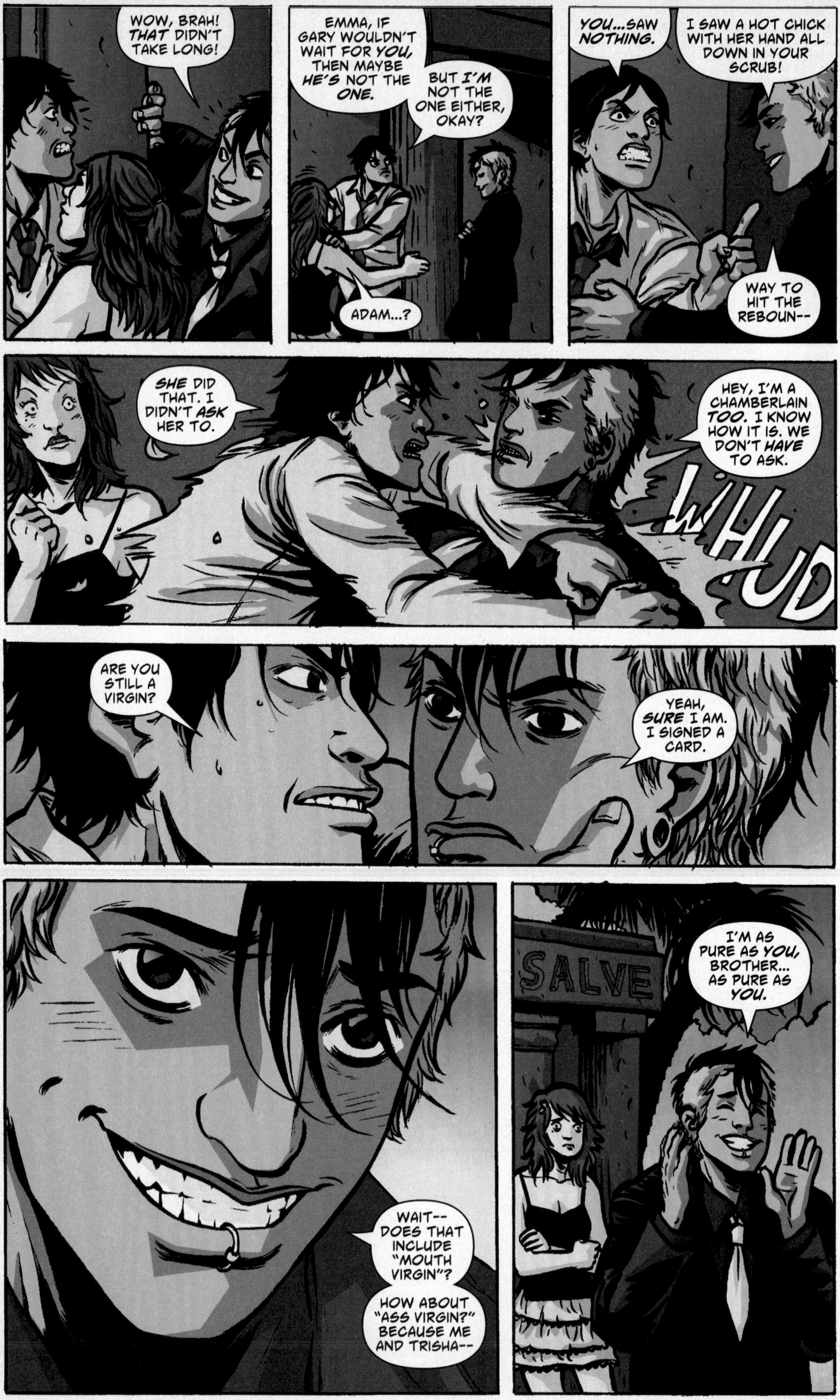
WOW, BRAH! THAT DIDN'T TAKE LONG!
EMMA, IF GARY WOULDN'T WAIT FOR YOU, THEN MAYBE HE'S NOT THE ONE.
BUT I'M NOT THE ONE EITHER, OKAY?
ADAM...?
YOU...SAW NOTHING.
I SAW A HOT CHICK WITH HER HAND ALL DOWN IN YOUR SCRUB!
WAY TO HIT THE REBOUN--
SHE DID THAT. I DIDN'T ASK HER TO.
HEY, I'M A CHAMBERLAIN TOO. I KNOW HOW IT IS. WE DON'T HAVE TO ASK.
WHUD
ARE YOU STILL A VIRGIN?
YEAH, SURE I AM. I SIGNED A CARD.
WAIT-- DOES THAT INCLUDE "MOUTH VIRGIN"?
HOW ABOUT "ASS VIRGIN?" BECAUSE ME AND TRISHA--
SALVE
I'M AS PURE AS YOU, BROTHER... AS PURE AS YOU.

9:45 pm.
The Chamberlain Mansion.

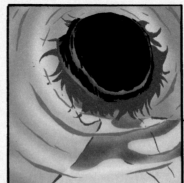

PUKT

HUH?!

WHO'S THERE--?

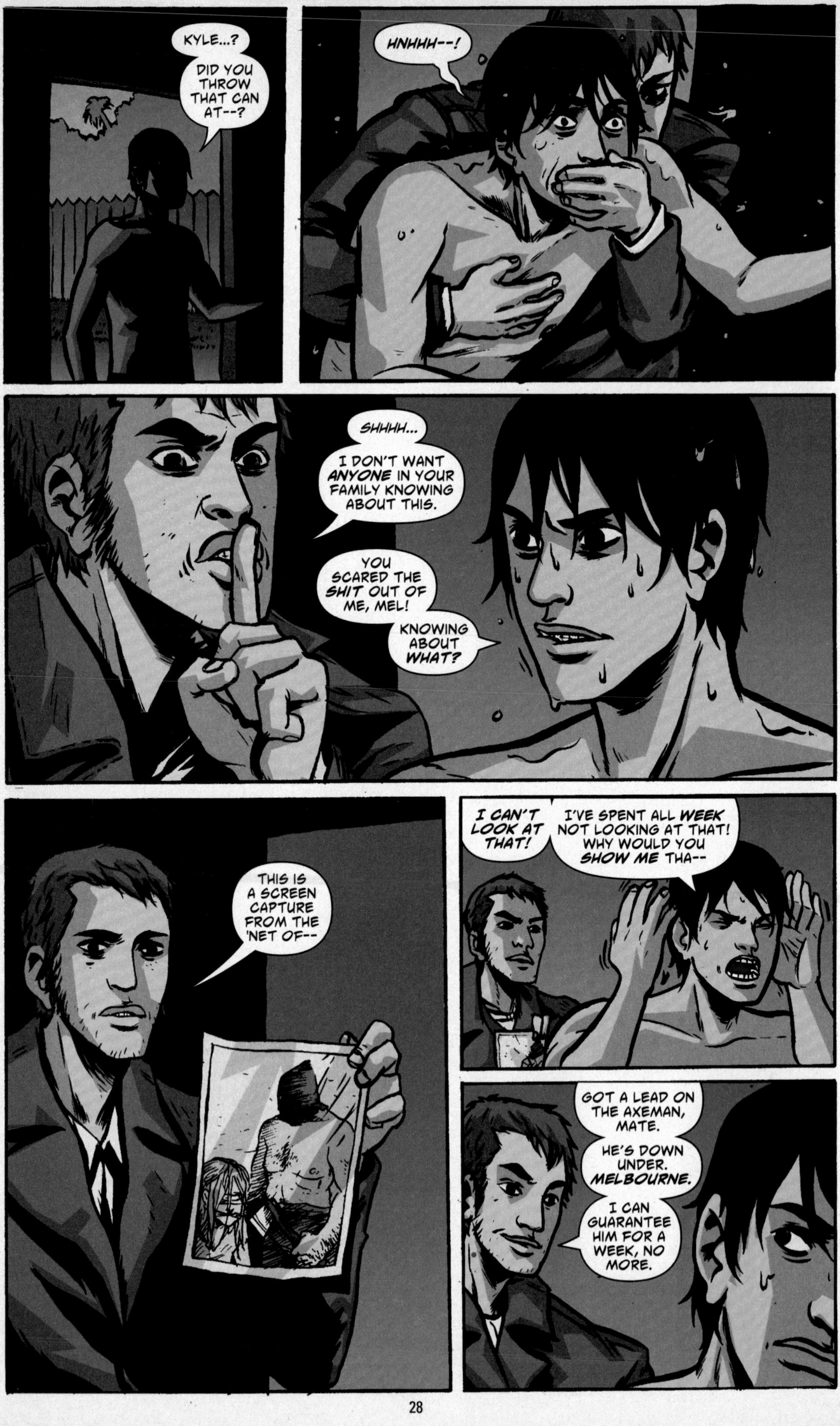
KYLE...?
DID YOU THROW THAT CAN AT--?
HNHHH--!
SHHHH...
I DON'T WANT ANYONE IN YOUR FAMILY KNOWING ABOUT THIS.
YOU SCARED THE SHIT OUT OF ME, MEL!
KNOWING ABOUT WHAT?
THIS IS A SCREEN CAPTURE FROM THE 'NET OF--
I CAN'T LOOK AT THAT!
I'VE SPENT ALL WEEK NOT LOOKING AT THAT! WHY WOULD YOU SHOW ME THA--
GOT A LEAD ON THE AXEMAN, MATE.
HE'S DOWN UNDER. MELBOURNE.
I CAN GUARANTEE HIM FOR A WEEK, NO MORE.

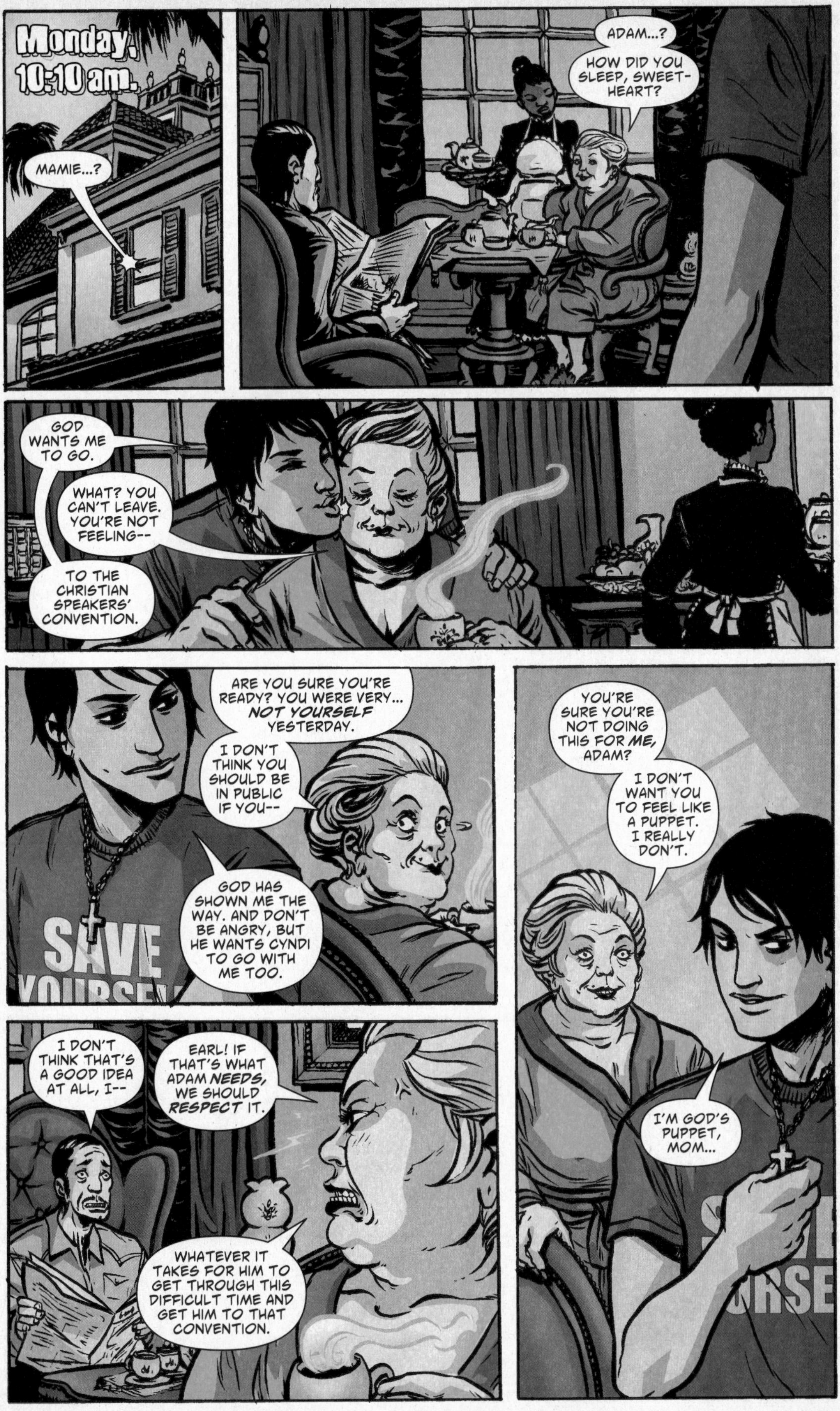
Monday, 10:10 am.
MAMIE...?
ADAM...?
HOW DID YOU SLEEP, SWEET-HEART?
GOD WANTS ME TO GO.
WHAT? YOU CAN'T LEAVE. YOU'RE NOT FEELING--
TO THE CHRISTIAN SPEAKERS' CONVENTION.
ARE YOU SURE YOU'RE READY? YOU WERE VERY... NOT YOURSELF YESTERDAY.
I DON'T THINK YOU SHOULD BE IN PUBLIC IF YOU--
GOD HAS SHOWN ME THE WAY. AND DON'T BE ANGRY, BUT HE WANTS CYNDI TO GO WITH ME TOO.
SAVE
YOU'RE SURE YOU'RE NOT DOING THIS FOR ME, ADAM?
I DON'T WANT YOU TO FEEL LIKE A PUPPET. I REALLY DON'T.
I DON'T THINK THAT'S A GOOD IDEA AT ALL, I--
EARL! IF THAT'S WHAT ADAM NEEDS, WE SHOULD RESPECT IT.
WHATEVER IT TAKES FOR HIM TO GET THROUGH THIS DIFFICULT TIME AND GET HIM TO THAT CONVENTION.
I'M GOD'S PUPPET, MOM...

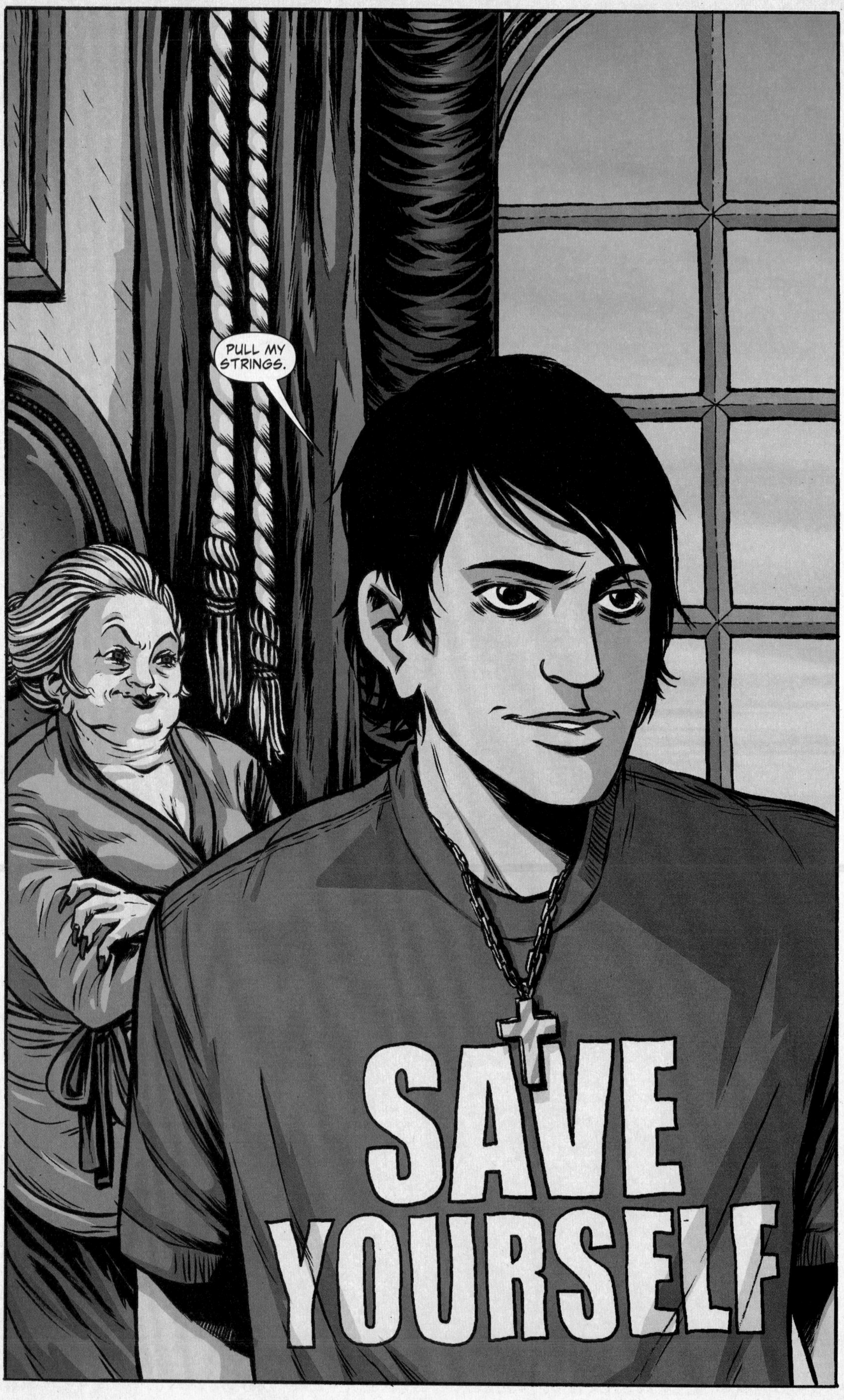
PULL MY STRINGS.
SAVE YOURSELF

CHAPTER TWO

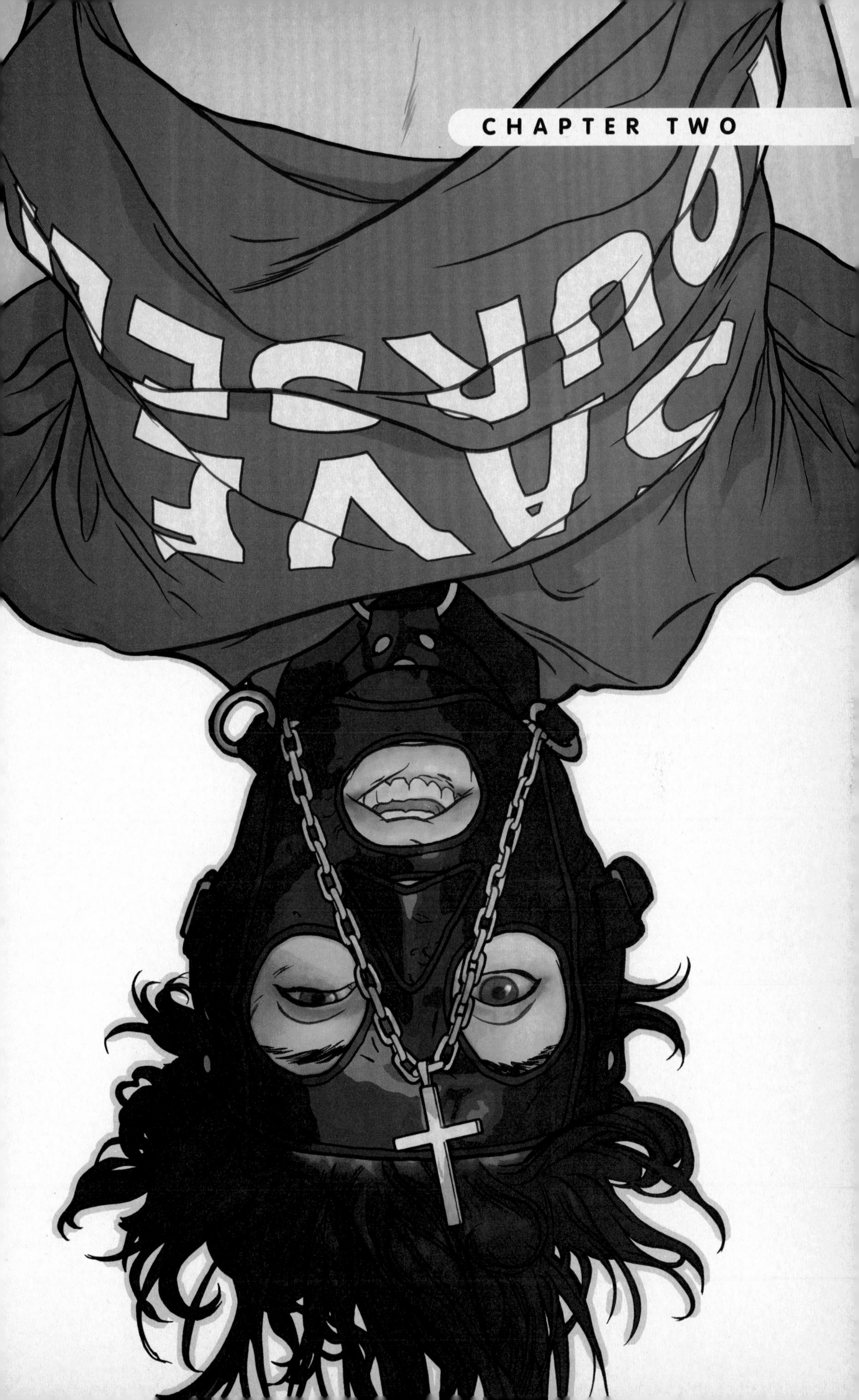

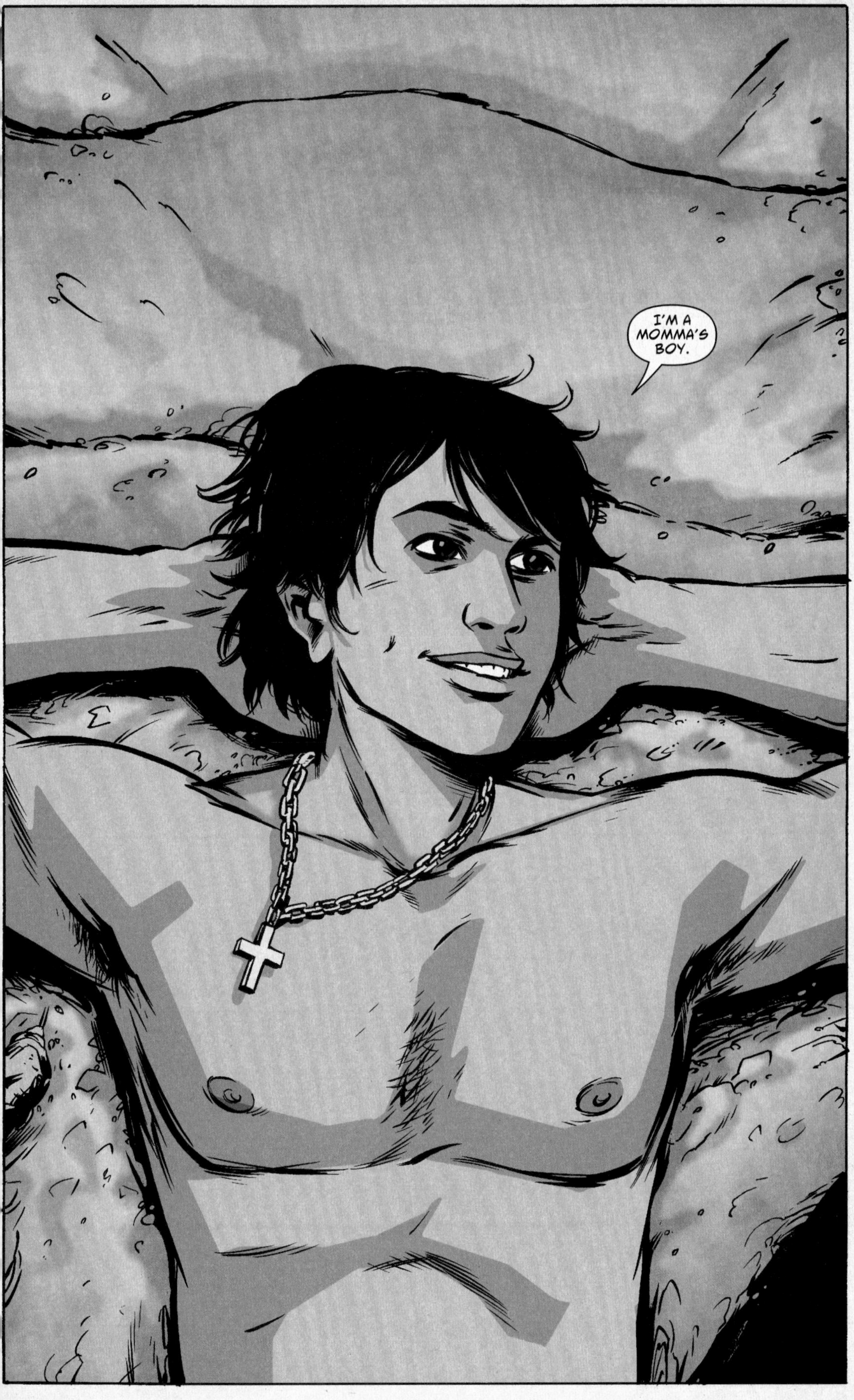
I'M A MOMMA'S BOY.

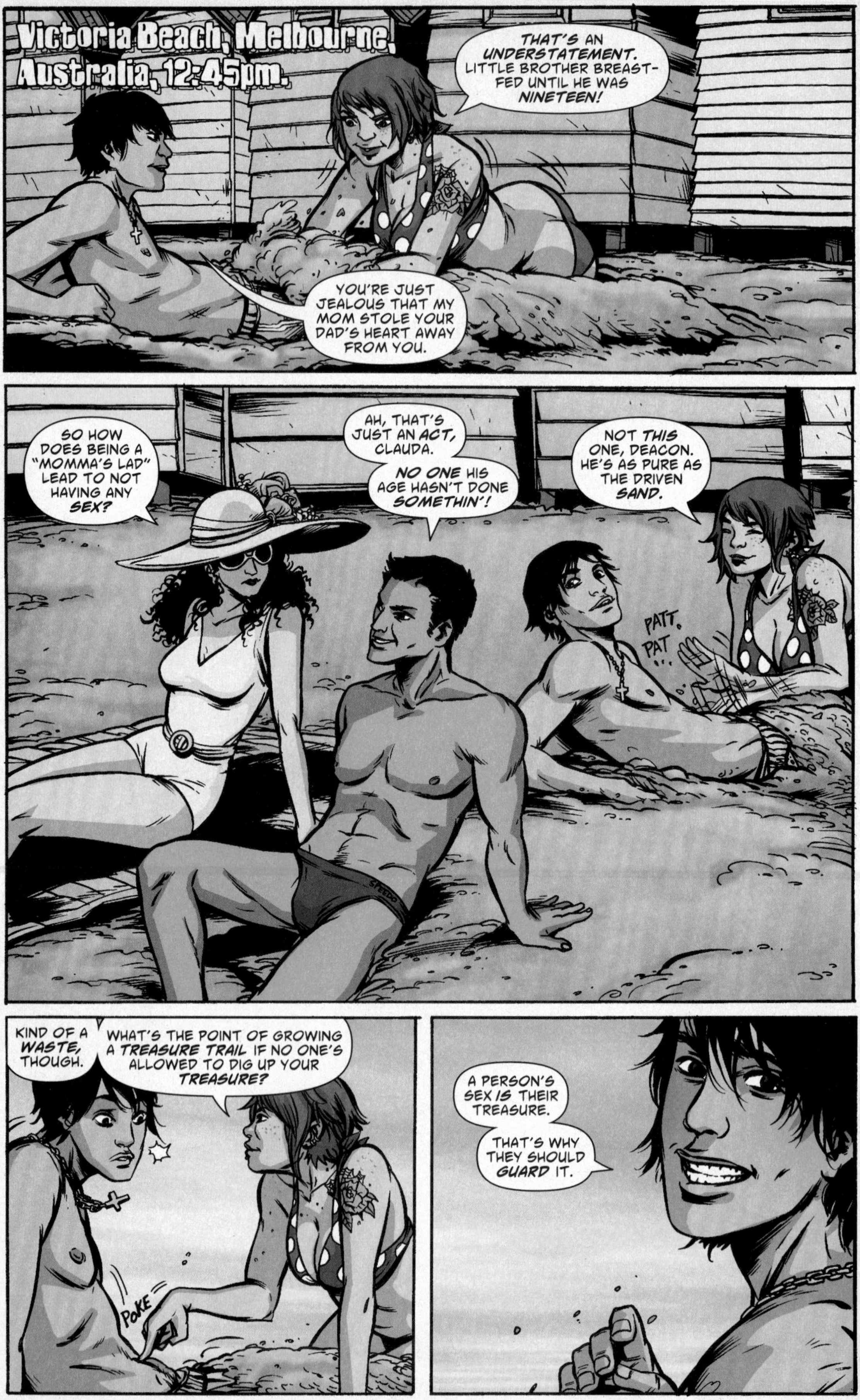

Victoria Beach, Melbourne, Australia, 12:45pm.
THAT'S AN UNDERSTATEMENT. LITTLE BROTHER BREAST-FED UNTIL HE WAS NINETEEN!
YOU'RE JUST JEALOUS THAT MY MOM STOLE YOUR DAD'S HEART AWAY FROM YOU.
SO HOW DOES BEING A "MOMMA'S LAD" LEAD TO NOT HAVING ANY SEX?
AH, THAT'S JUST AN ACT, CLAUDA.
NO ONE HIS AGE HASN'T DONE SOMETHIN'!
NOT THIS ONE, DEACON. HE'S AS PURE AS THE DRIVEN SAND.
PATT. PAT
SPEEDO
KIND OF A WASTE, THOUGH.
WHAT'S THE POINT OF GROWING A TREASURE TRAIL IF NO ONE'S ALLOWED TO DIG UP YOUR TREASURE?
POKE
A PERSON'S SEX IS THEIR TREASURE.
THAT'S WHY THEY SHOULD GUARD IT.

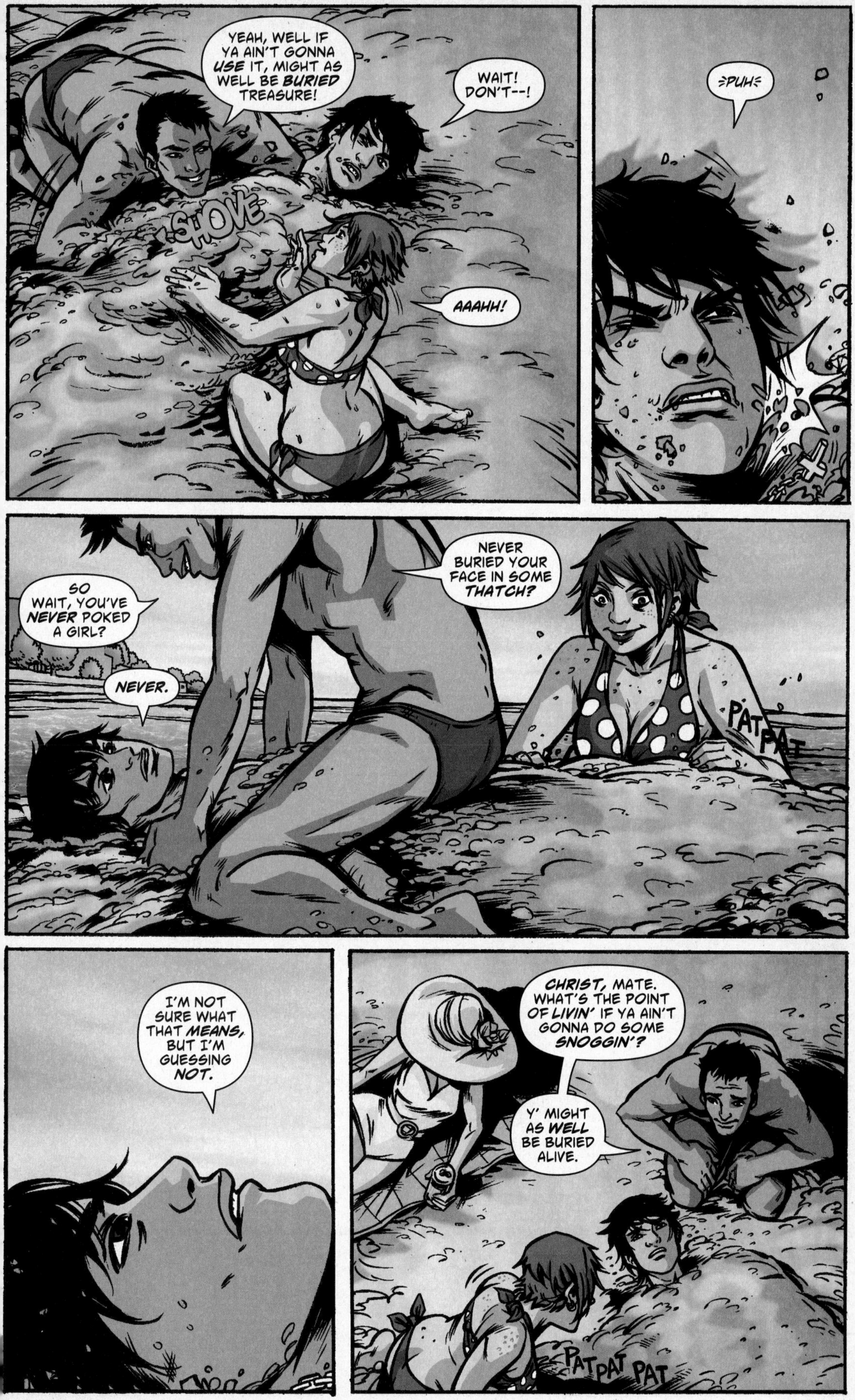
YEAH, WELL IF YA AIN'T GONNA USE IT, MIGHT AS WELL BE BURIED TREASURE!
WAIT! DON'T--!
SHOVE
AAAHH!
PUH
SO WAIT, YOU'VE NEVER POKED A GIRL?
NEVER.
NEVER BURIED YOUR FACE IN SOME THATCH?
PAT PAT
I'M NOT SURE WHAT THAT MEANS, BUT I'M GUESSING NOT.
CHRIST, MATE. WHAT'S THE POINT OF LIVIN' IF YA AIN'T GONNA DO SOME SNOGGIN'?
Y' MIGHT AS WELL BE BURIED ALIVE.
PAT PAT PAT

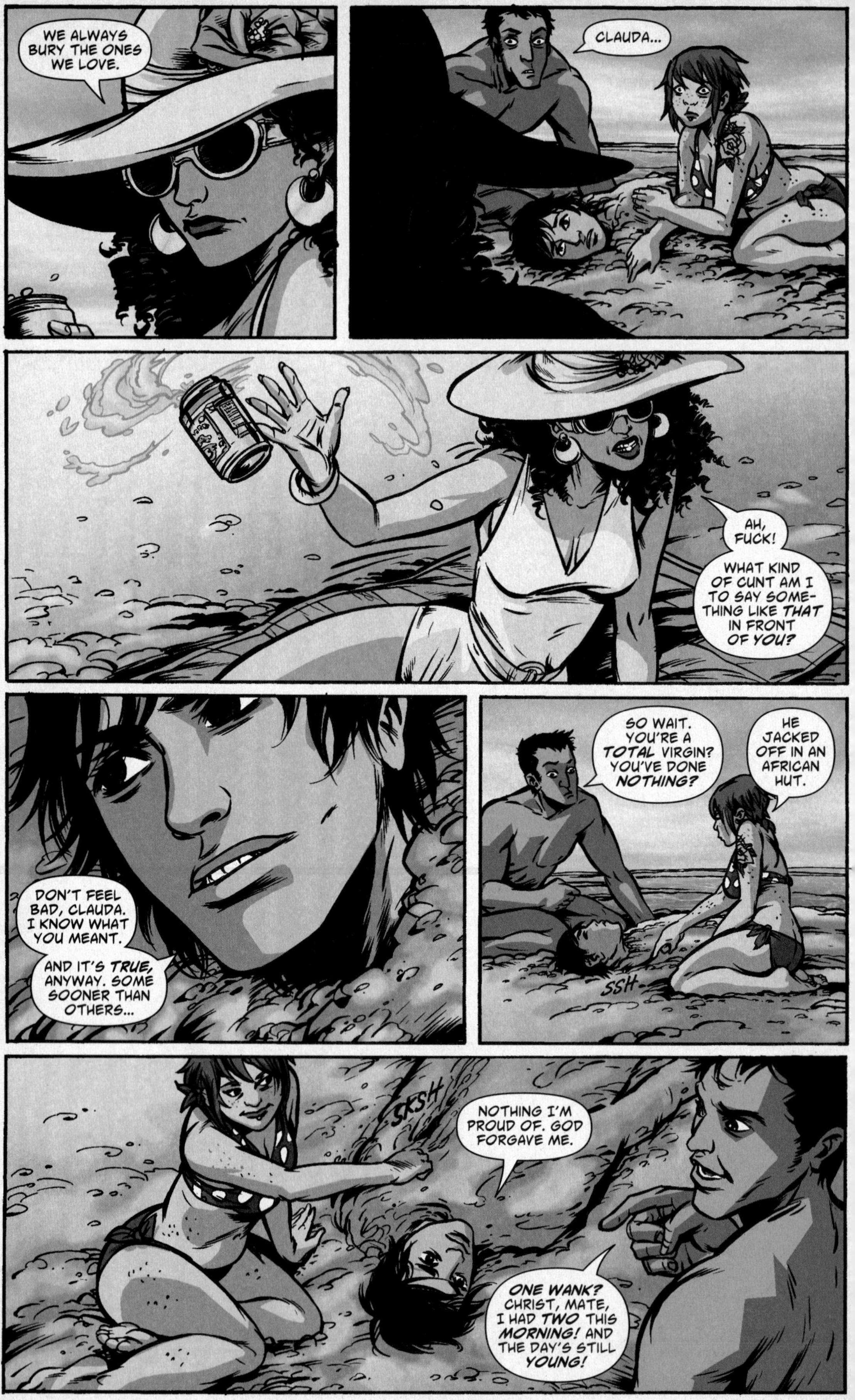
WE ALWAYS BURY THE ONES WE LOVE.
CLAUDA...
AH, FUCK!
WHAT KIND OF CUNT AM I TO SAY SOMETHING LIKE *THAT* IN FRONT OF *YOU?*
DON'T FEEL BAD, CLAUDA. I KNOW WHAT YOU MEANT.
AND IT'S *TRUE,* ANYWAY. SOME SOONER THAN OTHERS...
SO WAIT. YOU'RE A *TOTAL* VIRGIN? YOU'VE DONE *NOTHING?*
HE JACKED OFF IN AN AFRICAN HUT.
SSH
SKSH
NOTHING I'M PROUD OF. GOD FORGAVE ME.
ONE WANK? CHRIST, MATE, I HAD *TWO* THIS *MORNING!* AND THE DAY'S STILL *YOUNG!*

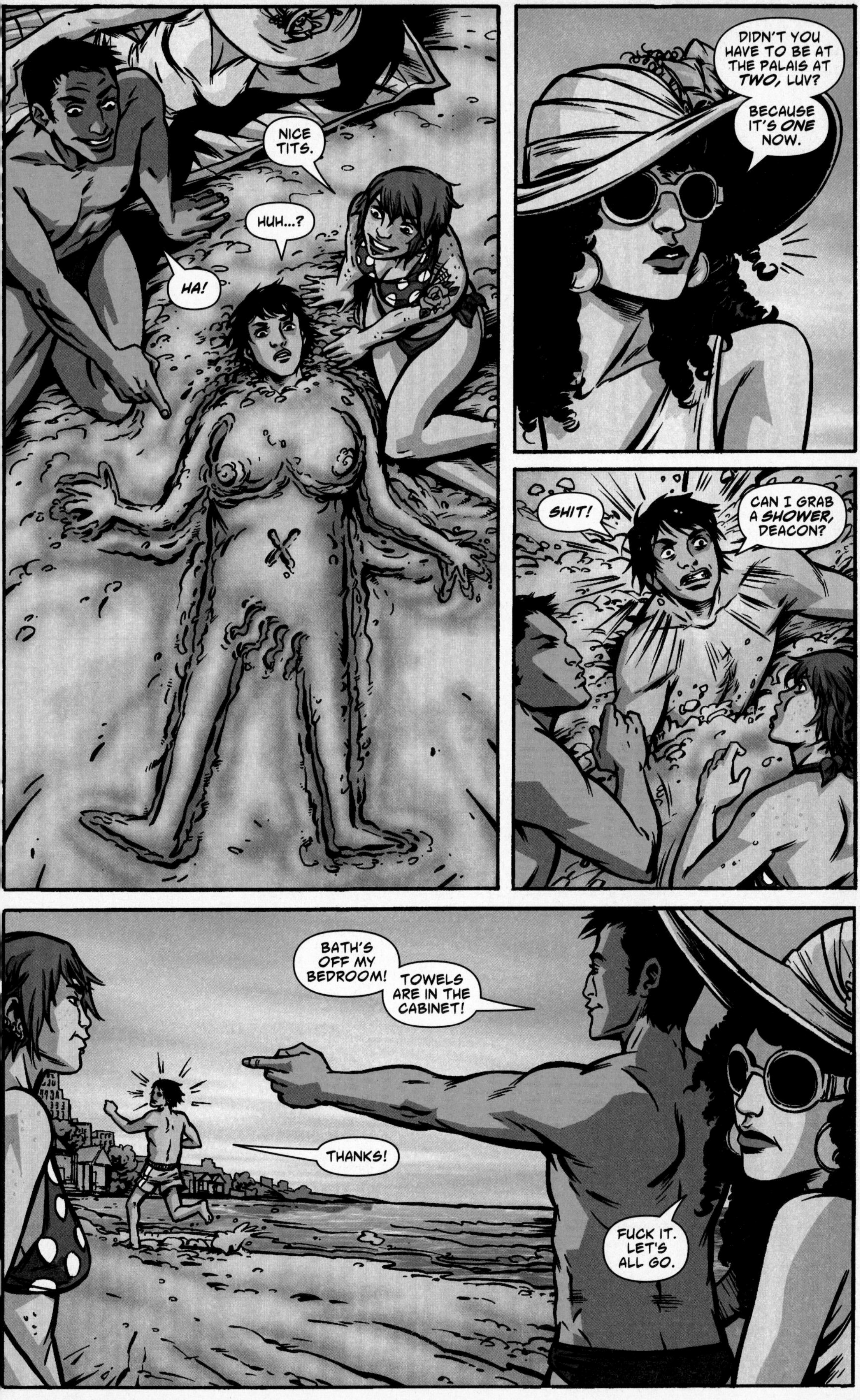
NICE TITS.
HUH...?
HA!
DIDN'T YOU HAVE TO BE AT THE PALAIS AT *TWO*, LUV?
BECAUSE IT'S *ONE* NOW.
SHIT!
CAN I GRAB A *SHOWER*, DEACON?
BATH'S OFF MY BEDROOM!
TOWELS ARE IN THE CABINET!
THANKS!
FUCK IT. LET'S ALL GO.

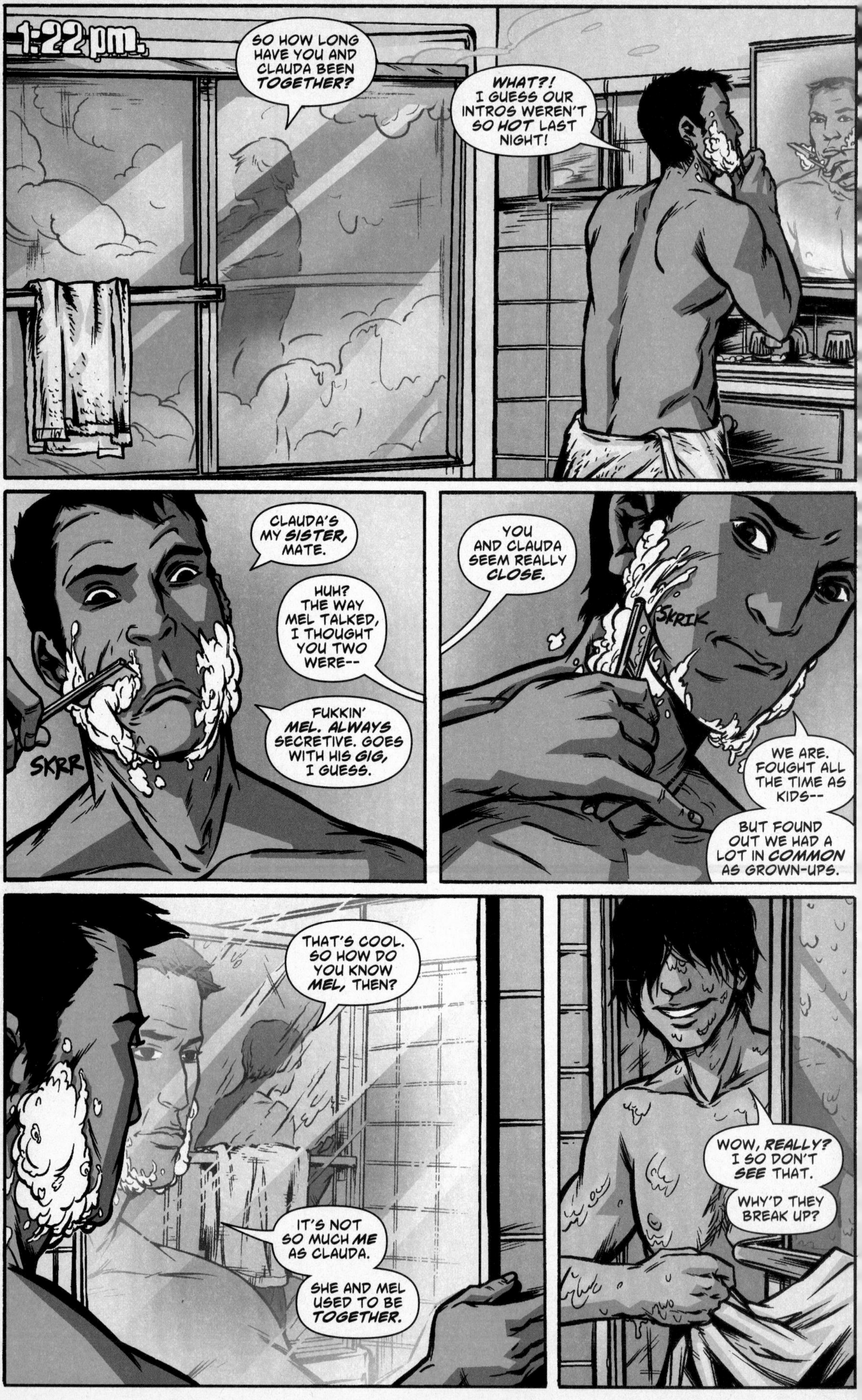
1:22 pm.
SO HOW LONG HAVE YOU AND CLAUDA BEEN TOGETHER?
WHAT?! I GUESS OUR INTROS WEREN'T SO HOT LAST NIGHT!
CLAUDA'S MY SISTER, MATE.
HUH? THE WAY MEL TALKED, I THOUGHT YOU TWO WERE--
FUKKIN' MEL. ALWAYS SECRETIVE. GOES WITH HIS GIG, I GUESS.
SKRR
YOU AND CLAUDA SEEM REALLY CLOSE.
SKRIK
WE ARE. FOUGHT ALL THE TIME AS KIDS--
BUT FOUND OUT WE HAD A LOT IN COMMON AS GROWN-UPS.
THAT'S COOL. SO HOW DO YOU KNOW MEL, THEN?
IT'S NOT SO MUCH ME AS CLAUDA.
SHE AND MEL USED TO BE TOGETHER.
WOW, REALLY? I SO DON'T SEE THAT.
WHY'D THEY BREAK UP?

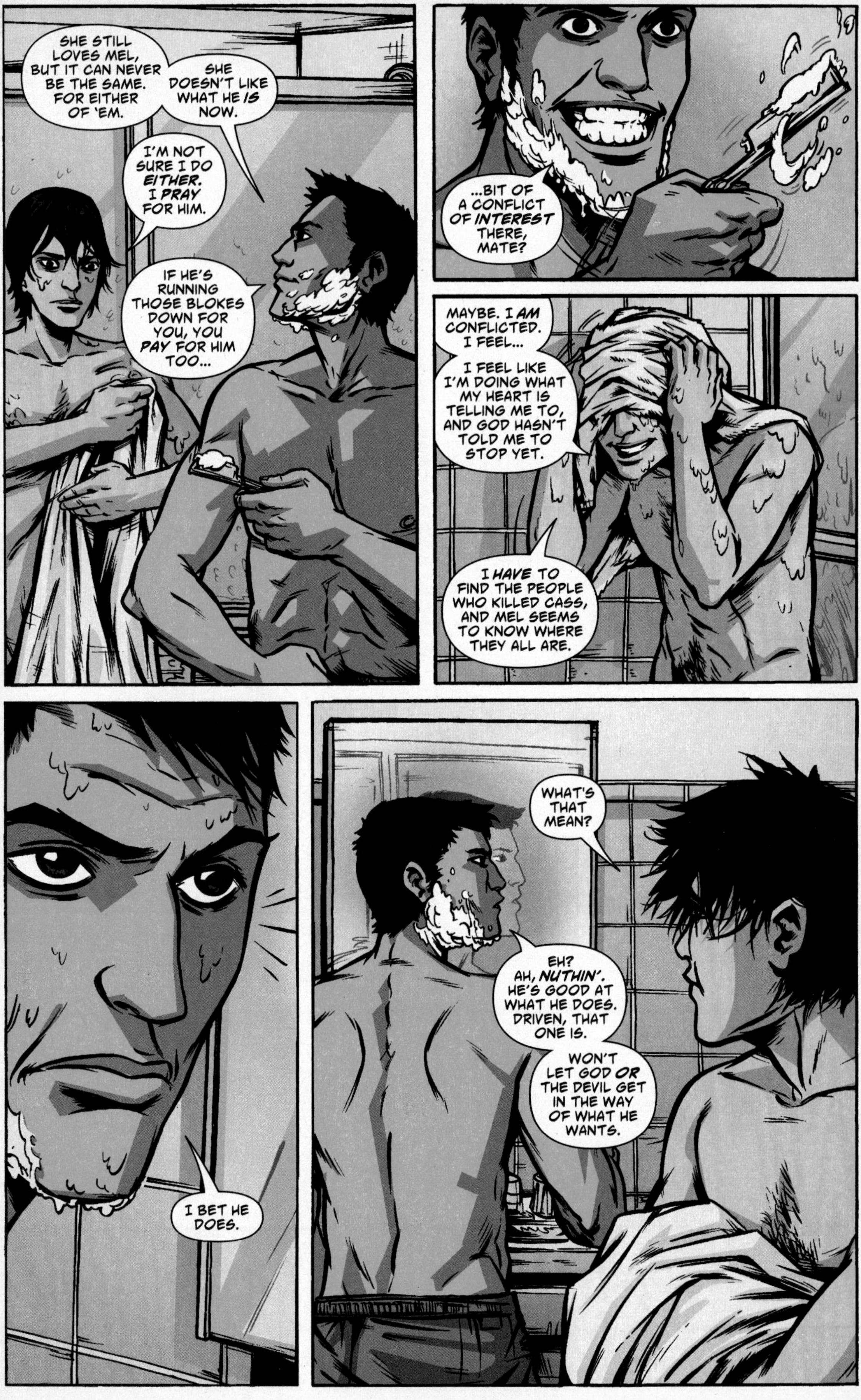
SHE STILL LOVES MEL, BUT IT CAN NEVER BE THE SAME. FOR EITHER OF 'EM.
SHE DOESN'T LIKE WHAT HE *IS* NOW.
I'M NOT SURE I DO *EITHER.* I *PRAY* FOR HIM.
IF HE'S RUNNING THOSE BLOKES DOWN FOR YOU, YOU *PAY* FOR HIM TOO...
...BIT OF A CONFLICT OF *INTEREST* THERE, MATE?
MAYBE. I *AM* CONFLICTED. I FEEL...
I FEEL LIKE I'M DOING WHAT MY HEART IS TELLING ME TO, AND GOD HASN'T TOLD ME TO STOP YET.
I *HAVE* TO FIND THE PEOPLE WHO KILLED CASS, AND MEL SEEMS TO KNOW WHERE THEY ALL ARE.
I BET HE DOES.
WHAT'S THAT MEAN?
EH? AH, *NUTHIN'*. HE'S GOOD AT WHAT HE DOES. DRIVEN, THAT ONE IS.
WON'T LET GOD *OR* THE DEVIL GET IN THE WAY OF WHAT HE WANTS.

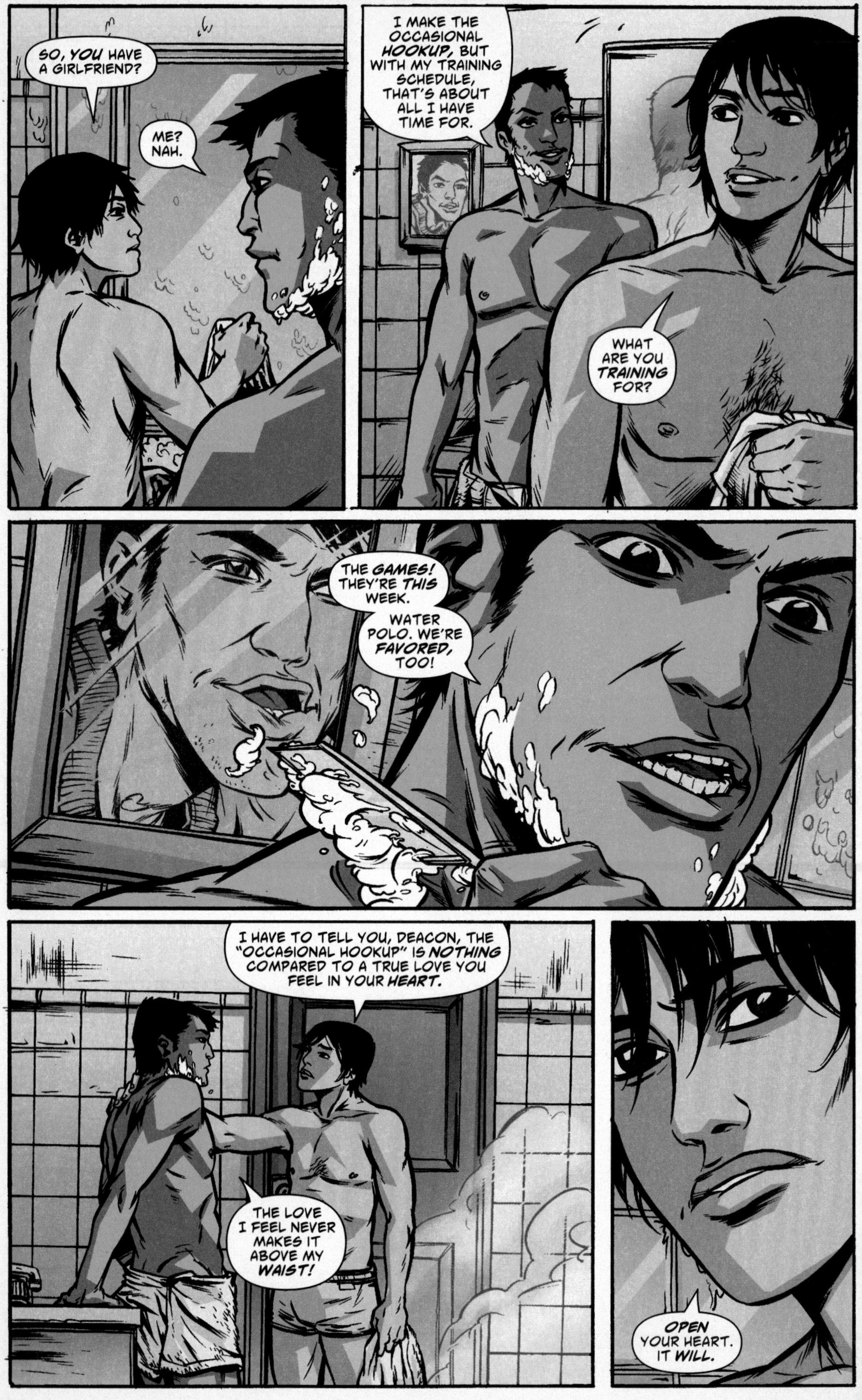
SO, YOU HAVE A GIRLFRIEND?
ME? NAH.
I MAKE THE OCCASIONAL HOOKUP, BUT WITH MY TRAINING SCHEDULE, THAT'S ABOUT ALL I HAVE TIME FOR.
WHAT ARE YOU TRAINING FOR?
THE GAMES! THEY'RE THIS WEEK.
WATER POLO. WE'RE FAVORED, TOO!
I HAVE TO TELL YOU, DEACON, THE "OCCASIONAL HOOKUP" IS NOTHING COMPARED TO A TRUE LOVE YOU FEEL IN YOUR HEART.
THE LOVE I FEEL NEVER MAKES IT ABOVE MY WAIST!
OPEN YOUR HEART. IT WILL.

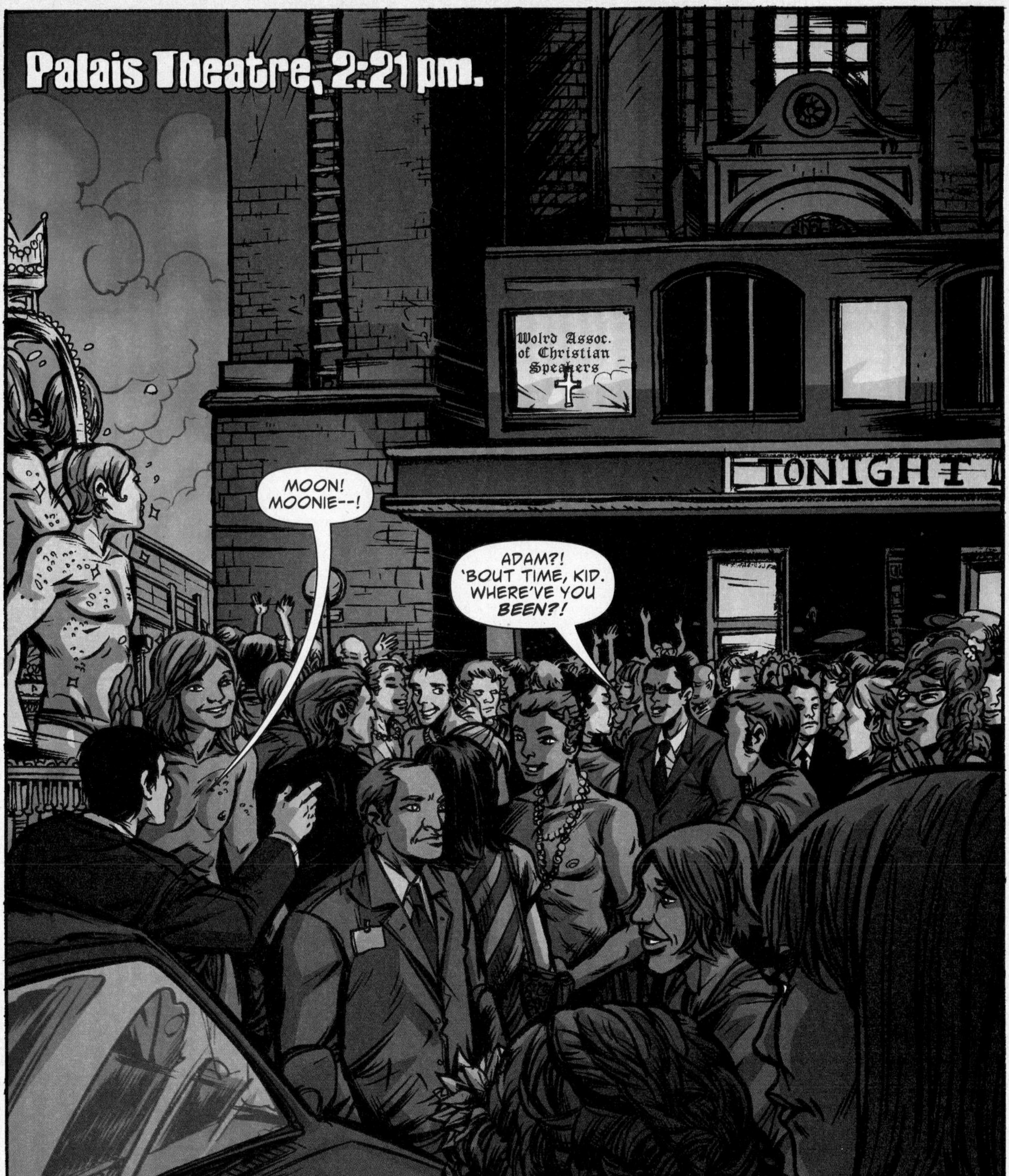
Palais Theatre, 2:21 pm.
Wolrd Assoc. of Christian Speakers
TONIGHT
MOON! MOONIE--!
ADAM?! 'BOUT TIME, KID. WHERE'VE YOU BEEN?!

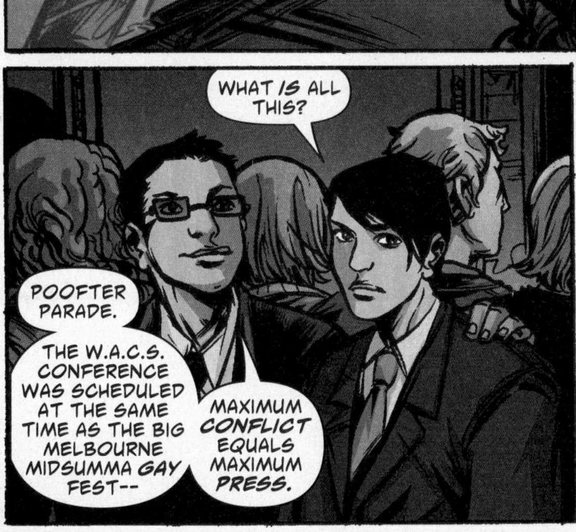
WHAT IS ALL THIS?
POOFTER PARADE.
THE W.A.C.S. CONFERENCE WAS SCHEDULED AT THE SAME TIME AS THE BIG MELBOURNE MIDSUMMA GAY FEST--
MAXIMUM CONFLICT EQUALS MAXIMUM PRESS.

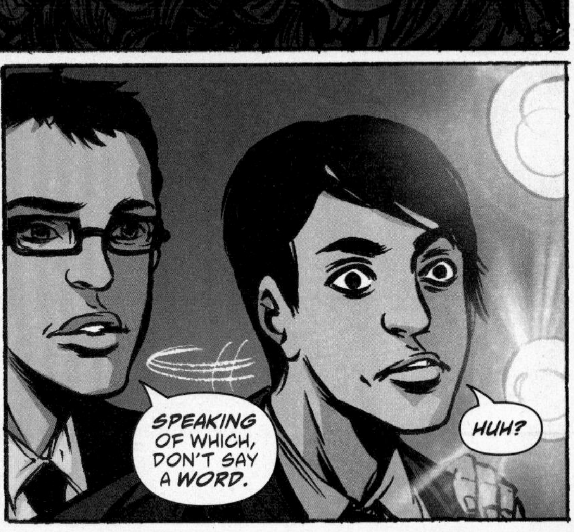
SPEAKING OF WHICH, DON'T SAY A WORD.
HUH?

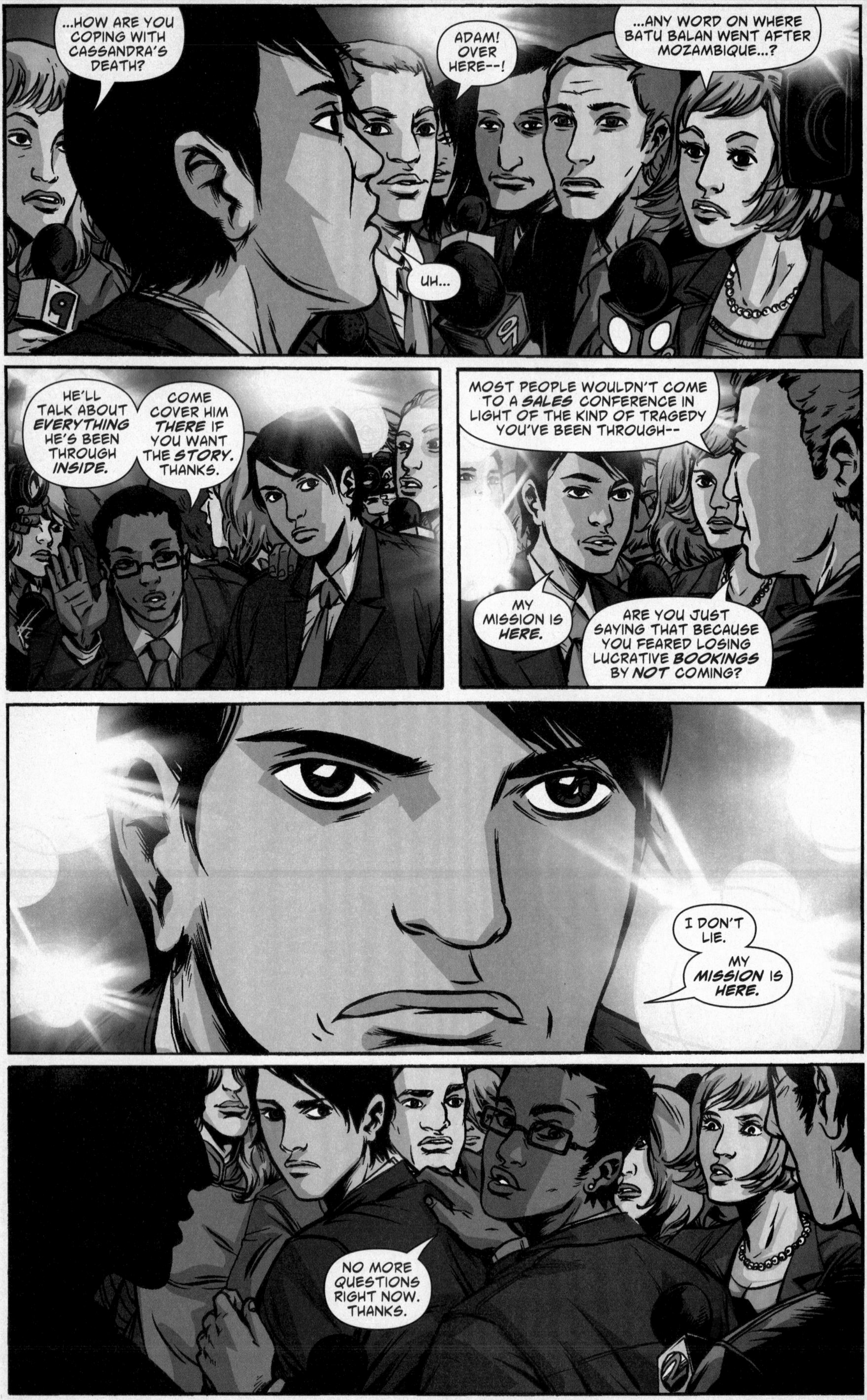
...HOW ARE YOU COPING WITH CASSANDRA'S DEATH?
ADAM! OVER HERE--!
...ANY WORD ON WHERE BATU BALAN WENT AFTER MOZAMBIQUE...?
UH...
HE'LL TALK ABOUT EVERYTHING HE'S BEEN THROUGH INSIDE.
COME COVER HIM THERE IF YOU WANT THE STORY. THANKS.
MOST PEOPLE WOULDN'T COME TO A SALES CONFERENCE IN LIGHT OF THE KIND OF TRAGEDY YOU'VE BEEN THROUGH--
MY MISSION IS HERE.
ARE YOU JUST SAYING THAT BECAUSE YOU FEARED LOSING LUCRATIVE BOOKINGS BY NOT COMING?
I DON'T LIE.
MY MISSION IS HERE.
NO MORE QUESTIONS RIGHT NOW. THANKS.

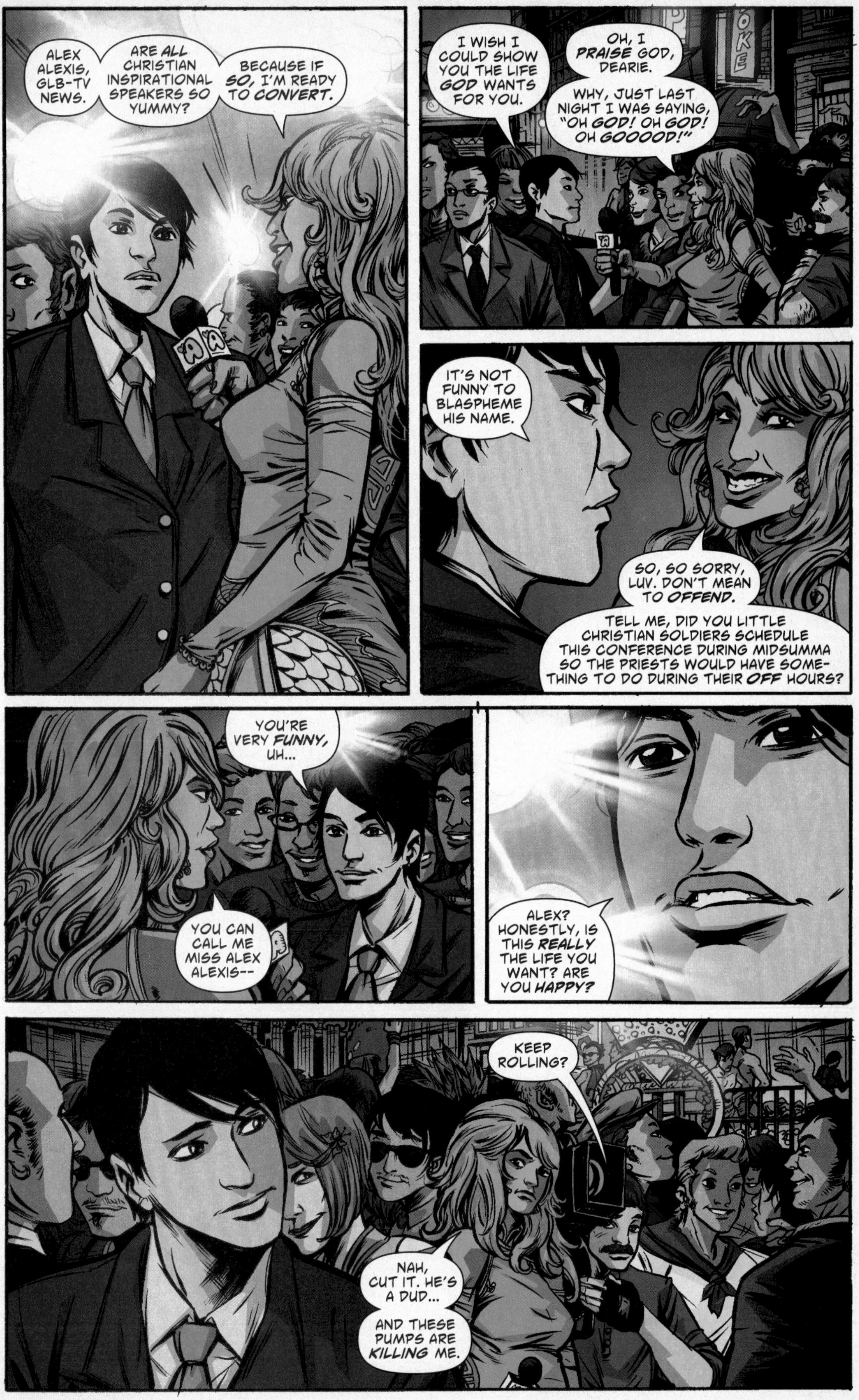
ALEX ALEXIS, GLB-TV NEWS.
ARE ALL CHRISTIAN INSPIRATIONAL SPEAKERS SO YUMMY?
BECAUSE IF SO, I'M READY TO CONVERT.
I WISH I COULD SHOW YOU THE LIFE GOD WANTS FOR YOU.
OH, I PRAISE GOD, DEARIE.
WHY, JUST LAST NIGHT I WAS SAYING, "OH GOD! OH GOD! OH GOOOOD!"
IT'S NOT FUNNY TO BLASPHEME HIS NAME.
SO, SO SORRY, LUV. DON'T MEAN TO OFFEND.
TELL ME, DID YOU LITTLE CHRISTIAN SOLDIERS SCHEDULE THIS CONFERENCE DURING MIDSUMMA SO THE PRIESTS WOULD HAVE SOME-THING TO DO DURING THEIR OFF HOURS?
YOU'RE VERY FUNNY, UH...
YOU CAN CALL ME MISS ALEX ALEXIS--
ALEX? HONESTLY, IS THIS REALLY THE LIFE YOU WANT? ARE YOU HAPPY?
KEEP ROLLING?
NAH, CUT IT. HE'S A DUD...
AND THESE PUMPS ARE KILLING ME.

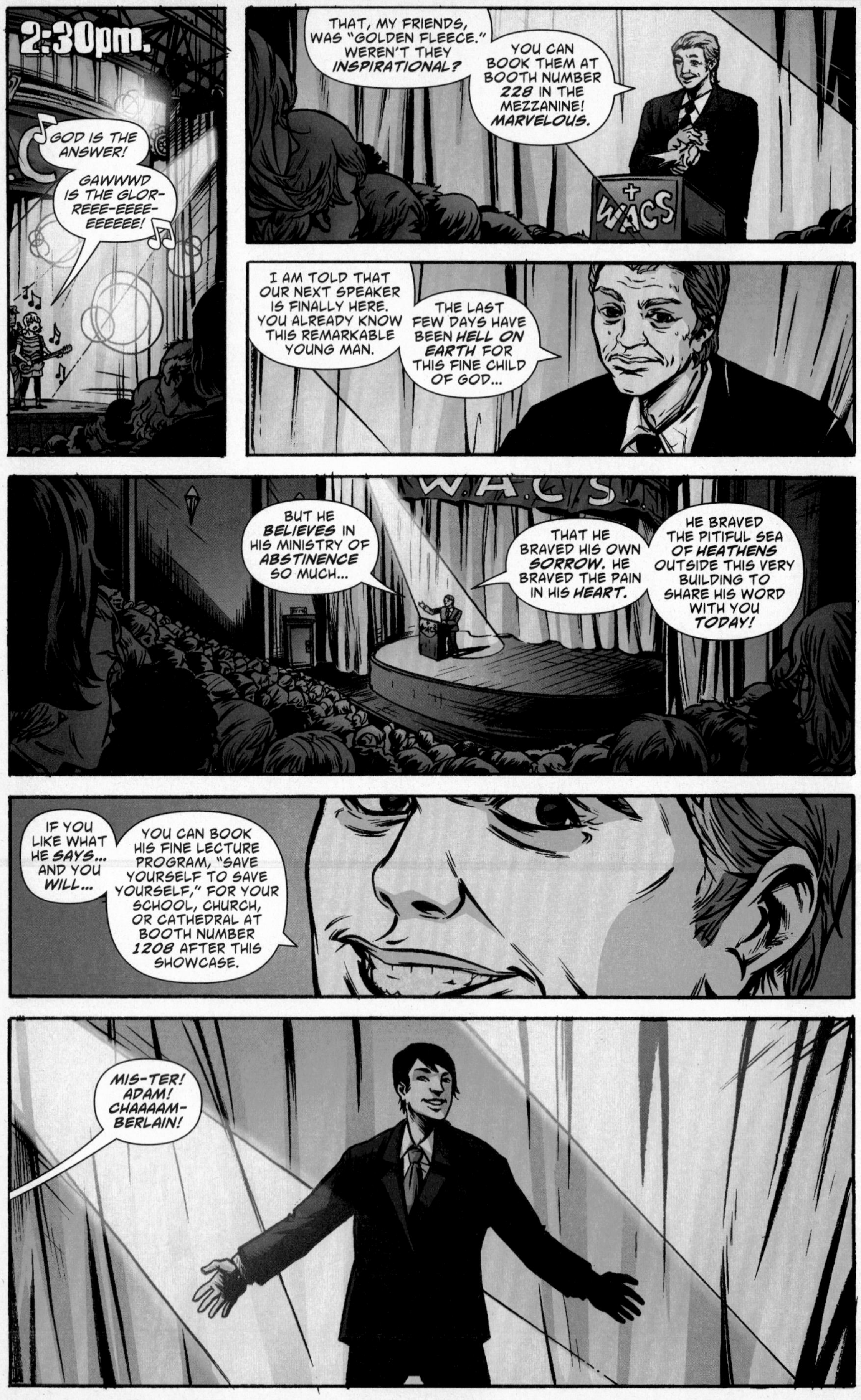
2:30pm.
GOD IS THE ANSWER!
GAWWWD IS THE GLOR-REEE-EEEE-EEEEEE!
THAT, MY FRIENDS, WAS "GOLDEN FLEECE." WEREN'T THEY INSPIRATIONAL?
YOU CAN BOOK THEM AT BOOTH NUMBER 228 IN THE MEZZANINE! MARVELOUS.
WACS
I AM TOLD THAT OUR NEXT SPEAKER IS FINALLY HERE. YOU ALREADY KNOW THIS REMARKABLE YOUNG MAN.
THE LAST FEW DAYS HAVE BEEN HELL ON EARTH FOR THIS FINE CHILD OF GOD...
W.A.C.S
BUT HE BELIEVES IN HIS MINISTRY OF ABSTINENCE SO MUCH...
THAT HE BRAVED HIS OWN SORROW. HE BRAVED THE PAIN IN HIS HEART.
HE BRAVED THE PITIFUL SEA OF HEATHENS OUTSIDE THIS VERY BUILDING TO SHARE HIS WORD WITH YOU TODAY!
IF YOU LIKE WHAT HE SAYS... AND YOU WILL...
YOU CAN BOOK HIS FINE LECTURE PROGRAM, "SAVE YOURSELF TO SAVE YOURSELF," FOR YOUR SCHOOL, CHURCH, OR CATHEDRAL AT BOOTH NUMBER 1208 AFTER THIS SHOWCASE.
MIS-TER! ADAM! CHAAAAM-BERLAIN!

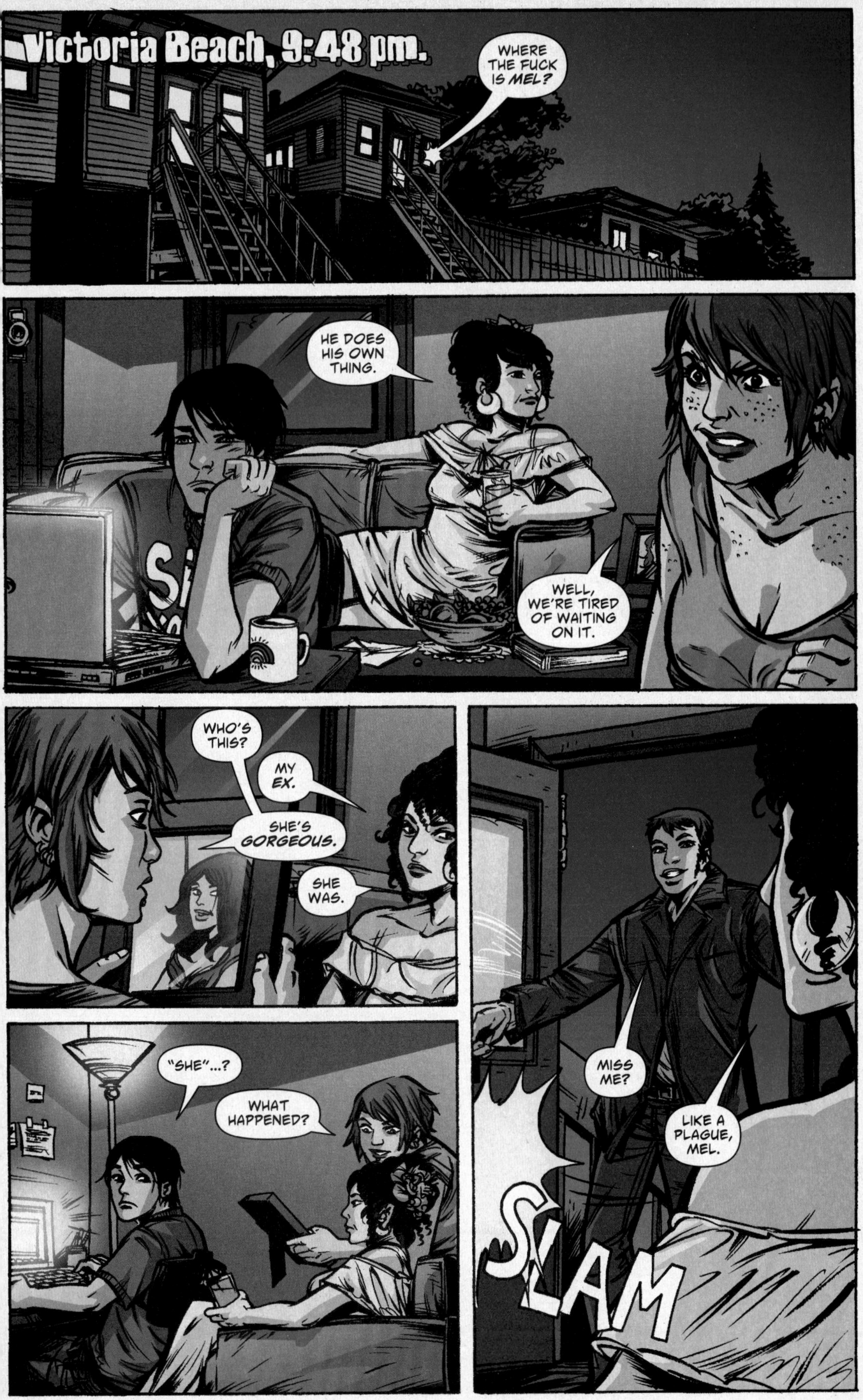

Victoria Beach, 9:48 pm.
WHERE THE FUCK IS MEL?
HE DOES HIS OWN THING.
WELL, WE'RE TIRED OF WAITING ON IT.
WHO'S THIS?
MY EX.
SHE'S GORGEOUS.
SHE WAS.
"SHE"...?
WHAT HAPPENED?
MISS ME?
LIKE A PLAGUE, MEL.
SLAM

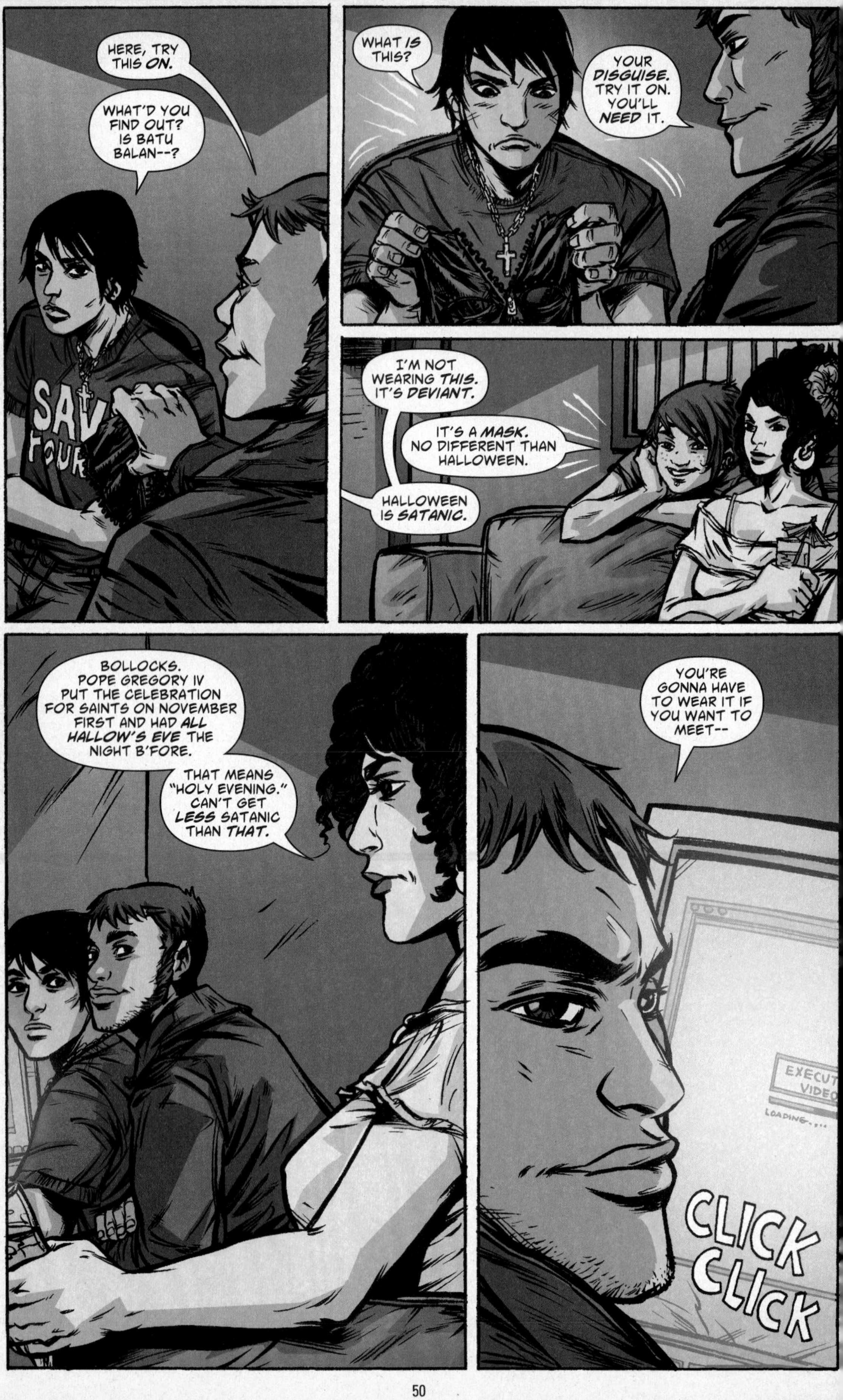
HERE, TRY THIS ON.
WHAT'D YOU FIND OUT? IS BATU BALAN--?
WHAT IS THIS?
YOUR DISGUISE. TRY IT ON. YOU'LL NEED IT.
I'M NOT WEARING THIS. IT'S DEVIANT.
IT'S A MASK. NO DIFFERENT THAN HALLOWEEN.
HALLOWEEN IS SATANIC.
BOLLOCKS. POPE GREGORY IV PUT THE CELEBRATION FOR SAINTS ON NOVEMBER FIRST AND HAD ALL HALLOW'S EVE THE NIGHT B'FORE.
THAT MEANS "HOLY EVENING." CAN'T GET LESS SATANIC THAN THAT.
YOU'RE GONNA HAVE TO WEAR IT IF YOU WANT TO MEET--
CLICK CLICK

HIM.

WHAT IS THIS, SOME KIND OF PORNO SITE YOU...?

WATCH.

WAIT... WHAT IS THAT...?

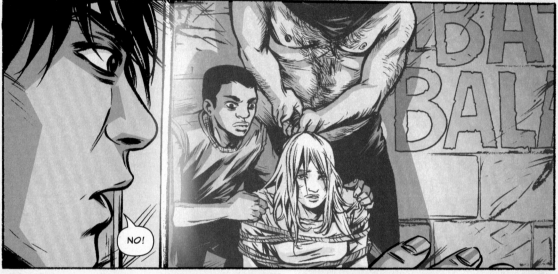

NO!

I CAN'T LOOK AT THAT!

ADAM...?

CASSIE...?

I DON'T WANT TO SEE THIS! IT'S *TOO REAL*.

IT'S NOT REAL AT ALL *UNTIL* YOU SEE IT.

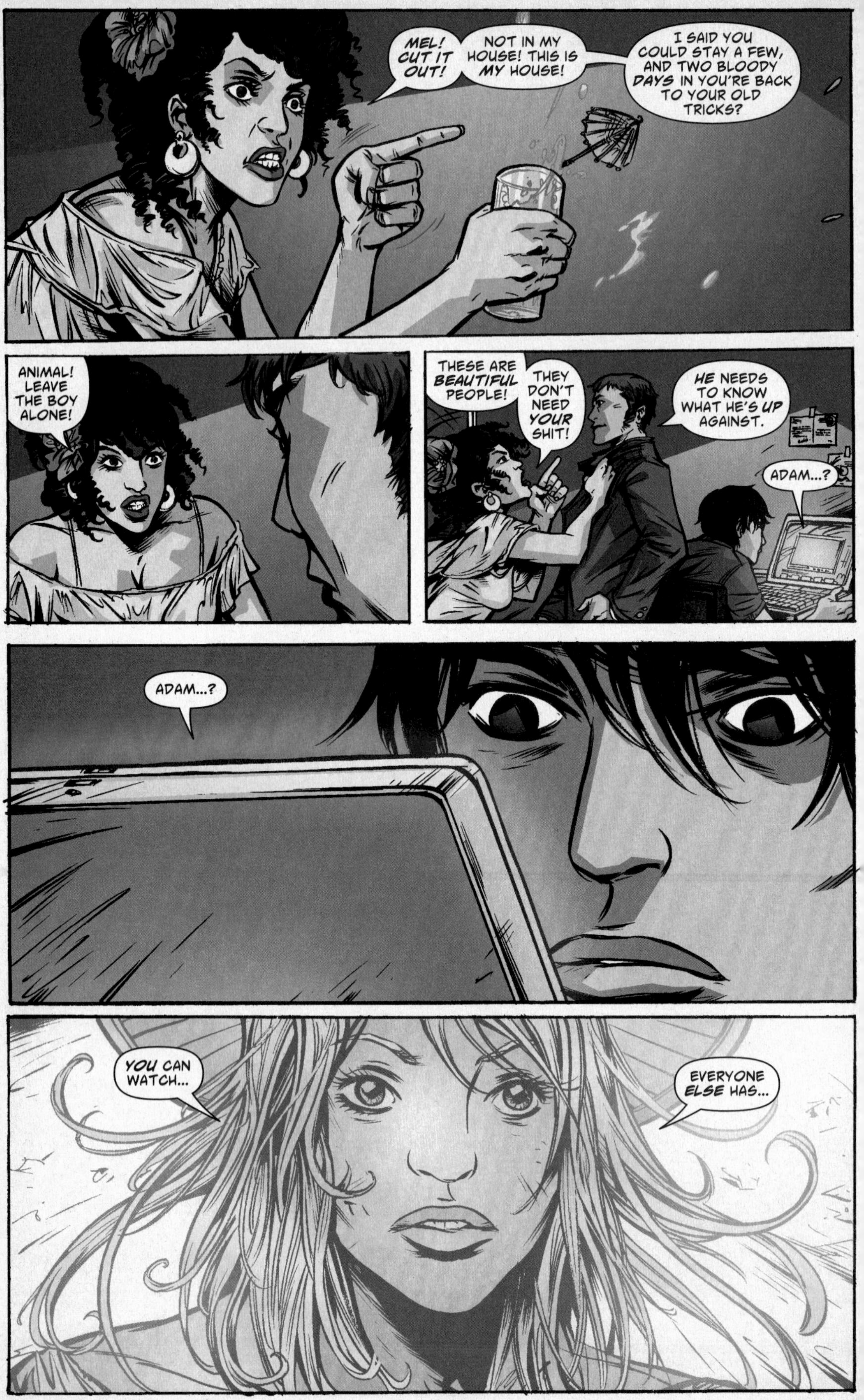
MEL! CUT IT OUT!
NOT IN MY HOUSE! THIS IS MY HOUSE!
I SAID YOU COULD STAY A FEW, AND TWO BLOODY DAYS IN YOU'RE BACK TO YOUR OLD TRICKS?
ANIMAL! LEAVE THE BOY ALONE!
THESE ARE BEAUTIFUL PEOPLE!
THEY DON'T NEED YOUR SHIT!
HE NEEDS TO KNOW WHAT HE'S UP AGAINST.
ADAM...?
ADAM...?
YOU CAN WATCH...
EVERYONE ELSE HAS...

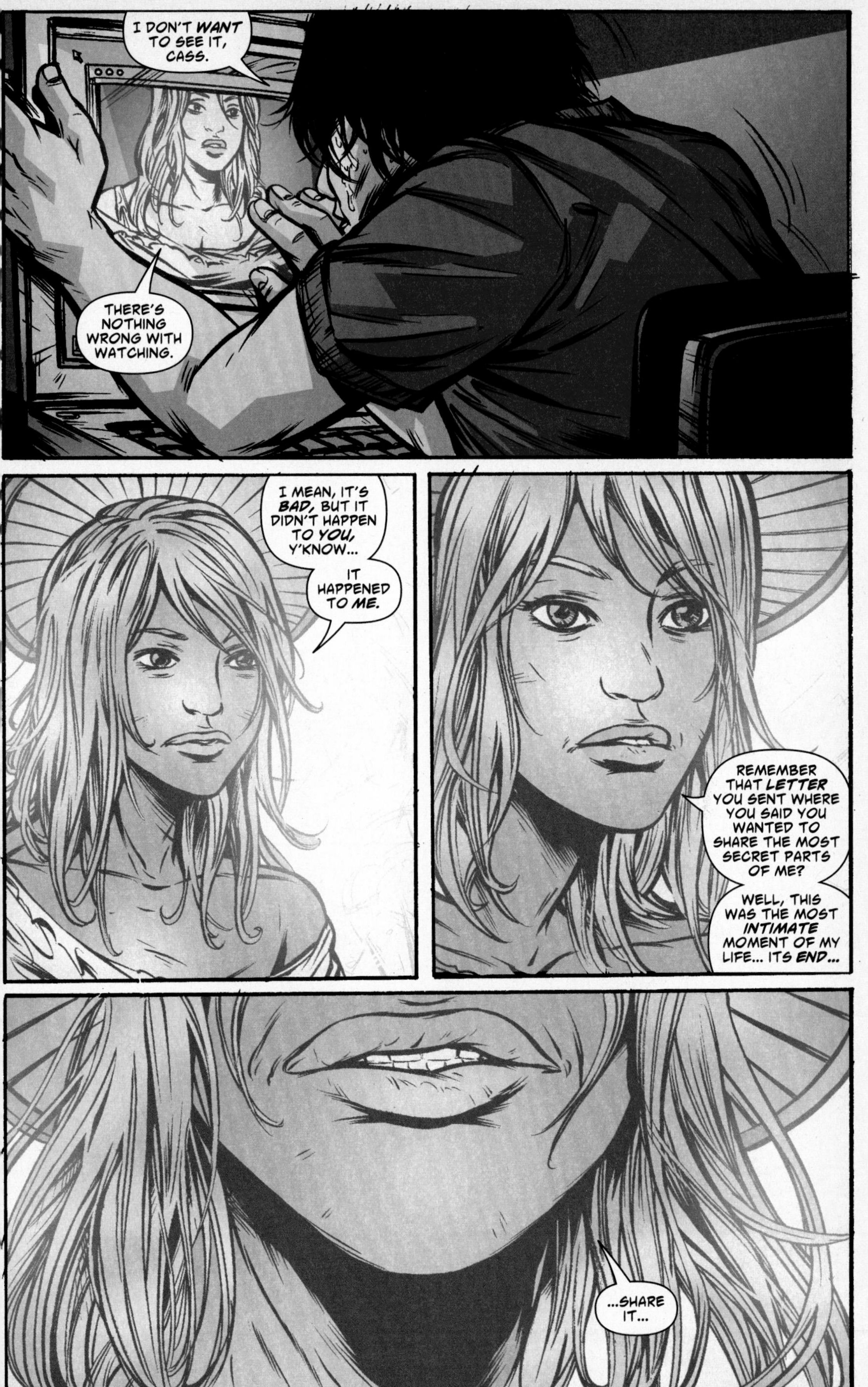
I DON'T WANT TO SEE IT, CASS.
THERE'S NOTHING WRONG WITH WATCHING.
I MEAN, IT'S BAD, BUT IT DIDN'T HAPPEN TO YOU, Y'KNOW...
IT HAPPENED TO ME.
REMEMBER THAT LETTER YOU SENT WHERE YOU SAID YOU WANTED TO SHARE THE MOST SECRET PARTS OF ME?
WELL, THIS WAS THE MOST INTIMATE MOMENT OF MY LIFE... ITS END...
...SHARE IT...

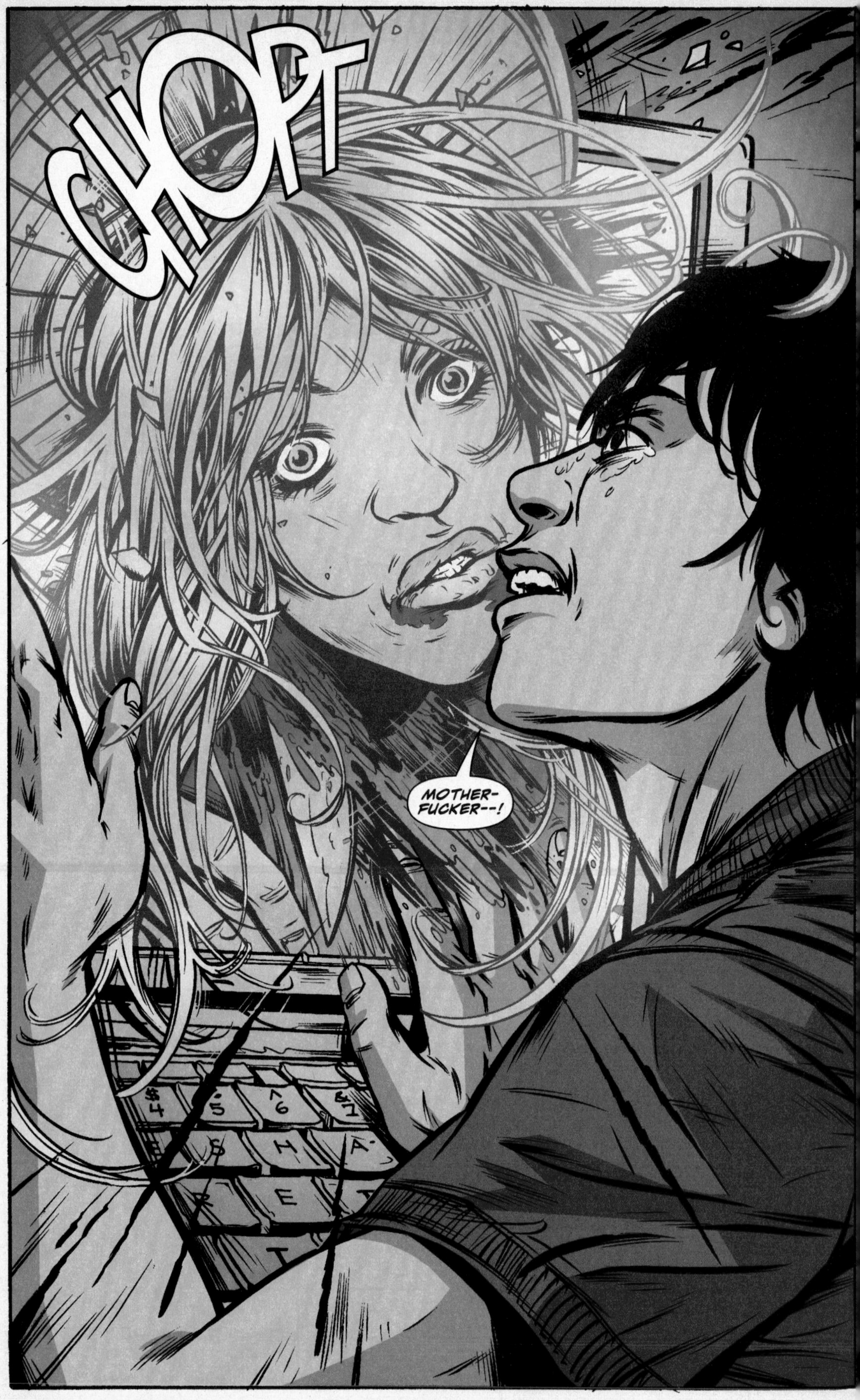
CHOP!
MOTHER-FUCKER--!

CHAPTER THREE

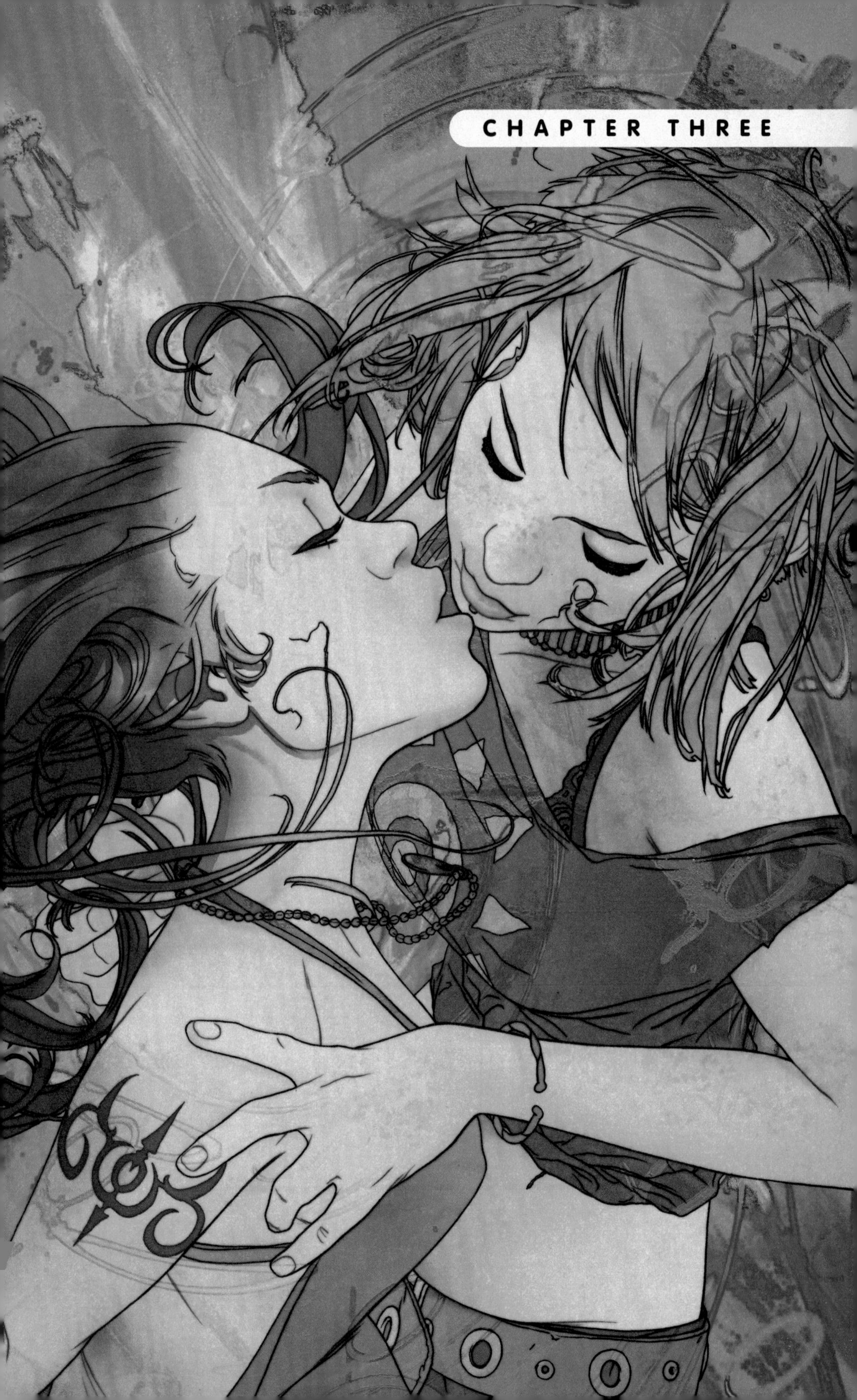

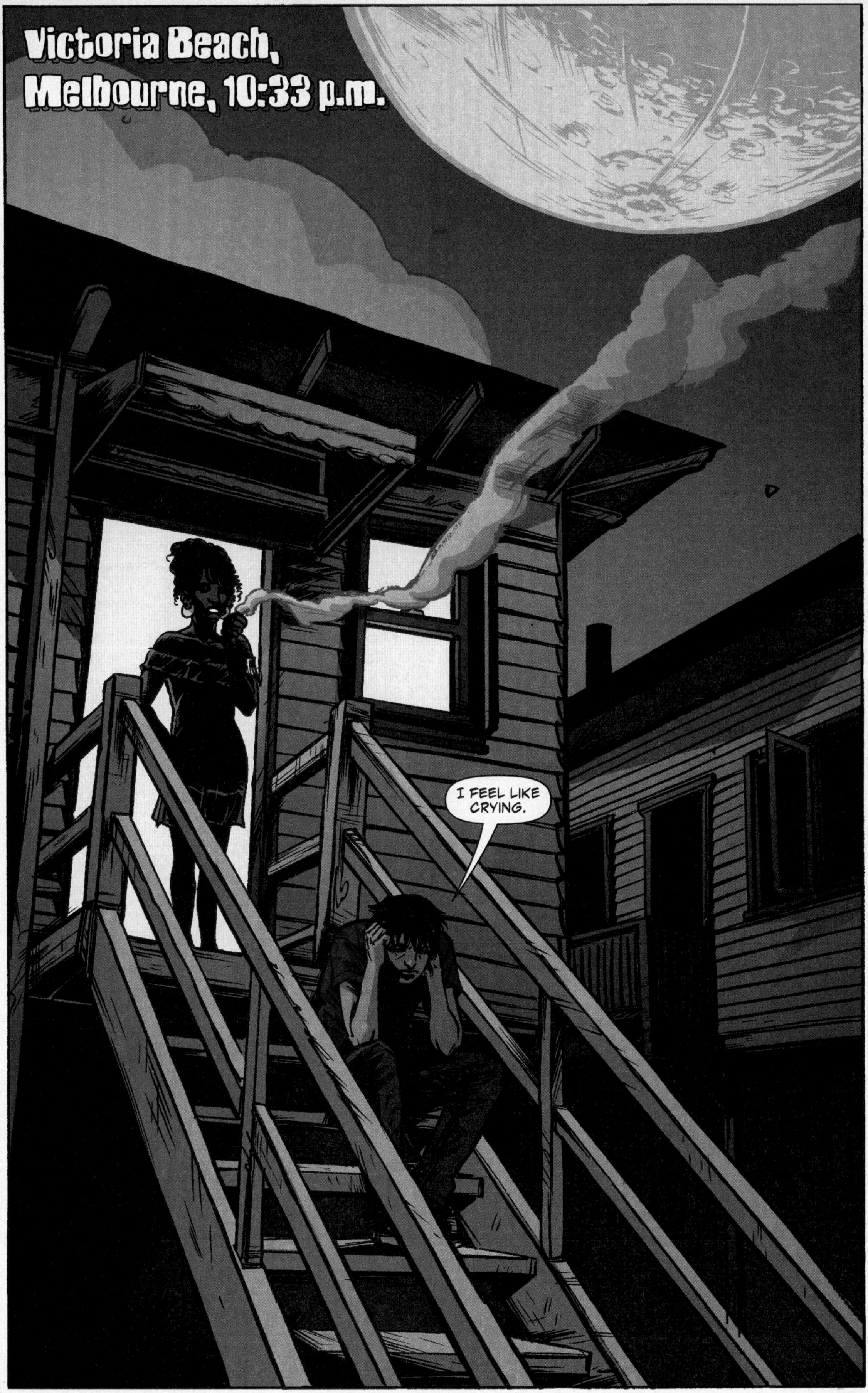
Victoria Beach, Melbourne, 10:33 p.m.
I FEEL LIKE CRYING.

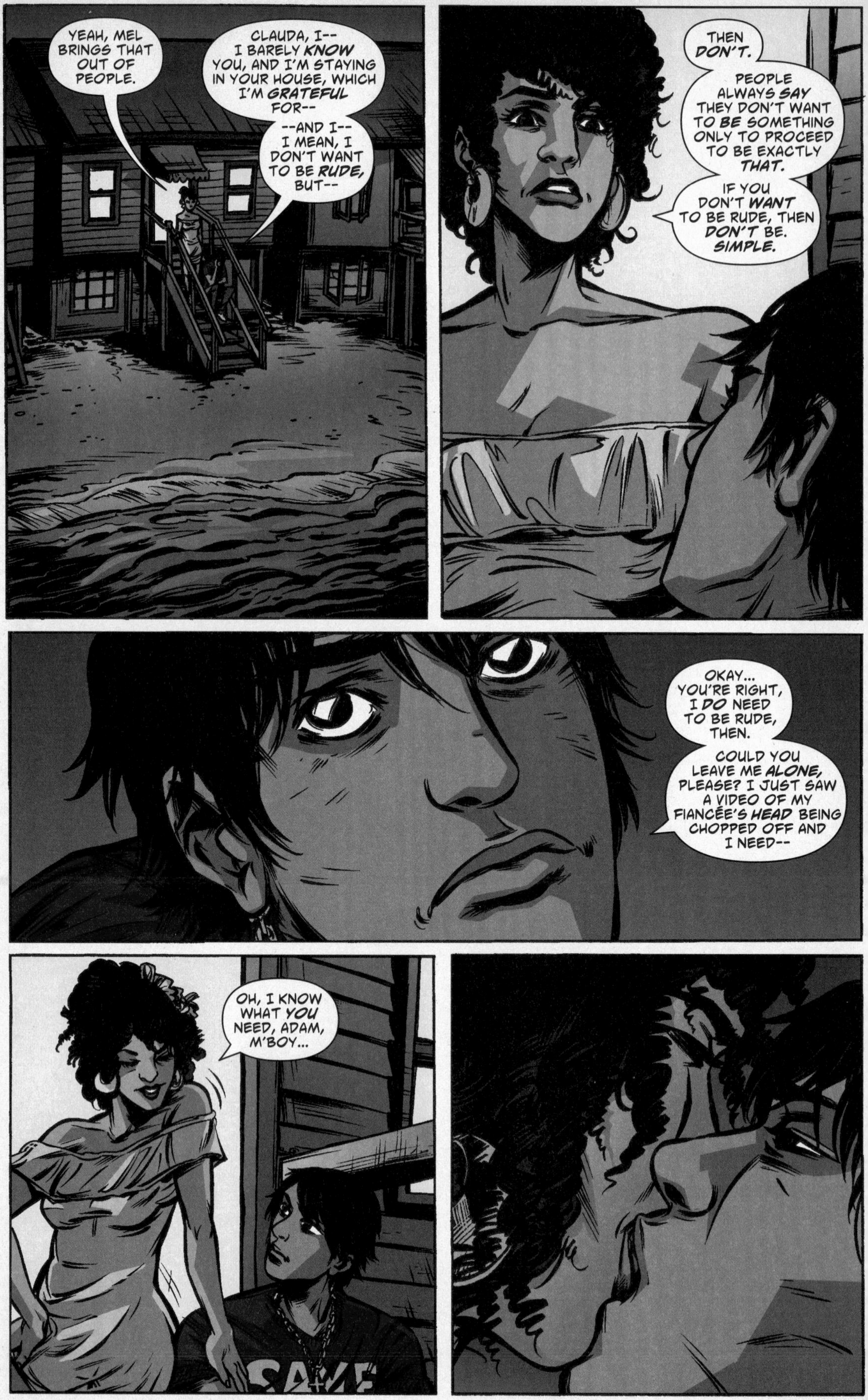
YEAH, MEL BRINGS THAT OUT OF PEOPLE.
CLAUDA, I-- I BARELY KNOW YOU, AND I'M STAYING IN YOUR HOUSE, WHICH I'M GRATEFUL FOR--
--AND I-- I MEAN, I DON'T WANT TO BE RUDE, BUT--
THEN DON'T.
PEOPLE ALWAYS SAY THEY DON'T WANT TO BE SOMETHING ONLY TO PROCEED TO BE EXACTLY THAT.
IF YOU DON'T WANT TO BE RUDE, THEN DON'T BE. SIMPLE.
OKAY... YOU'RE RIGHT, I DO NEED TO BE RUDE, THEN.
COULD YOU LEAVE ME ALONE, PLEASE? I JUST SAW A VIDEO OF MY FIANCÉE'S HEAD BEING CHOPPED OFF AND I NEED--
OH, I KNOW WHAT YOU NEED, ADAM, M'BOY...

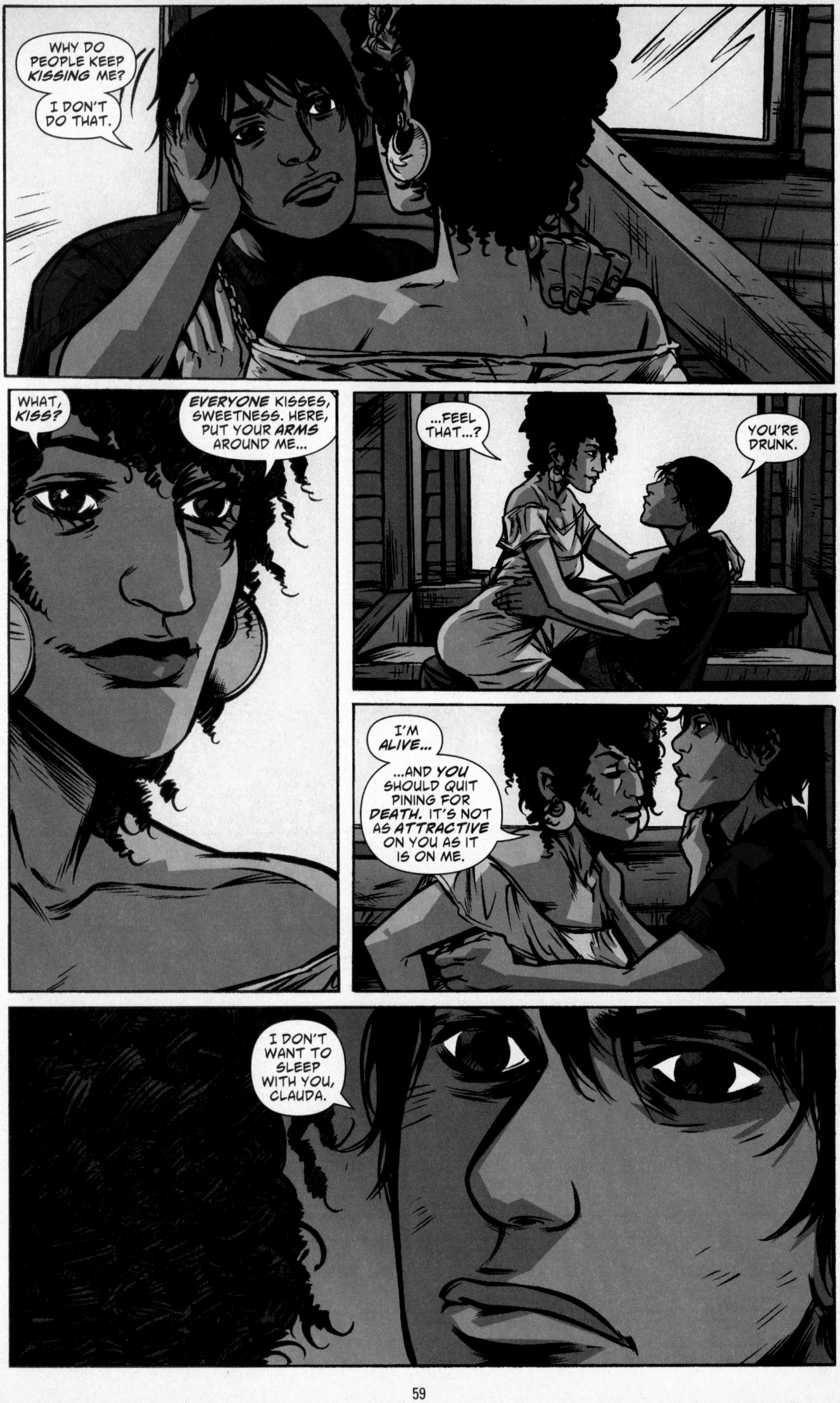
WHY DO PEOPLE KEEP KISSING ME?
I DON'T DO THAT.
WHAT, KISS?
EVERYONE KISSES, SWEETNESS. HERE, PUT YOUR ARMS AROUND ME...
...FEEL THAT...?
YOU'RE DRUNK.
I'M ALIVE...
...AND YOU SHOULD QUIT PINING FOR DEATH. IT'S NOT AS ATTRACTIVE ON YOU AS IT IS ON ME.
I DON'T WANT TO SLEEP WITH YOU, CLAUDA.

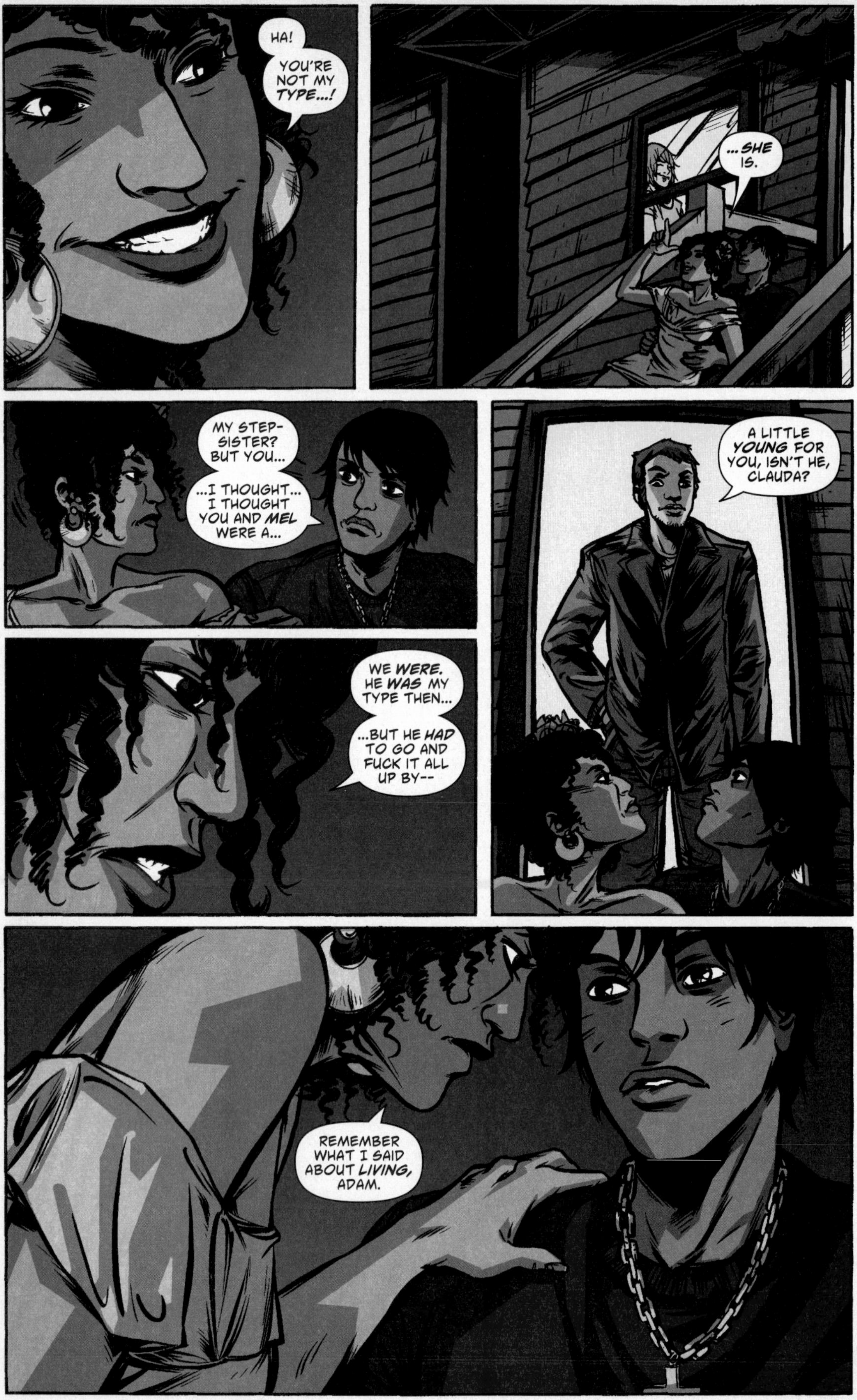
HA!
YOU'RE NOT MY *TYPE...!*
...*SHE* IS.
MY STEP-SISTER? BUT YOU...
...I THOUGHT... I THOUGHT YOU AND *MEL* WERE A...
A LITTLE *YOUNG* FOR YOU, ISN'T HE, CLAUDA?
WE *WERE.* HE *WAS* MY TYPE THEN...
...BUT HE *HAD* TO GO AND FUCK IT ALL UP BY--
REMEMBER WHAT I SAID ABOUT *LIVING,* ADAM.

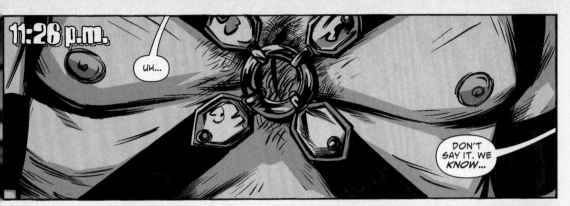

UH...

DON'T SAY IT. WE *KNOW*...

...YOU FEEL LIKE A *TWAT*.

...I JUST CAN'T BELIEVE WE'RE FINALLY GONNA GET OUT AND *PARTY*.

OF COURSE, JUST *MY* LUCK-- I'M GOING TO A CLUB WHERE *NO ONE* WILL HIT ON ME-- WHICH IS KINDA JUST LIKE *MIAMI*...

...BUT *YOU*, BROTHER MINE, YOU'RE GOING TO BE THE BELLE OF THE BALL!

AND BY "BALL," I *DO* MEAN *TESTICLE*.

INHALE.

AHH! CYNDI, IT'S TOO *TIGHT*!

THAT'S WHAT *SHE* SAID...

TUG

NOW, I'M TOO KNOWN AROUND THE CLUB, SO I WON'T BE INSIDE WITH YOU.

YOU'RE SENDING ME INTO A GAY CLUB DRESSED LIKE THIS *ALONE*?

NOT ALONE--

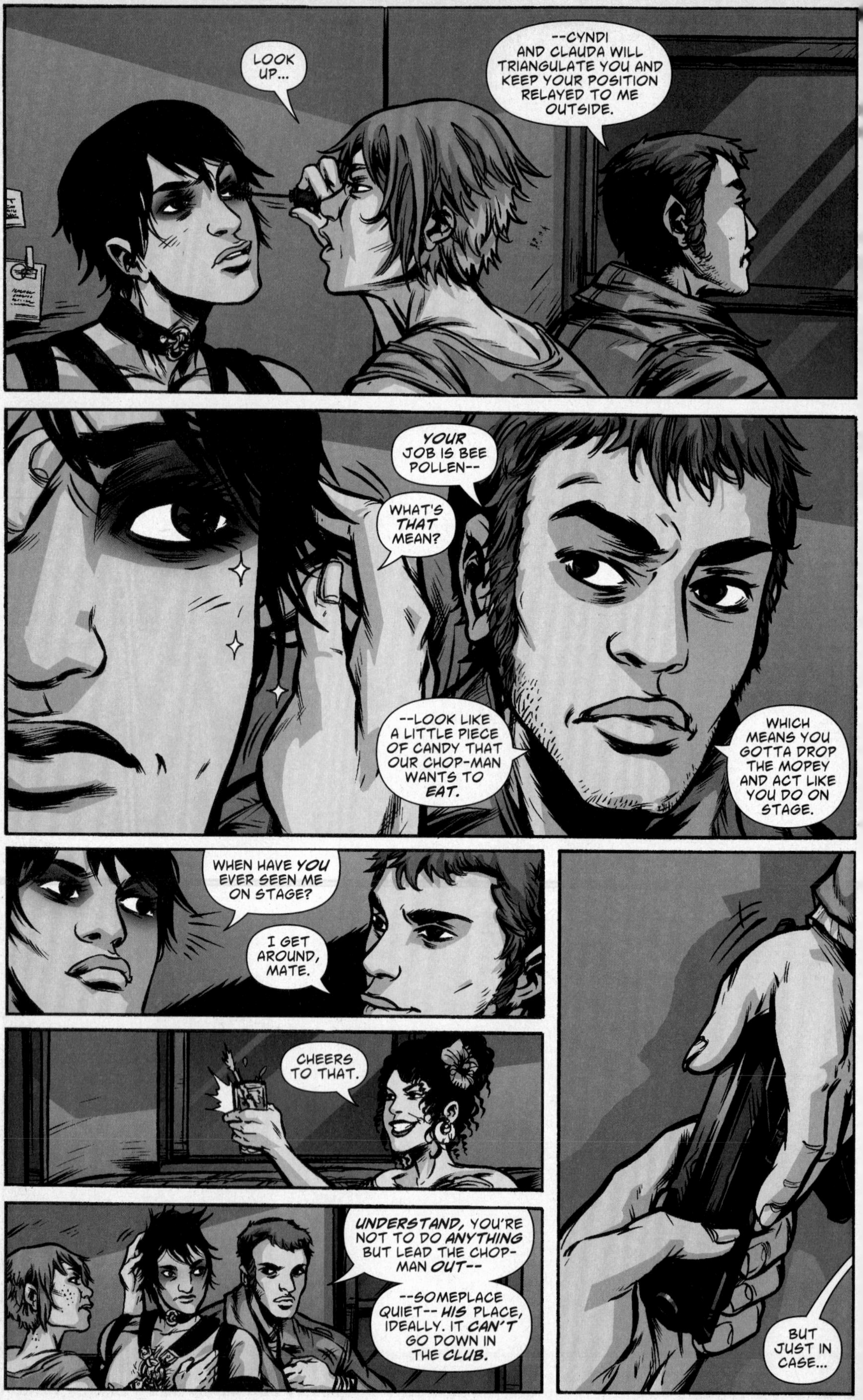
LOOK UP...
--CYNDI AND CLAUDA WILL TRIANGULATE YOU AND KEEP YOUR POSITION RELAYED TO ME OUTSIDE.
YOUR JOB IS BEE POLLEN--
WHAT'S THAT MEAN?
--LOOK LIKE A LITTLE PIECE OF CANDY THAT OUR CHOP-MAN WANTS TO EAT.
WHICH MEANS YOU GOTTA DROP THE MOPEY AND ACT LIKE YOU DO ON STAGE.
WHEN HAVE YOU EVER SEEN ME ON STAGE?
I GET AROUND, MATE.
CHEERS TO THAT.
UNDERSTAND, YOU'RE NOT TO DO ANYTHING BUT LEAD THE CHOP-MAN OUT--
--SOMEPLACE QUIET-- HIS PLACE, IDEALLY. IT CAN'T GO DOWN IN THE CLUB.
BUT JUST IN CASE...

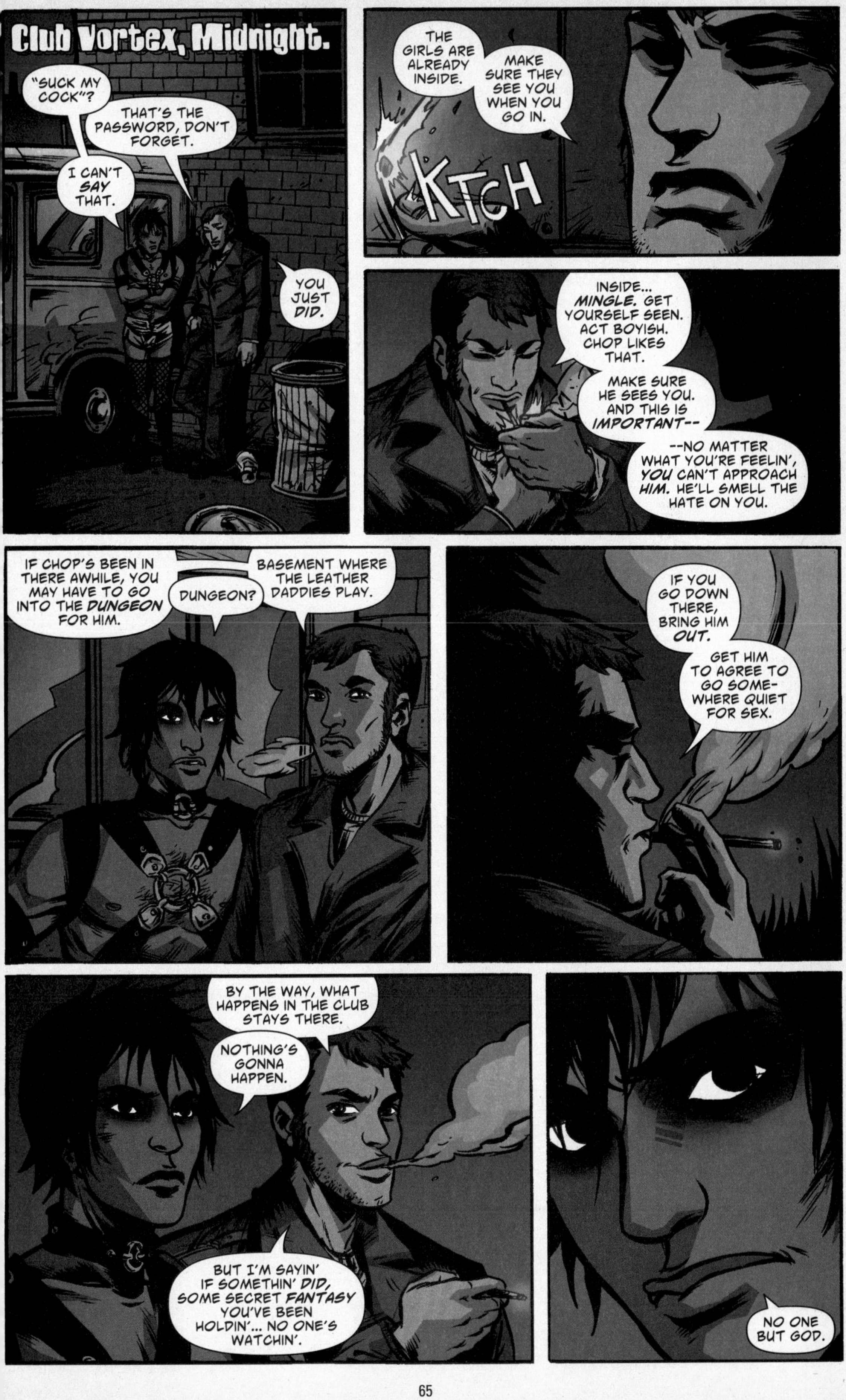
Club Vortex, Midnight.
"SUCK MY COCK"?
THAT'S THE PASSWORD, DON'T FORGET.
I CAN'T SAY THAT.
YOU JUST DID.
THE GIRLS ARE ALREADY INSIDE.
MAKE SURE THEY SEE YOU WHEN YOU GO IN.
KTCH
INSIDE... MINGLE. GET YOURSELF SEEN. ACT BOYISH. CHOP LIKES THAT.
MAKE SURE HE SEES YOU. AND THIS IS IMPORTANT--
--NO MATTER WHAT YOU'RE FEELIN', YOU CAN'T APPROACH HIM. HE'LL SMELL THE HATE ON YOU.
IF CHOP'S BEEN IN THERE AWHILE, YOU MAY HAVE TO GO INTO THE DUNGEON FOR HIM.
DUNGEON?
BASEMENT WHERE THE LEATHER DADDIES PLAY.
IF YOU GO DOWN THERE, BRING HIM OUT.
GET HIM TO AGREE TO GO SOME-WHERE QUIET FOR SEX.
BY THE WAY, WHAT HAPPENS IN THE CLUB STAYS THERE.
NOTHING'S GONNA HAPPEN.
BUT I'M SAYIN' IF SOMETHIN' DID, SOME SECRET FANTASY YOU'VE BEEN HOLDIN'... NO ONE'S WATCHIN'.
NO ONE BUT GOD.

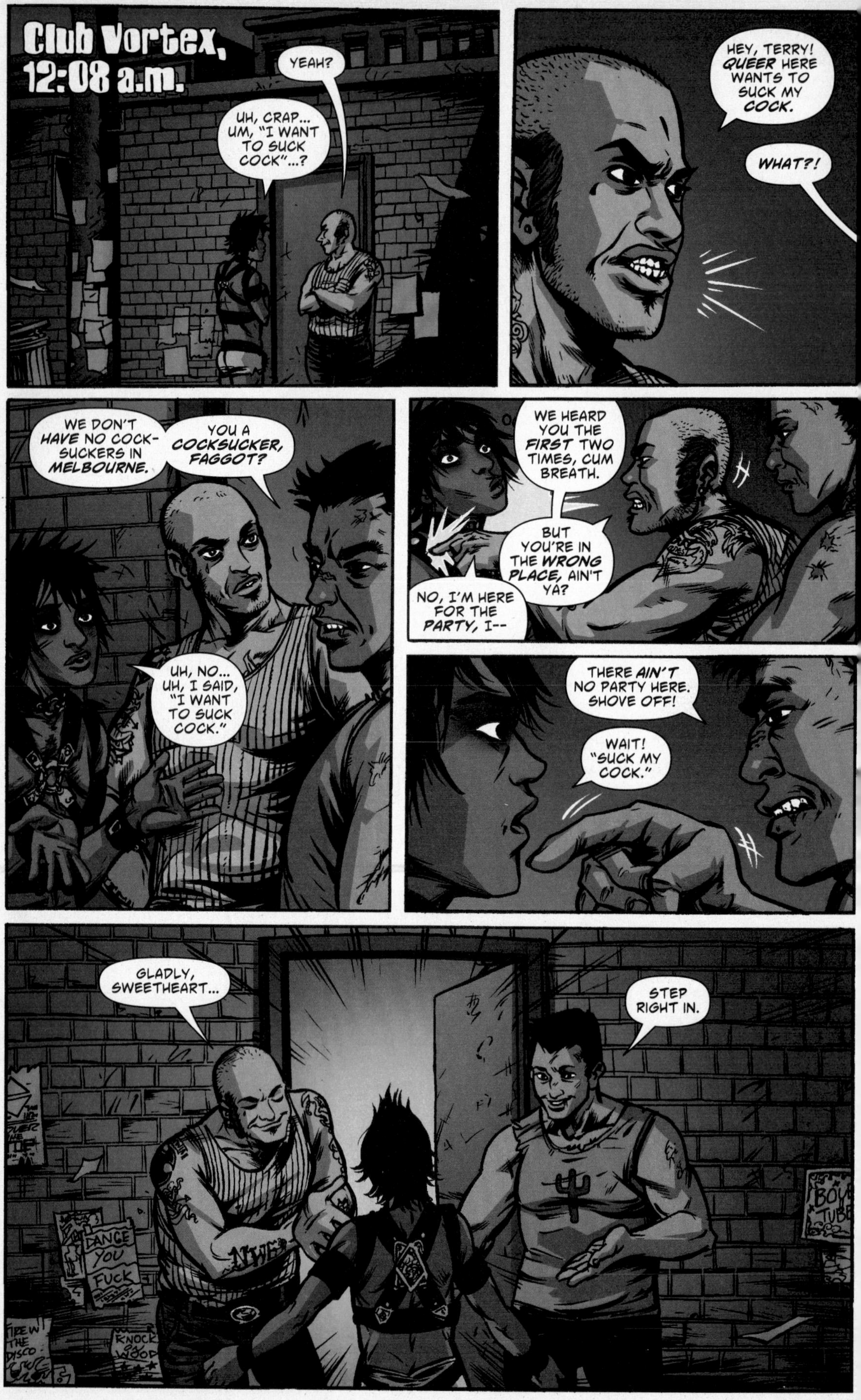
Club Vortex,
12:08 a.m.
YEAH?
UH, CRAP... UM, "I WANT TO SUCK COCK"...?
HEY, TERRY! QUEER HERE WANTS TO SUCK MY COCK.
WHAT?!
WE DON'T HAVE NO COCK-SUCKERS IN MELBOURNE.
YOU A COCKSUCKER, FAGGOT?
UH, NO... UH, I SAID, "I WANT TO SUCK COCK."
WE HEARD YOU THE FIRST TWO TIMES, CUM BREATH.
BUT YOU'RE IN THE WRONG PLACE, AIN'T YA?
NO, I'M HERE FOR THE PARTY, I--
THERE AIN'T NO PARTY HERE. SHOVE OFF!
WAIT! "SUCK MY COCK."
GLADLY, SWEETHEART...
STEP RIGHT IN.
DANCE YOU FUCK
KNOCK ON WOOD

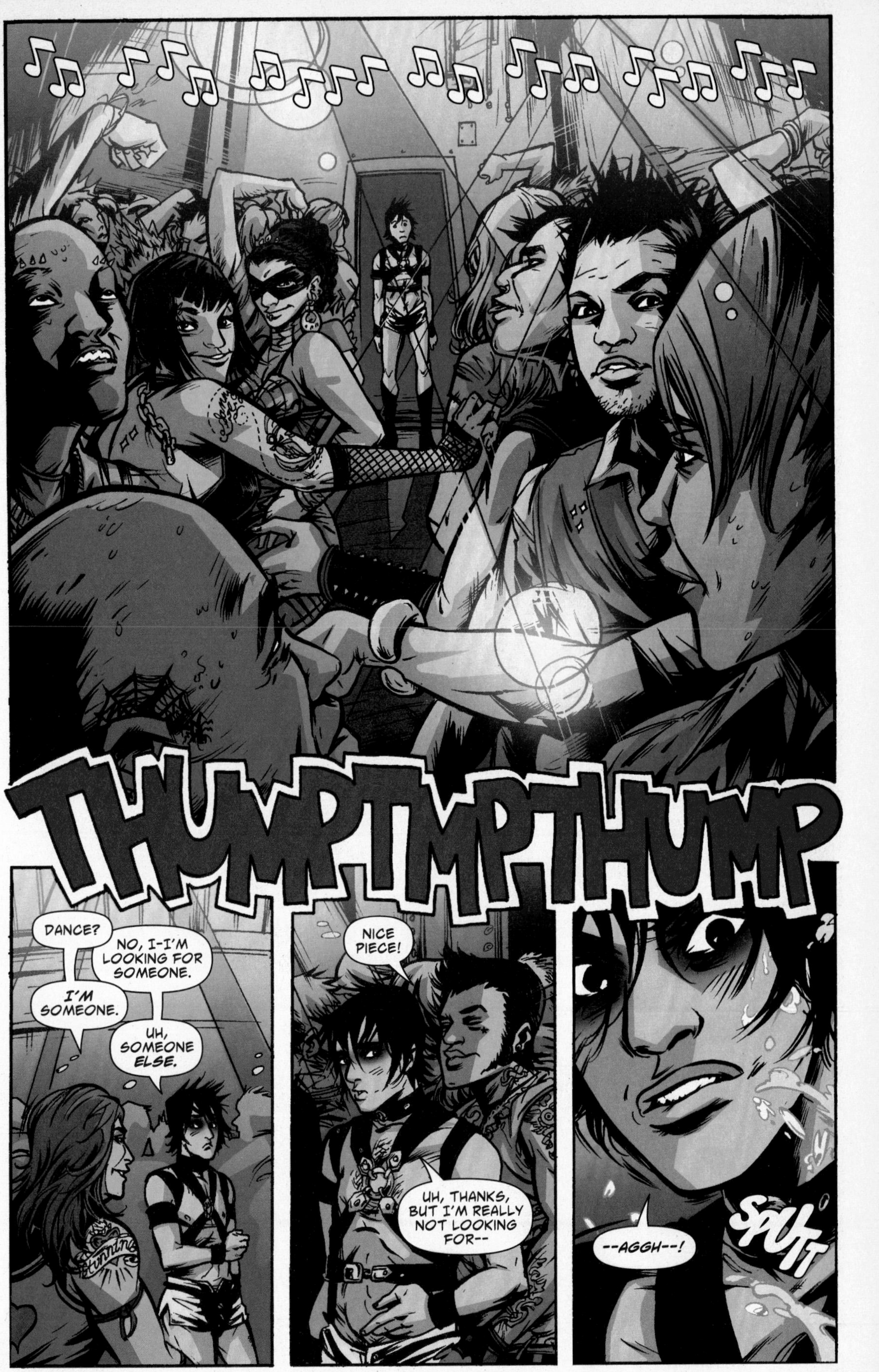
THUMPTMPTHUMP
DANCE?
NO, I-I'M LOOKING FOR SOMEONE.
I'M SOMEONE.
UH, SOMEONE ELSE.
NICE PIECE!
UH, THANKS, BUT I'M REALLY NOT LOOKING FOR--
--AGGH--!
SPUTT

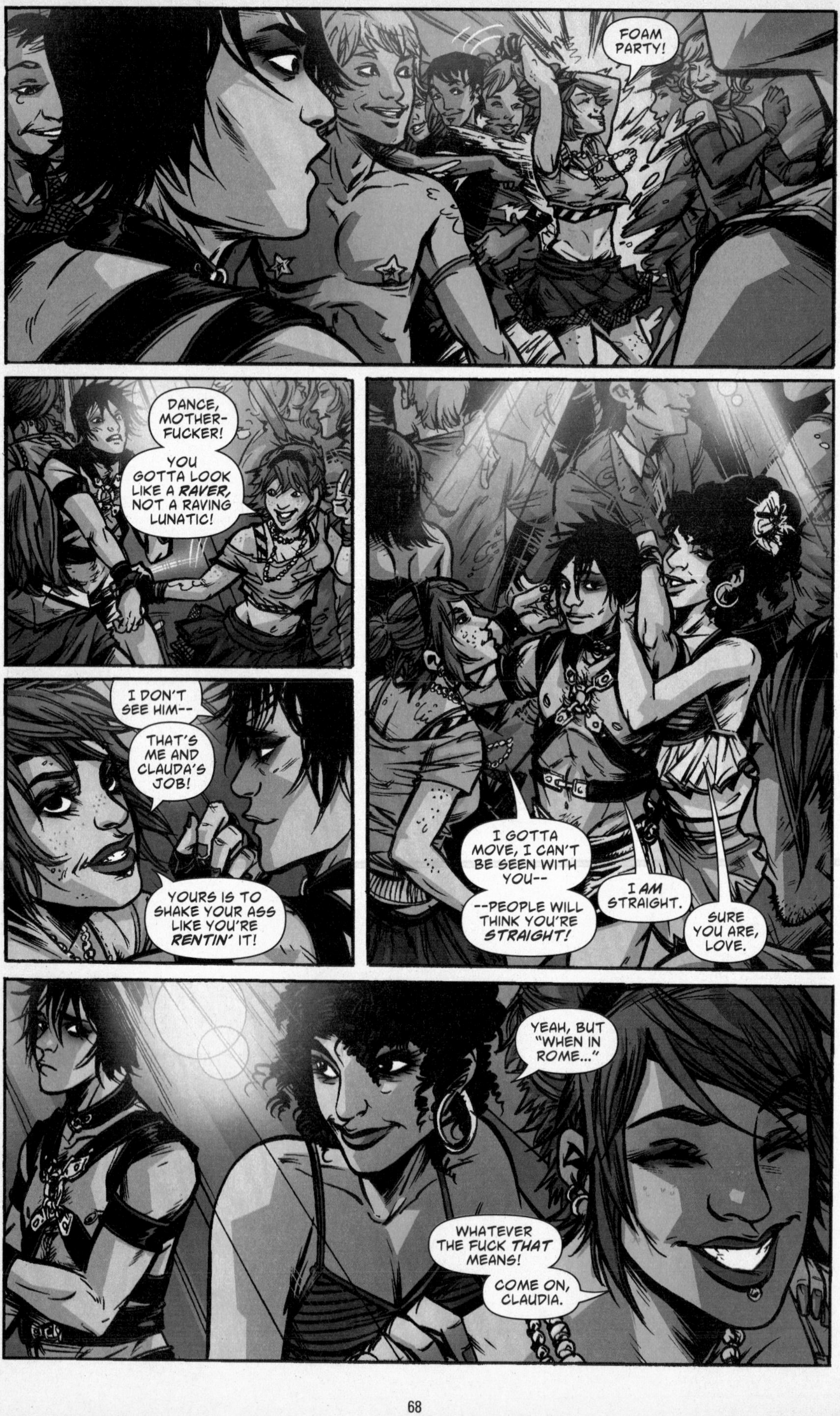
FOAM PARTY!
DANCE, MOTHER-FUCKER!
YOU GOTTA LOOK LIKE A *RAVER*, NOT A RAVING LUNATIC!
I GOTTA MOVE, I CAN'T BE SEEN WITH YOU--
--PEOPLE WILL THINK YOU'RE *STRAIGHT!*
I *AM* STRAIGHT.
SURE YOU ARE, LOVE.
I DON'T SEE HIM--
THAT'S ME AND CLAUDA'S JOB!
YOURS IS TO SHAKE YOUR ASS LIKE YOU'RE *RENTIN'* IT!
YEAH, BUT "WHEN IN ROME..."
WHATEVER THE FUCK *THAT* MEANS!
COME ON, CLAUDIA.

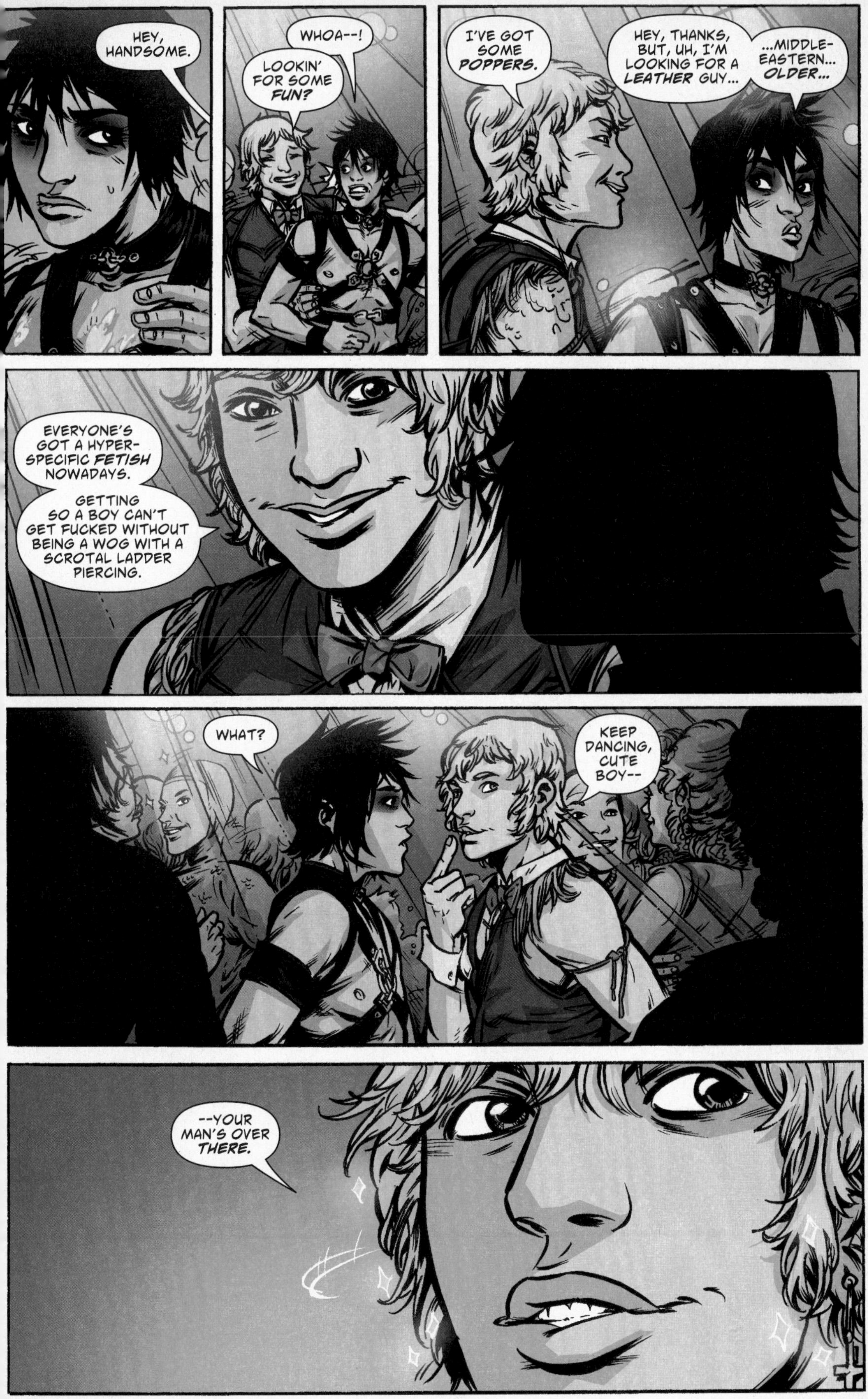
HEY, HANDSOME.
WHOA--!
LOOKIN' FOR SOME FUN?
I'VE GOT SOME POPPERS.
HEY, THANKS, BUT, UH, I'M LOOKING FOR A LEATHER GUY...
...MIDDLE-EASTERN... OLDER...
EVERYONE'S GOT A HYPER-SPECIFIC FETISH NOWADAYS.
GETTING SO A BOY CAN'T GET FUCKED WITHOUT BEING A WOG WITH A SCROTAL LADDER PIERCING.
WHAT?
KEEP DANCING, CUTE BOY--
--YOUR MAN'S OVER THERE.

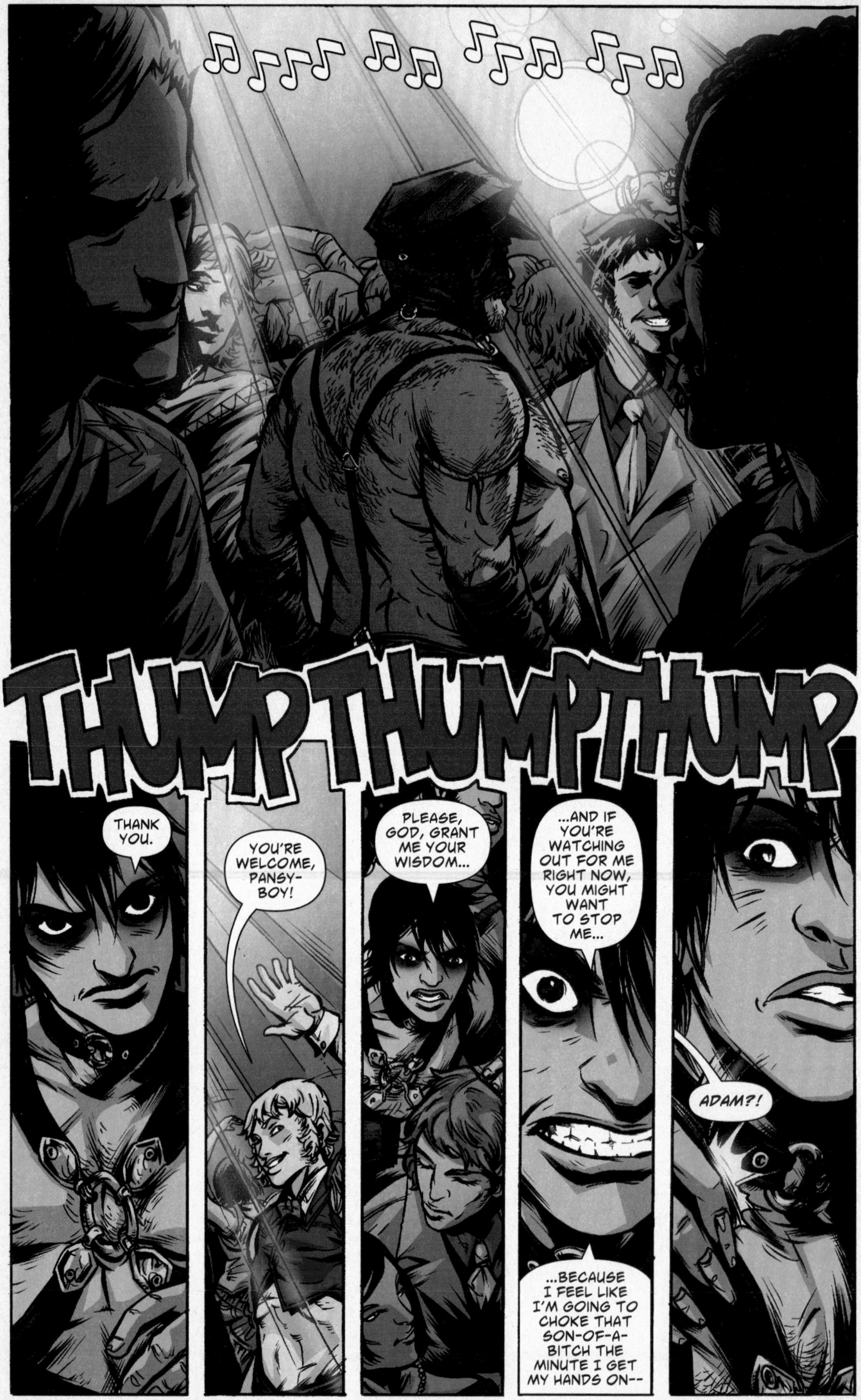
THUMP THUMP THUMP
THANK YOU.
YOU'RE WELCOME, PANSY-BOY!
PLEASE, GOD, GRANT ME YOUR WISDOM...
...AND IF YOU'RE WATCHING OUT FOR ME RIGHT NOW, YOU MIGHT WANT TO STOP ME...
...BECAUSE I FEEL LIKE I'M GOING TO CHOKE THAT SON-OF-A-BITCH THE MINUTE I GET MY HANDS ON--
ADAM?!

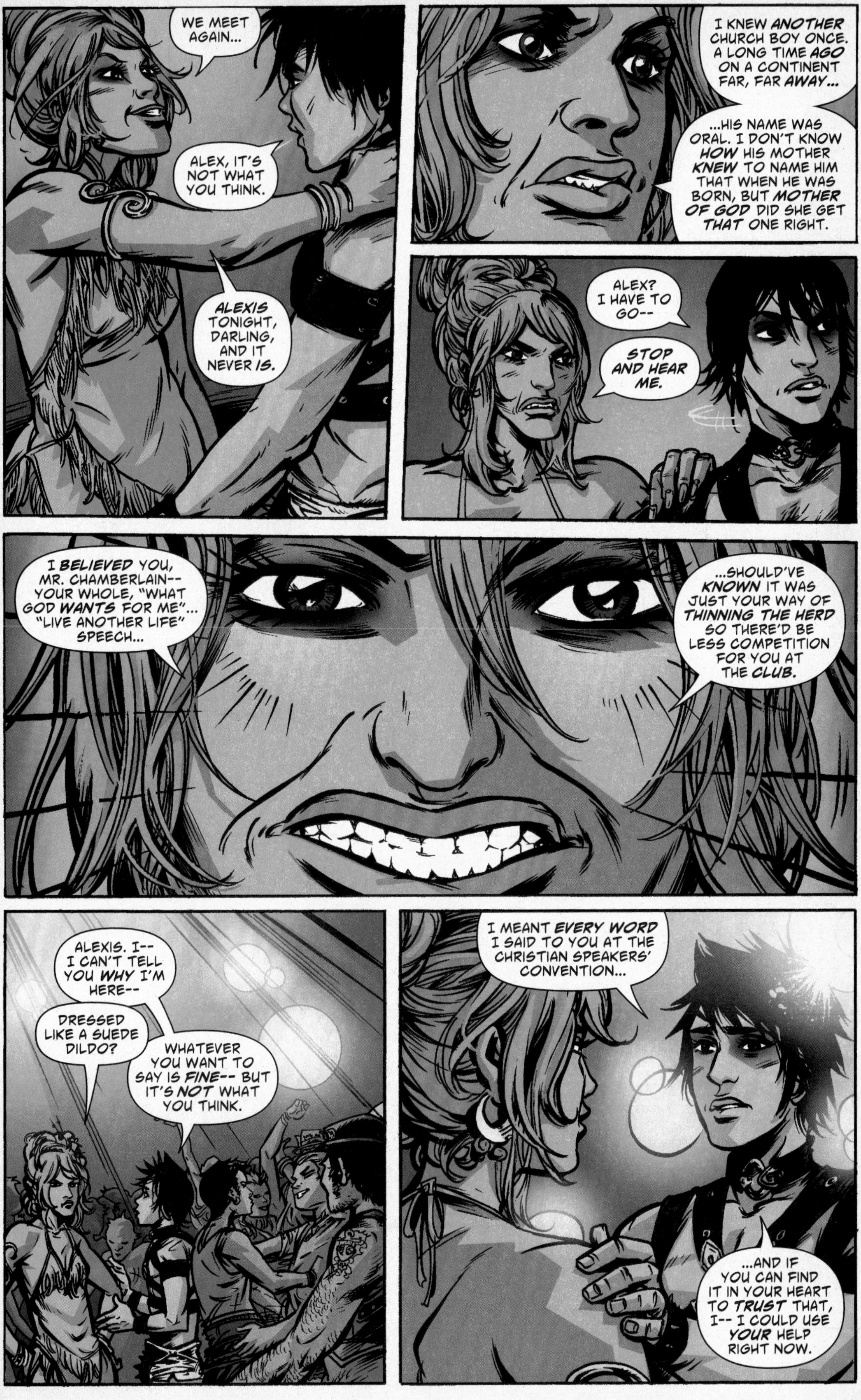
WE MEET AGAIN...
ALEX, IT'S NOT WHAT YOU THINK.
ALEXIS TONIGHT, DARLING, AND IT NEVER IS.
I KNEW ANOTHER CHURCH BOY ONCE. A LONG TIME AGO ON A CONTINENT FAR, FAR AWAY...
...HIS NAME WAS ORAL. I DON'T KNOW HOW HIS MOTHER KNEW TO NAME HIM THAT WHEN HE WAS BORN, BUT MOTHER OF GOD DID SHE GET THAT ONE RIGHT.
ALEX? I HAVE TO GO--
STOP AND HEAR ME.
I BELIEVED YOU, MR. CHAMBERLAIN-- YOUR WHOLE, "WHAT GOD WANTS FOR ME"... "LIVE ANOTHER LIFE" SPEECH...
...SHOULD'VE KNOWN IT WAS JUST YOUR WAY OF THINNING THE HERD SO THERE'D BE LESS COMPETITION FOR YOU AT THE CLUB.
ALEXIS. I-- I CAN'T TELL YOU WHY I'M HERE--
DRESSED LIKE A SUEDE DILDO?
WHATEVER YOU WANT TO SAY IS FINE-- BUT IT'S NOT WHAT YOU THINK.
I MEANT EVERY WORD I SAID TO YOU AT THE CHRISTIAN SPEAKERS' CONVENTION...
...AND IF YOU CAN FIND IT IN YOUR HEART TO TRUST THAT, I-- I COULD USE YOUR HELP RIGHT NOW.

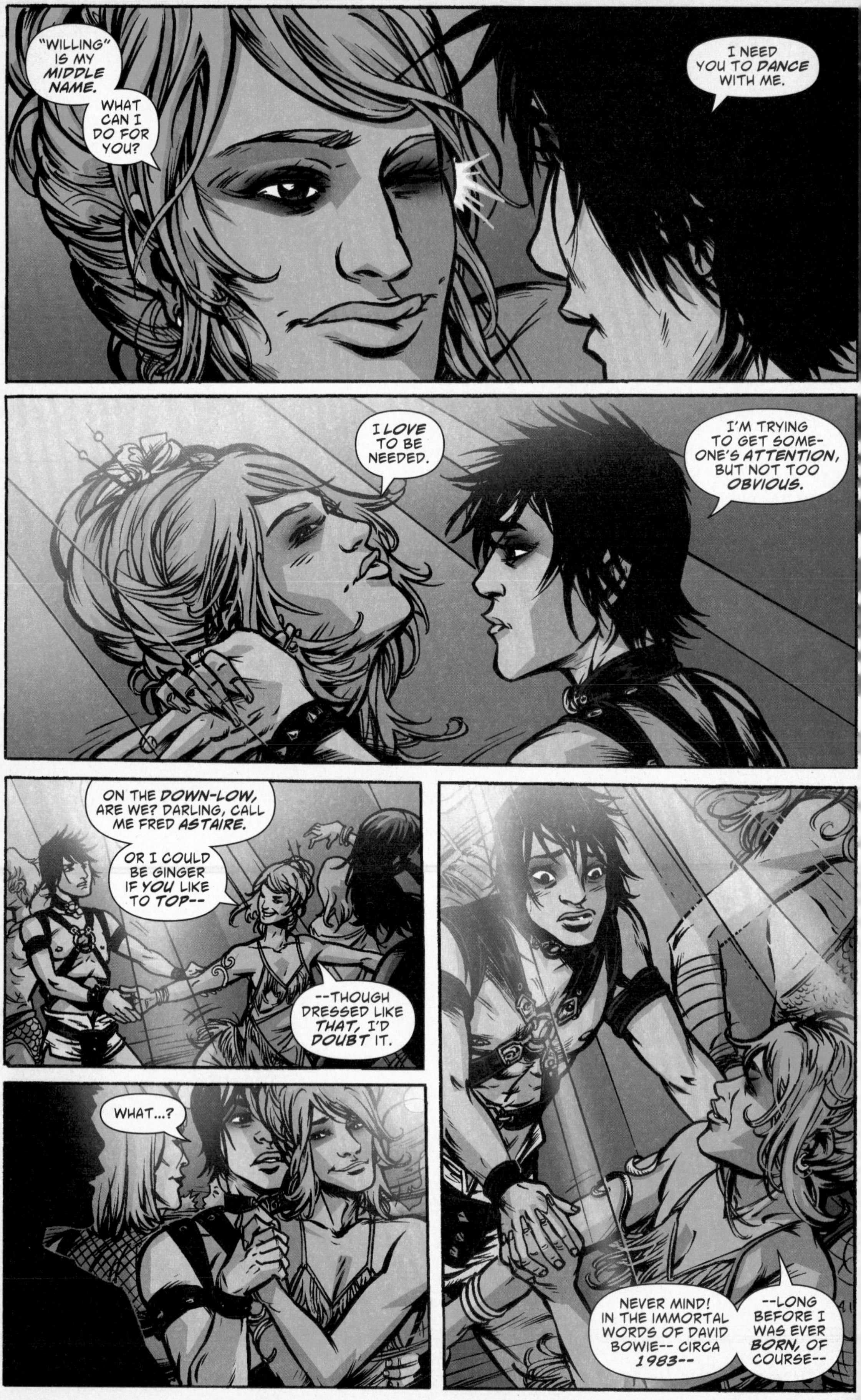
"WILLING" IS MY MIDDLE NAME.
WHAT CAN I DO FOR YOU?
I NEED YOU TO DANCE WITH ME.
I LOVE TO BE NEEDED.
I'M TRYING TO GET SOME-ONE'S ATTENTION, BUT NOT TOO OBVIOUS.
ON THE DOWN-LOW, ARE WE? DARLING, CALL ME FRED ASTAIRE.
OR I COULD BE GINGER IF YOU LIKE TO TOP--
--THOUGH DRESSED LIKE THAT, I'D DOUBT IT.
WHAT...?
NEVER MIND! IN THE IMMORTAL WORDS OF DAVID BOWIE-- CIRCA 1983--
--LONG BEFORE I WAS EVER BORN, OF COURSE--

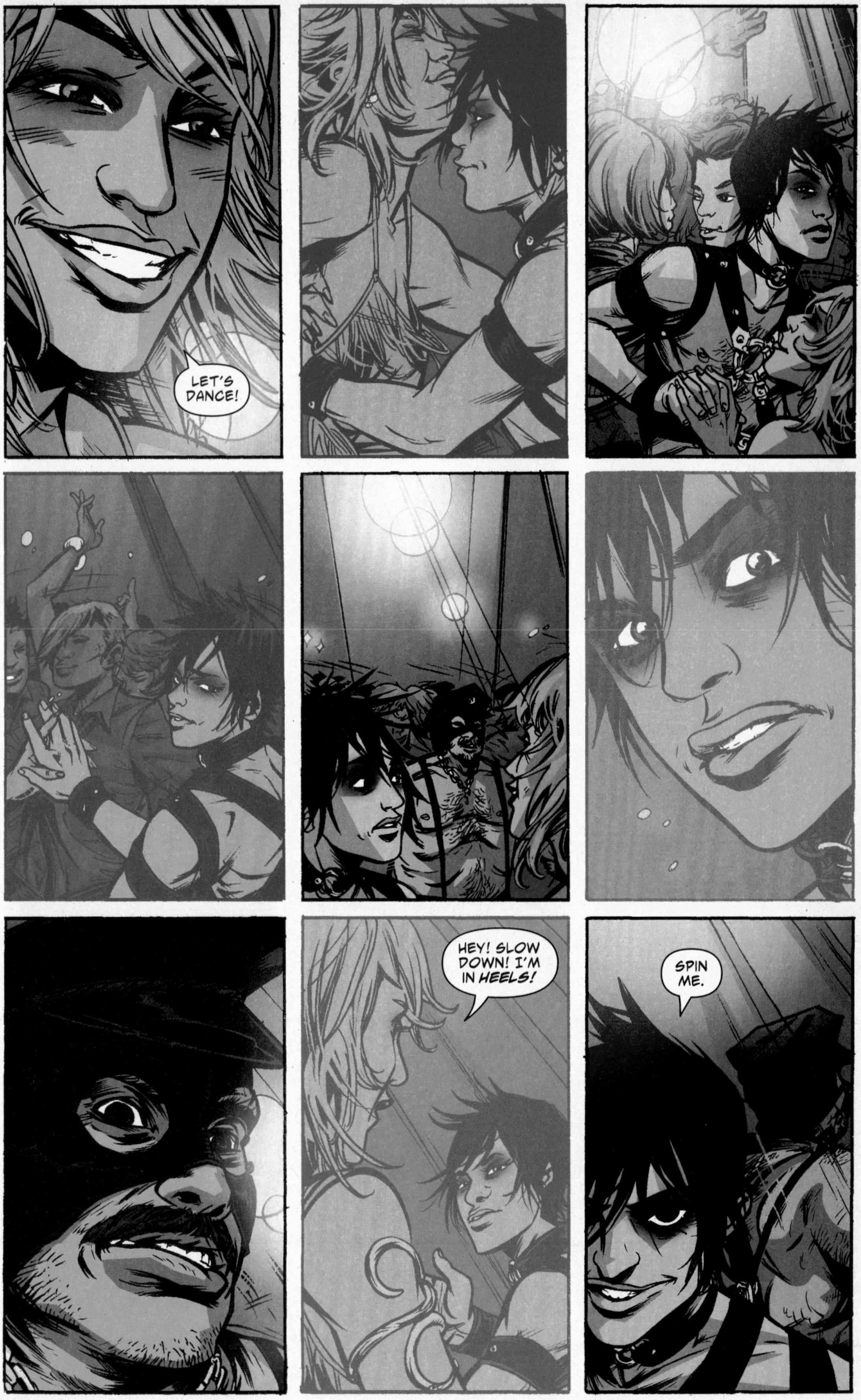
LET'S DANCE!
HEY! SLOW DOWN! I'M IN HEELS!
SPIN ME.

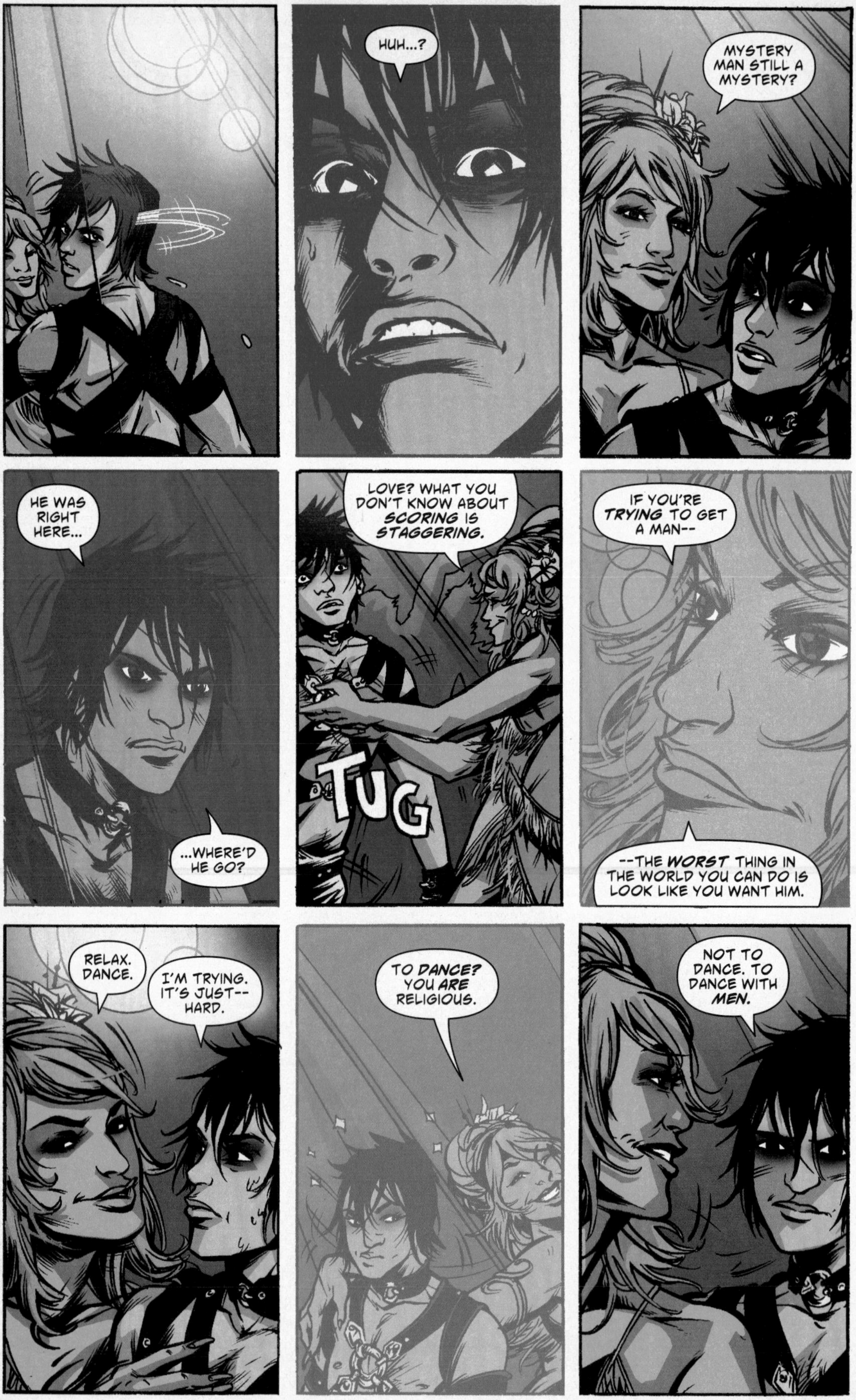
HUH...?
MYSTERY MAN STILL A MYSTERY?
HE WAS RIGHT HERE...
...WHERE'D HE GO?
LOVE? WHAT YOU DON'T KNOW ABOUT SCORING IS STAGGERING.
TUG
IF YOU'RE TRYING TO GET A MAN--
--THE WORST THING IN THE WORLD YOU CAN DO IS LOOK LIKE YOU WANT HIM.
RELAX. DANCE.
I'M TRYING. IT'S JUST--HARD.
TO DANCE? YOU ARE RELIGIOUS.
NOT TO DANCE. TO DANCE WITH MEN.

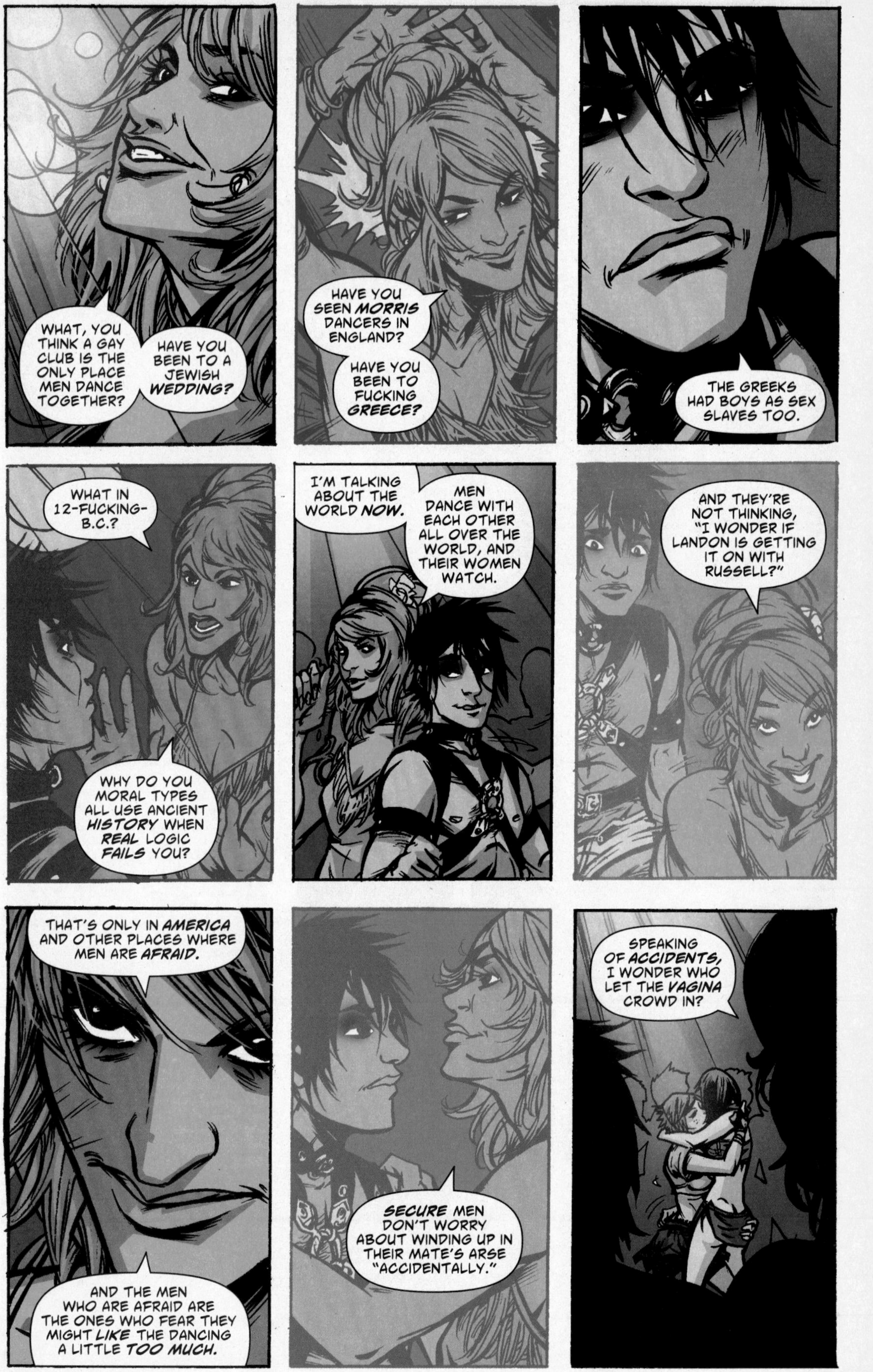
WHAT, YOU THINK A GAY CLUB IS THE ONLY PLACE MEN DANCE TOGETHER?
HAVE YOU BEEN TO A JEWISH WEDDING?
HAVE YOU SEEN MORRIS DANCERS IN ENGLAND?
HAVE YOU BEEN TO FUCKING GREECE?
THE GREEKS HAD BOYS AS SEX SLAVES TOO.
WHAT IN 12-FUCKING-B.C.?
WHY DO YOU MORAL TYPES ALL USE ANCIENT HISTORY WHEN REAL LOGIC FAILS YOU?
I'M TALKING ABOUT THE WORLD NOW.
MEN DANCE WITH EACH OTHER ALL OVER THE WORLD, AND THEIR WOMEN WATCH.
AND THEY'RE NOT THINKING, "I WONDER IF LANDON IS GETTING IT ON WITH RUSSELL?"
THAT'S ONLY IN AMERICA AND OTHER PLACES WHERE MEN ARE AFRAID.
AND THE MEN WHO ARE AFRAID ARE THE ONES WHO FEAR THEY MIGHT LIKE THE DANCING A LITTLE TOO MUCH.
SECURE MEN DON'T WORRY ABOUT WINDING UP IN THEIR MATE'S ARSE "ACCIDENTALLY."
SPEAKING OF ACCIDENTS, I WONDER WHO LET THE VAGINA CROWD IN?

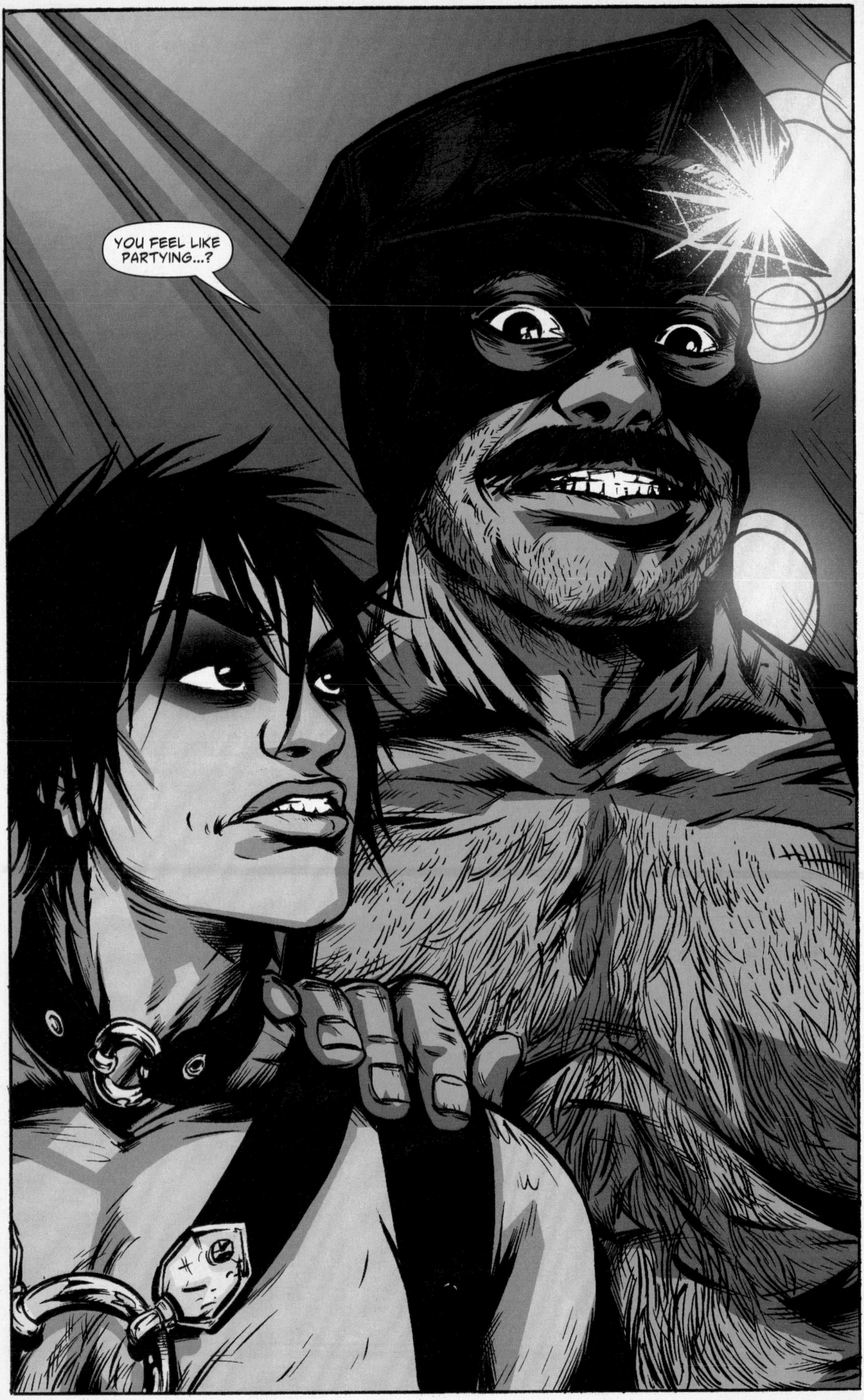
YOU FEEL LIKE PARTYING...?

CHAPTER FOUR

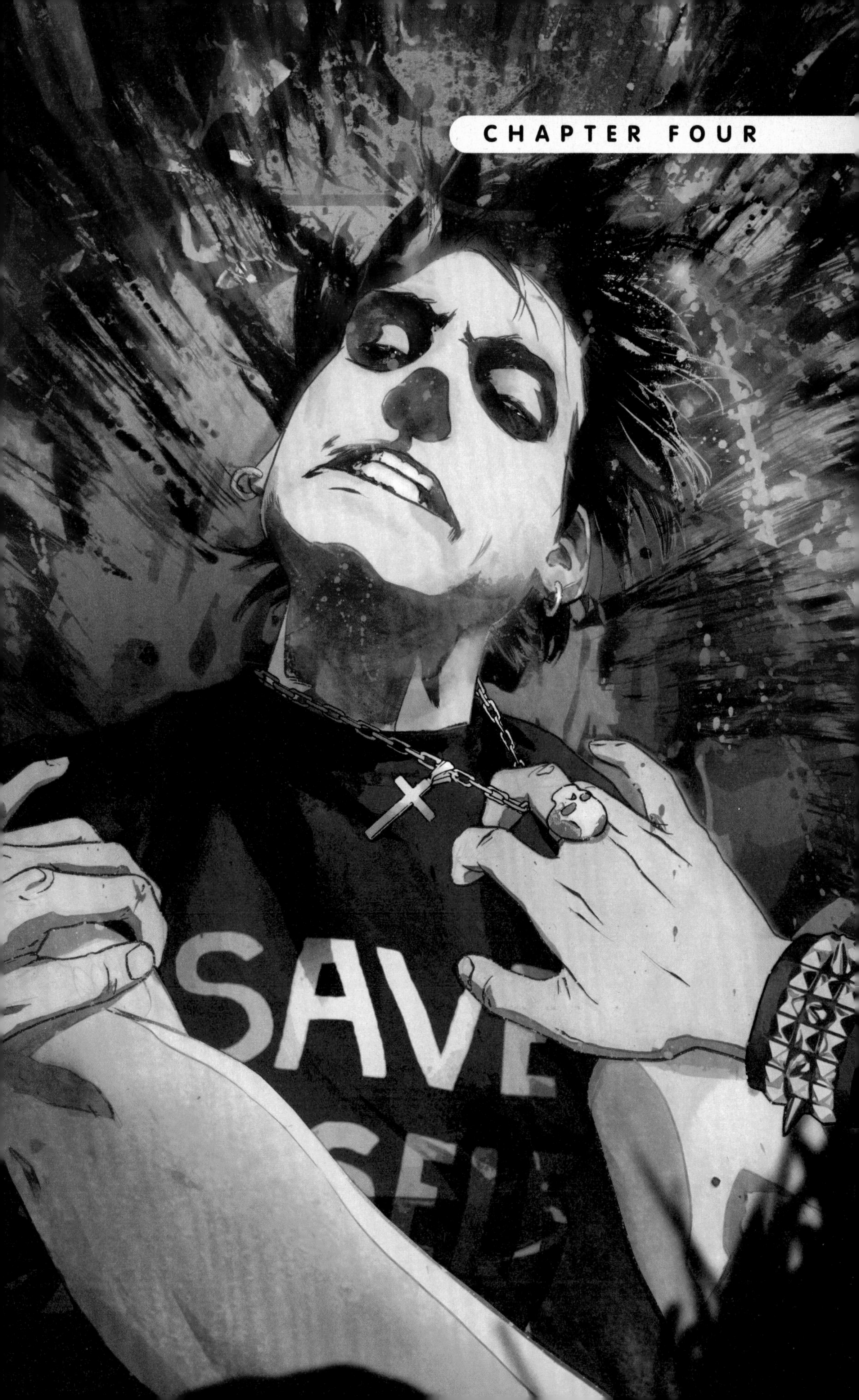
SAVE

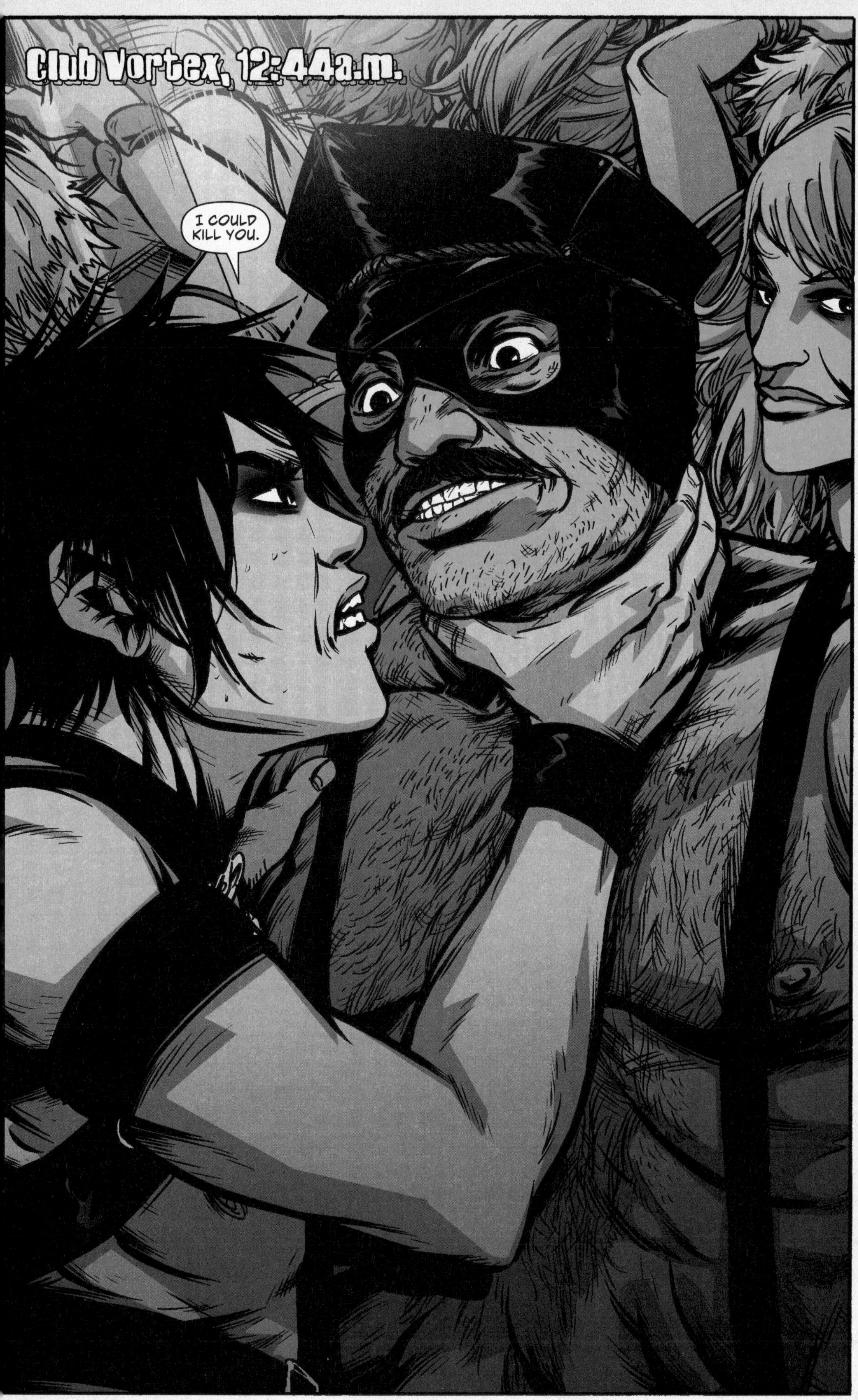
Club Vortex, 12:44a.m.
I COULD KILL YOU.

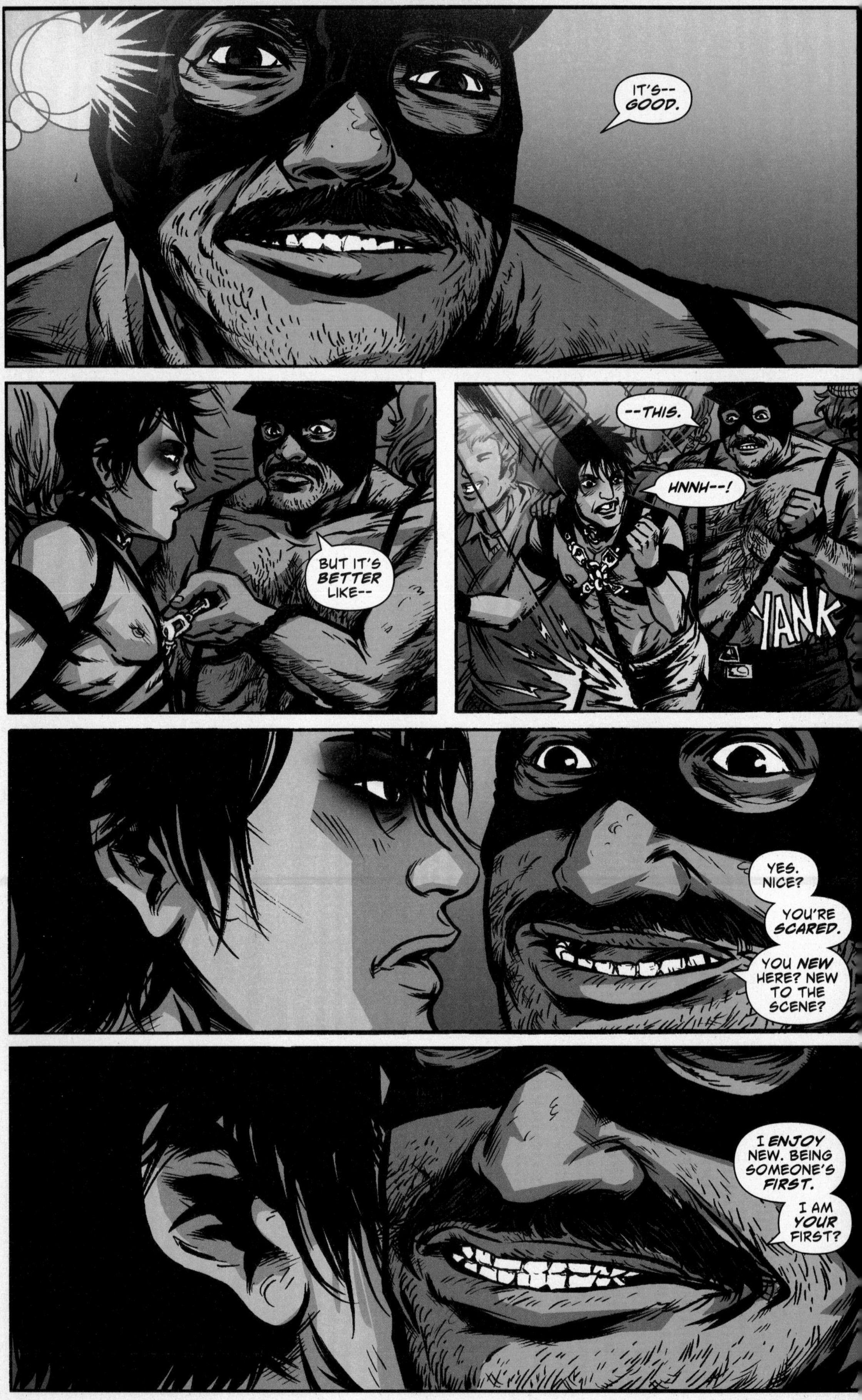
IT'S--
GOOD.
BUT IT'S BETTER LIKE--
--THIS.
HNNH--!
YANK
YES. NICE?
YOU'RE SCARED.
YOU NEW HERE? NEW TO THE SCENE?
I ENJOY NEW. BEING SOMEONE'S FIRST.
I AM YOUR FIRST?

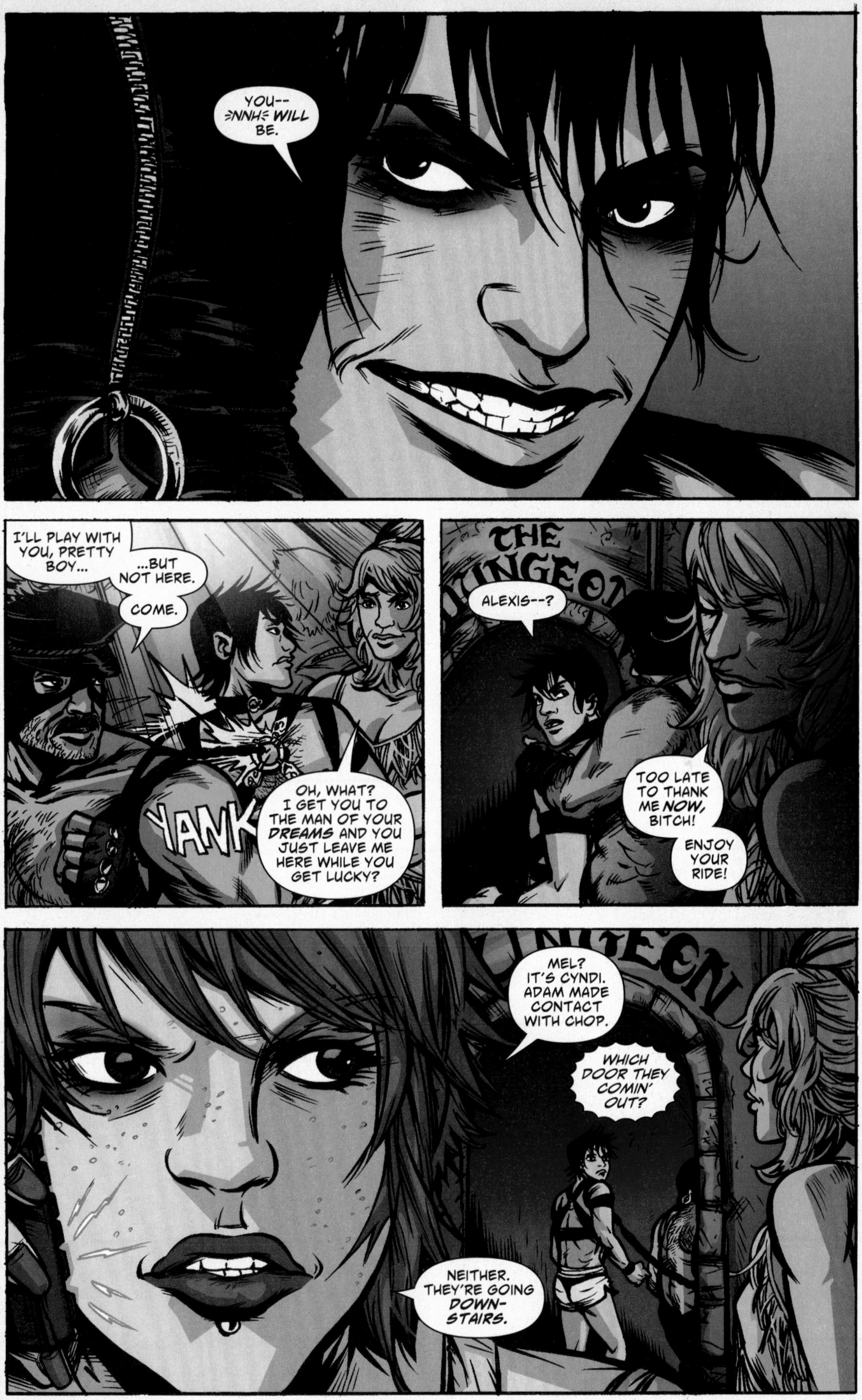

YOU-- ≥NNH≤ WILL BE.
I'LL PLAY WITH YOU, PRETTY BOY...
...BUT NOT HERE.
COME.
YANK
OH, WHAT? I GET YOU TO THE MAN OF YOUR DREAMS AND YOU JUST LEAVE ME HERE WHILE YOU GET LUCKY?
THE DUNGEON
ALEXIS--?
TOO LATE TO THANK ME NOW, BITCH!
ENJOY YOUR RIDE!
MEL? IT'S CYNDI. ADAM MADE CONTACT WITH CHOP.
WHICH DOOR THEY COMIN' OUT?
NEITHER. THEY'RE GOING DOWN-STAIRS.

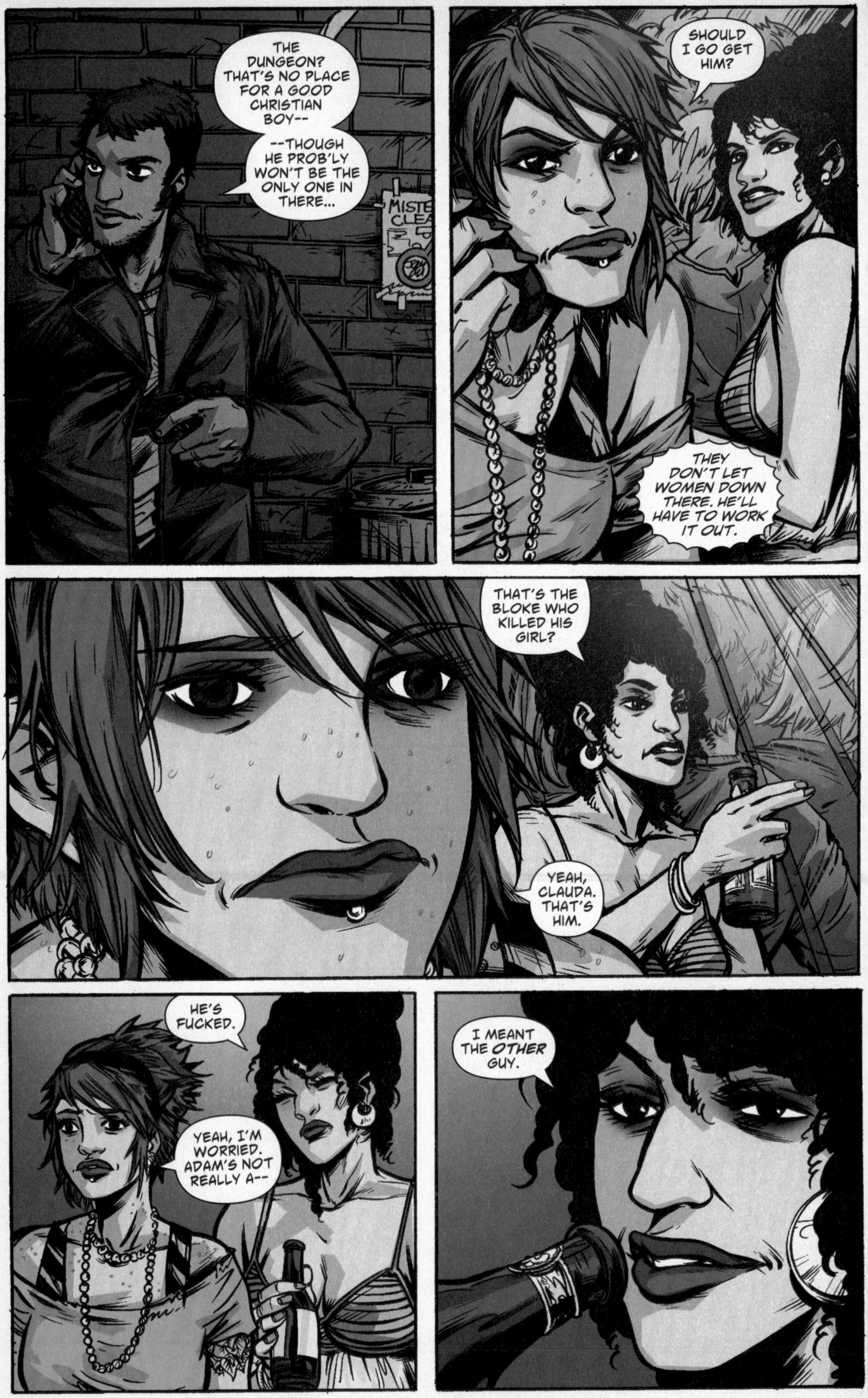
THE DUNGEON? THAT'S NO PLACE FOR A GOOD CHRISTIAN BOY--
--THOUGH HE PROB'LY WON'T BE THE ONLY ONE IN THERE...
SHOULD I GO GET HIM?
THEY DON'T LET WOMEN DOWN THERE. HE'LL HAVE TO WORK IT OUT.
THAT'S THE BLOKE WHO KILLED HIS GIRL?
YEAH, CLAUDA. THAT'S HIM.
HE'S FUCKED.
YEAH, I'M WORRIED. ADAM'S NOT REALLY A--
I MEANT THE OTHER GUY.

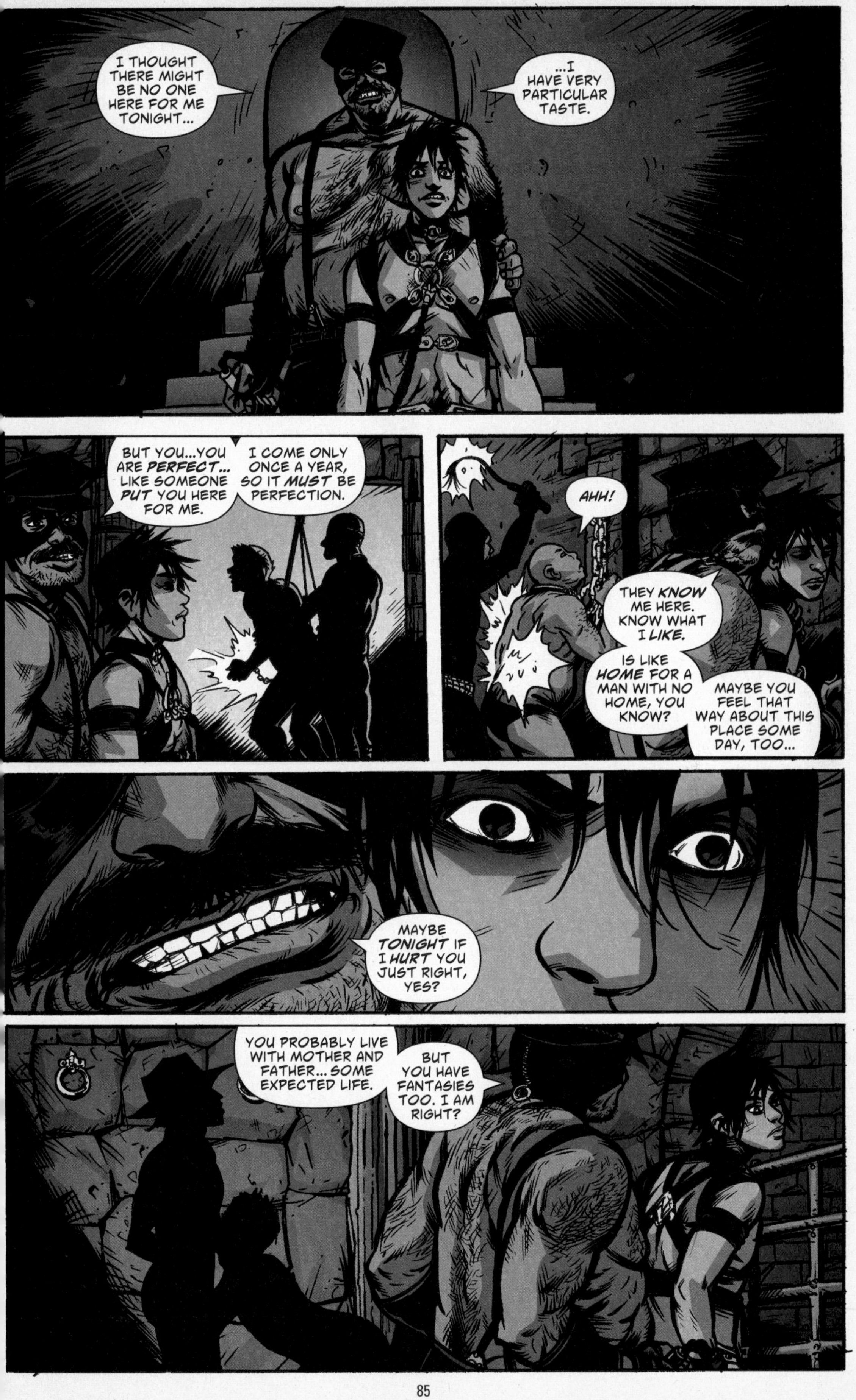
I THOUGHT THERE MIGHT BE NO ONE HERE FOR ME TONIGHT...
...I HAVE VERY PARTICULAR TASTE.
BUT YOU...YOU ARE PERFECT... LIKE SOMEONE PUT YOU HERE FOR ME.
I COME ONLY ONCE A YEAR, SO IT MUST BE PERFECTION.
AHH!
THEY KNOW ME HERE. KNOW WHAT I LIKE.
IS LIKE HOME FOR A MAN WITH NO HOME, YOU KNOW?
MAYBE YOU FEEL THAT WAY ABOUT THIS PLACE SOME DAY, TOO...
MAYBE TONIGHT IF I HURT YOU JUST RIGHT, YES?
YOU PROBABLY LIVE WITH MOTHER AND FATHER... SOME EXPECTED LIFE.
BUT YOU HAVE FANTASIES TOO. I AM RIGHT?

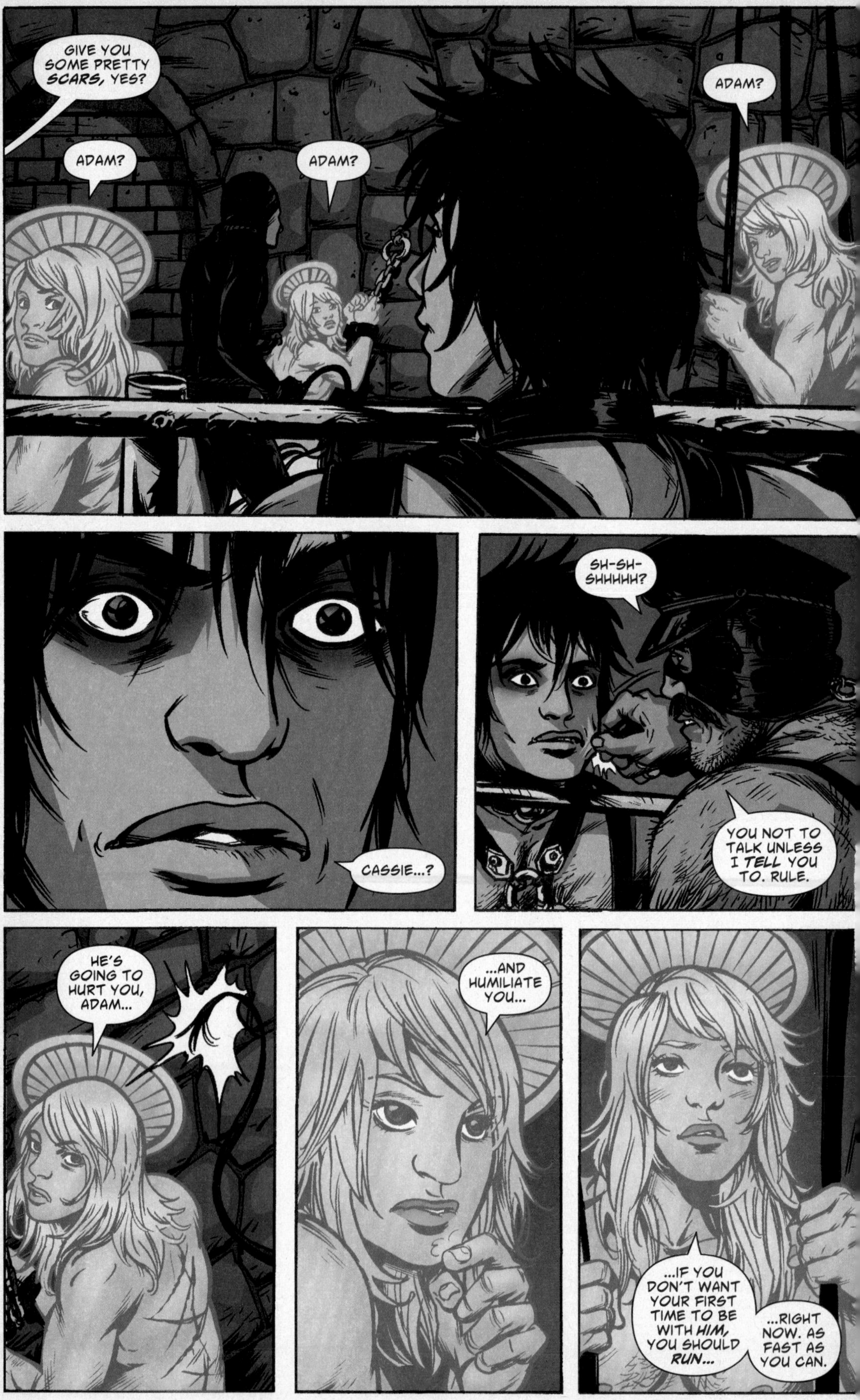
GIVE YOU SOME PRETTY SCARS, YES?
ADAM?
ADAM?
ADAM?
CASSIE...?
SH-SH-SHHHHH?
YOU NOT TO TALK UNLESS I TELL YOU TO. RULE.
HE'S GOING TO HURT YOU, ADAM...
...AND HUMILIATE YOU...
...IF YOU DON'T WANT YOUR FIRST TIME TO BE WITH HIM, YOU SHOULD RUN...
...RIGHT NOW. AS FAST AS YOU CAN.

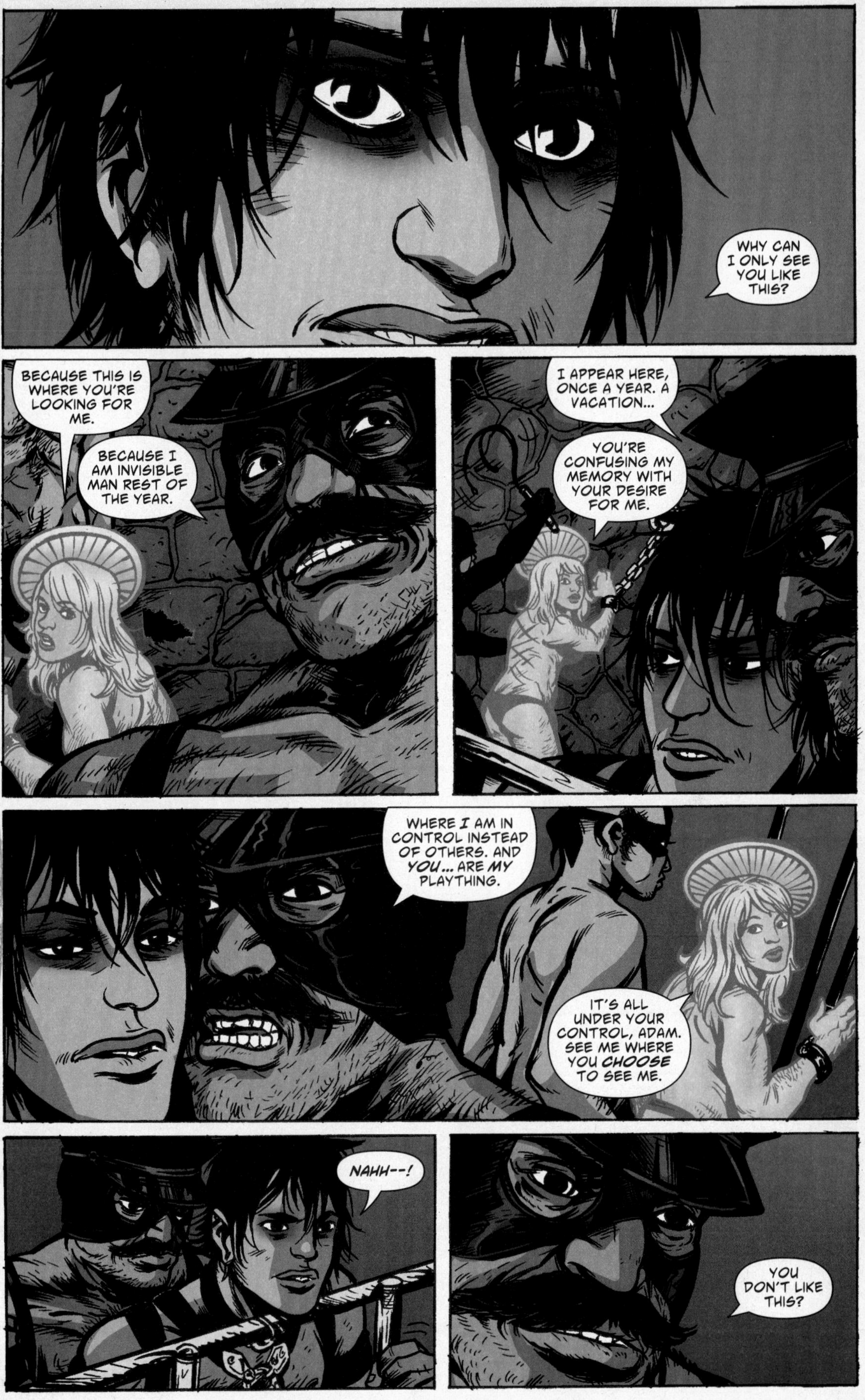
WHY CAN I ONLY SEE YOU LIKE THIS?
BECAUSE THIS IS WHERE YOU'RE LOOKING FOR ME.
BECAUSE I AM INVISIBLE MAN REST OF THE YEAR.
I APPEAR HERE, ONCE A YEAR. A VACATION...
YOU'RE CONFUSING MY MEMORY WITH YOUR DESIRE FOR ME.
WHERE *I* AM IN CONTROL INSTEAD OF OTHERS. AND *YOU*... ARE *MY* PLAYTHING.
IT'S ALL UNDER YOUR CONTROL, ADAM. SEE ME WHERE YOU *CHOOSE* TO SEE ME.
NAHH--!
YOU DON'T LIKE THIS?

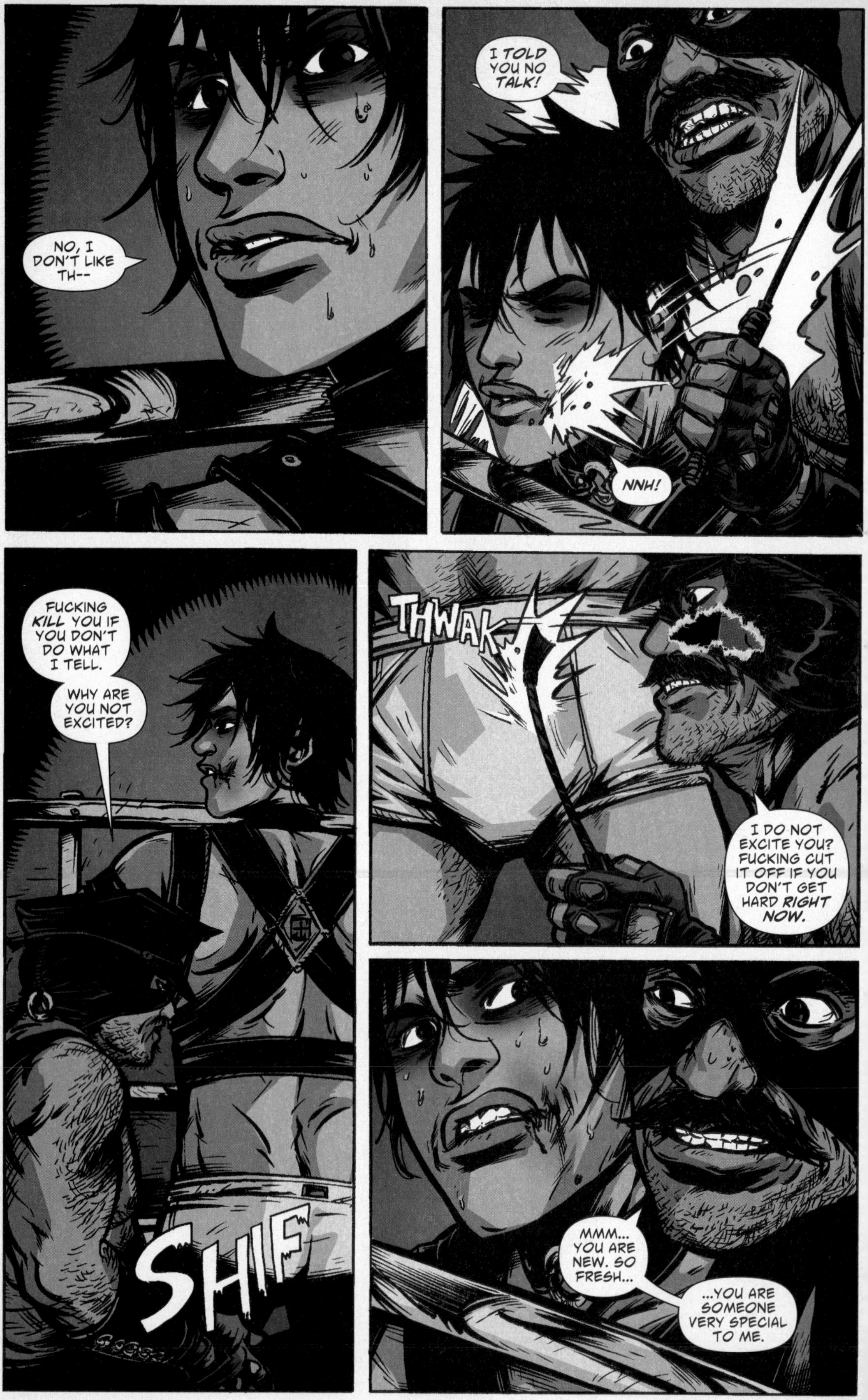
NO, I DON'T LIKE TH--
I TOLD YOU NO TALK!
NNH!
FUCKING KILL YOU IF YOU DON'T DO WHAT I TELL.
WHY ARE YOU NOT EXCITED?
SHIF
THWAK
I DO NOT EXCITE YOU? FUCKING CUT IT OFF IF YOU DON'T GET HARD RIGHT NOW.
MMM... YOU ARE NEW. SO FRESH...
...YOU ARE SOMEONE VERY SPECIAL TO ME.

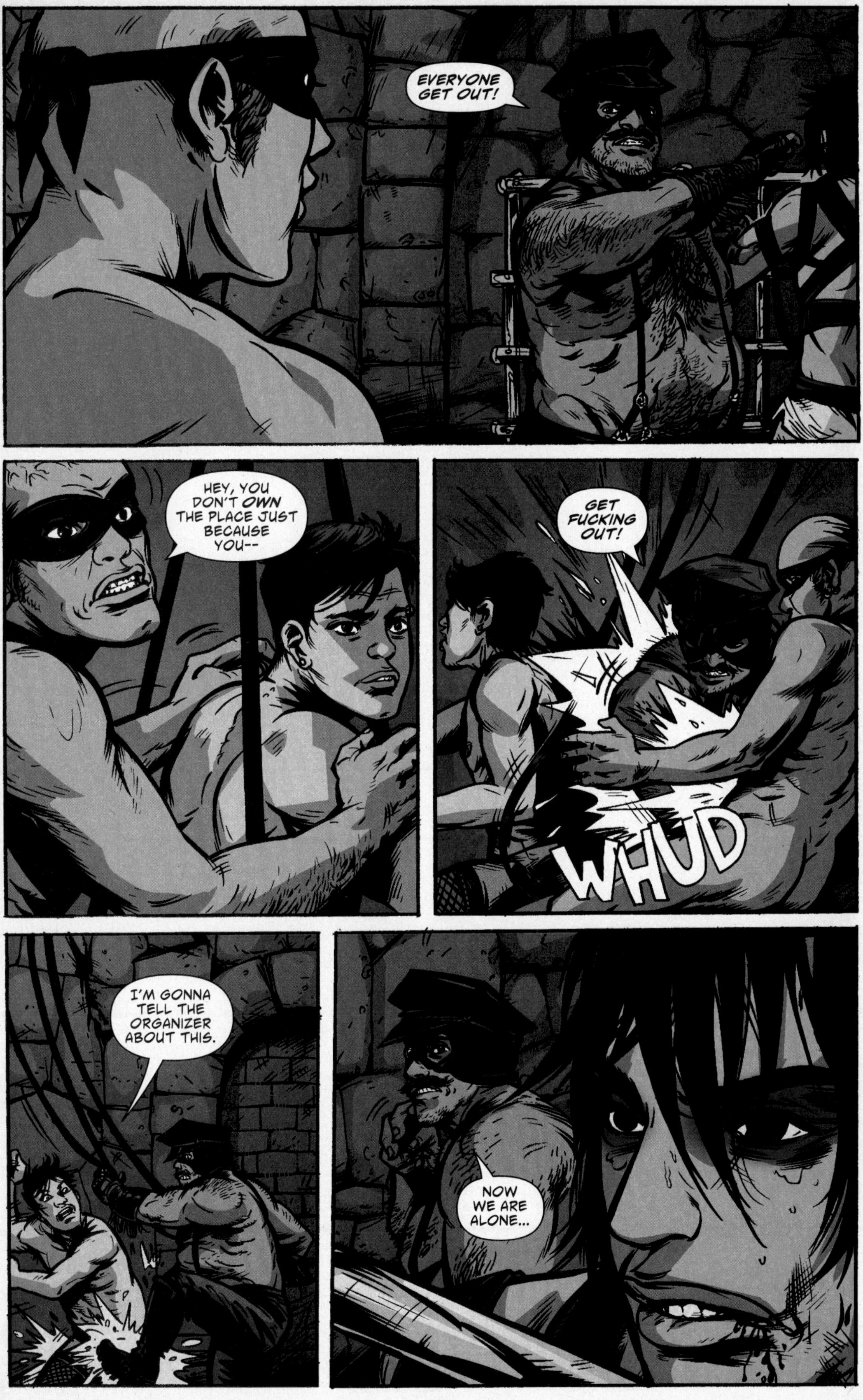
EVERYONE GET OUT!
HEY, YOU DON'T OWN THE PLACE JUST BECAUSE YOU--
GET FUCKING OUT!
WHUD
I'M GONNA TELL THE ORGANIZER ABOUT THIS.
NOW WE ARE ALONE...

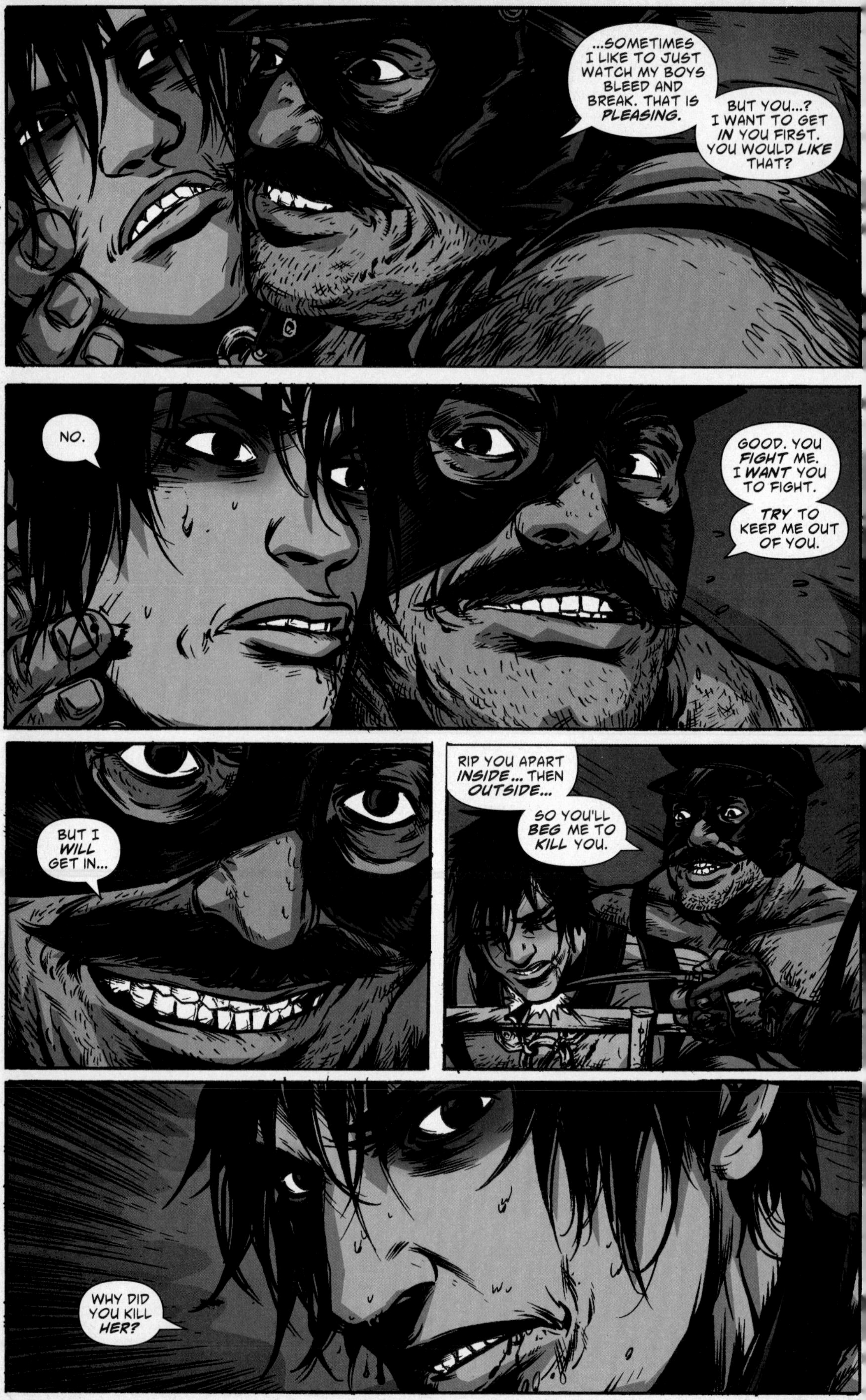
...SOMETIMES I LIKE TO JUST WATCH MY BOYS BLEED AND BREAK. THAT IS PLEASING.
BUT YOU...? I WANT TO GET IN YOU FIRST. YOU WOULD LIKE THAT?
NO.
GOOD. YOU FIGHT ME. I WANT YOU TO FIGHT.
TRY TO KEEP ME OUT OF YOU.
BUT I WILL GET IN...
RIP YOU APART INSIDE... THEN OUTSIDE...
SO YOU'LL BEG ME TO KILL YOU.
WHY DID YOU KILL HER?

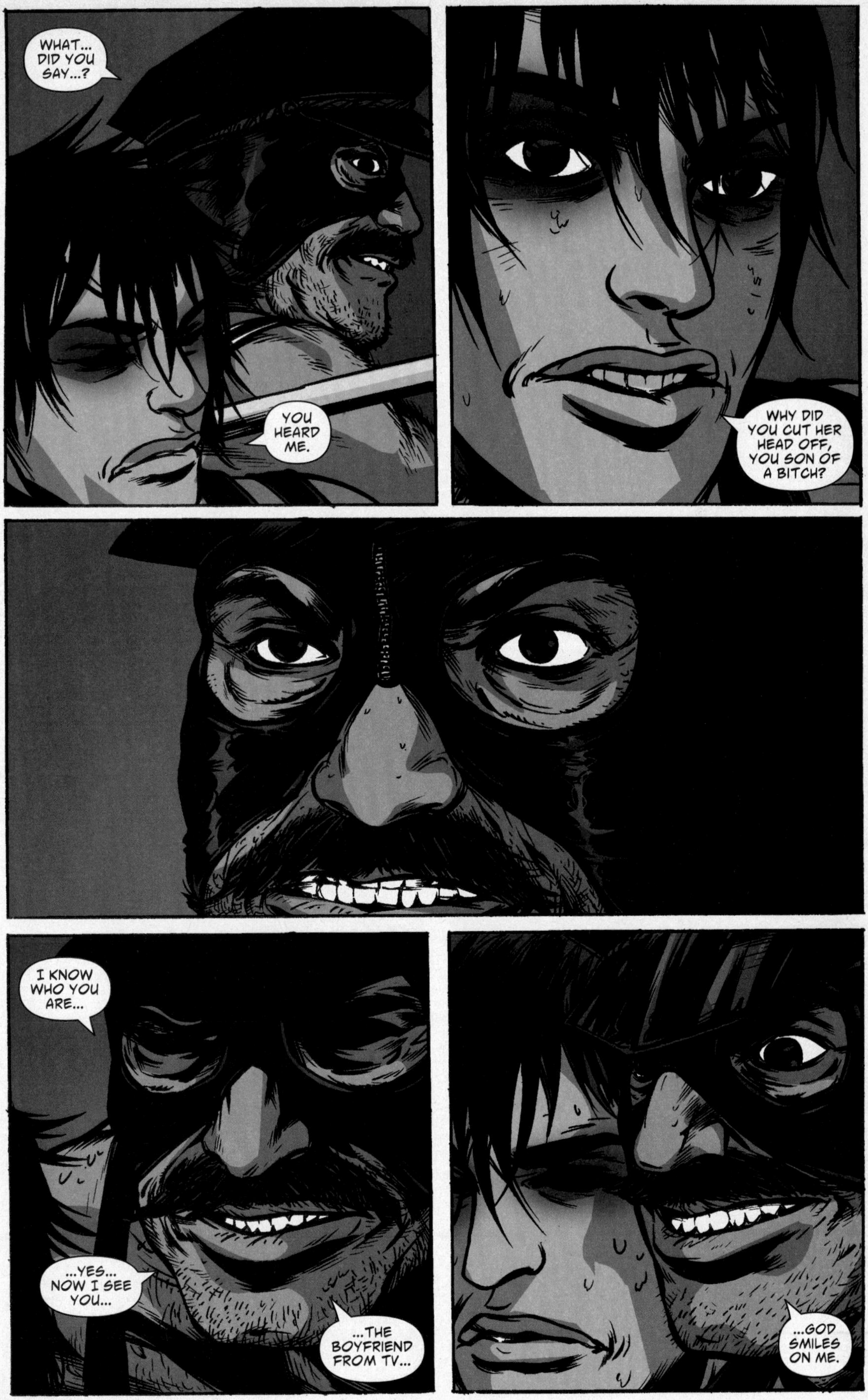
WHAT... DID YOU SAY...?
YOU HEARD ME.
WHY DID YOU CUT HER HEAD OFF, YOU SON OF A BITCH?
I KNOW WHO YOU ARE...
...YES... NOW I SEE YOU...
...THE BOYFRIEND FROM TV...
...GOD SMILES ON ME.

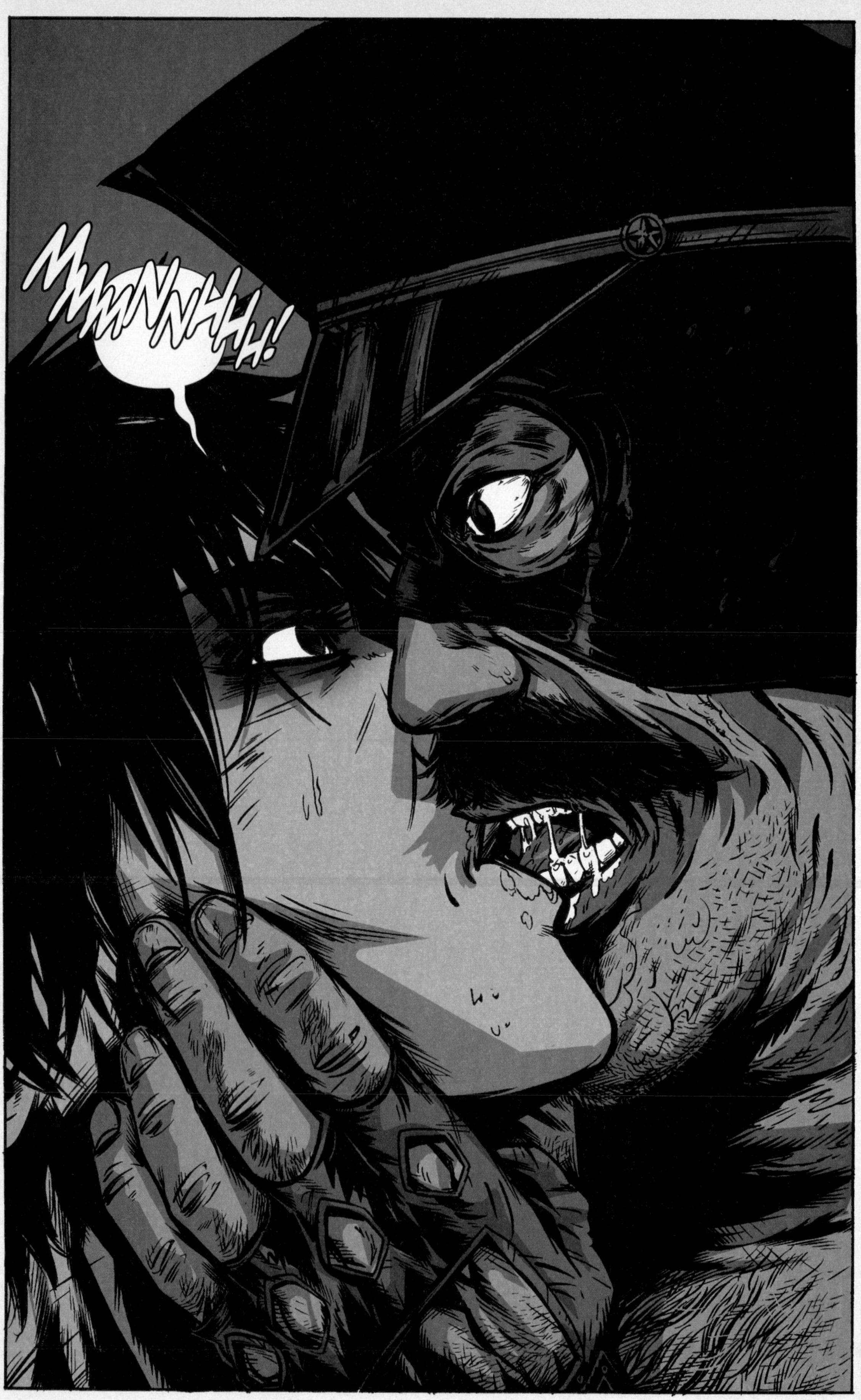
MMMNNHHH!

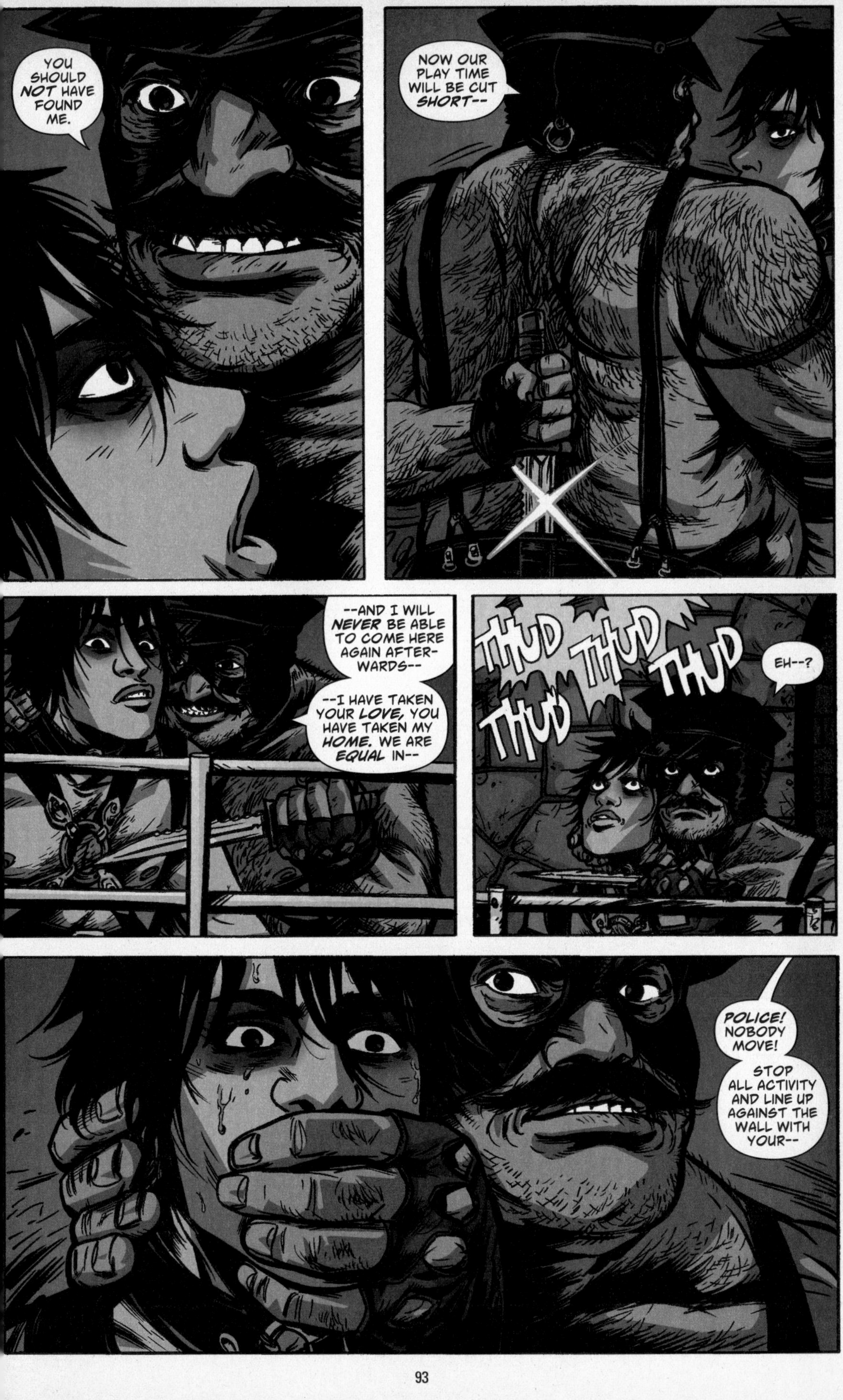
YOU SHOULD NOT HAVE FOUND ME.
NOW OUR PLAY TIME WILL BE CUT SHORT--
--AND I WILL NEVER BE ABLE TO COME HERE AGAIN AFTER-WARDS--
--I HAVE TAKEN YOUR LOVE, YOU HAVE TAKEN MY HOME. WE ARE EQUAL IN--
THUD THUD THUD THUD
EH--?
POLICE! NOBODY MOVE!
STOP ALL ACTIVITY AND LINE UP AGAINST THE WALL WITH YOUR--

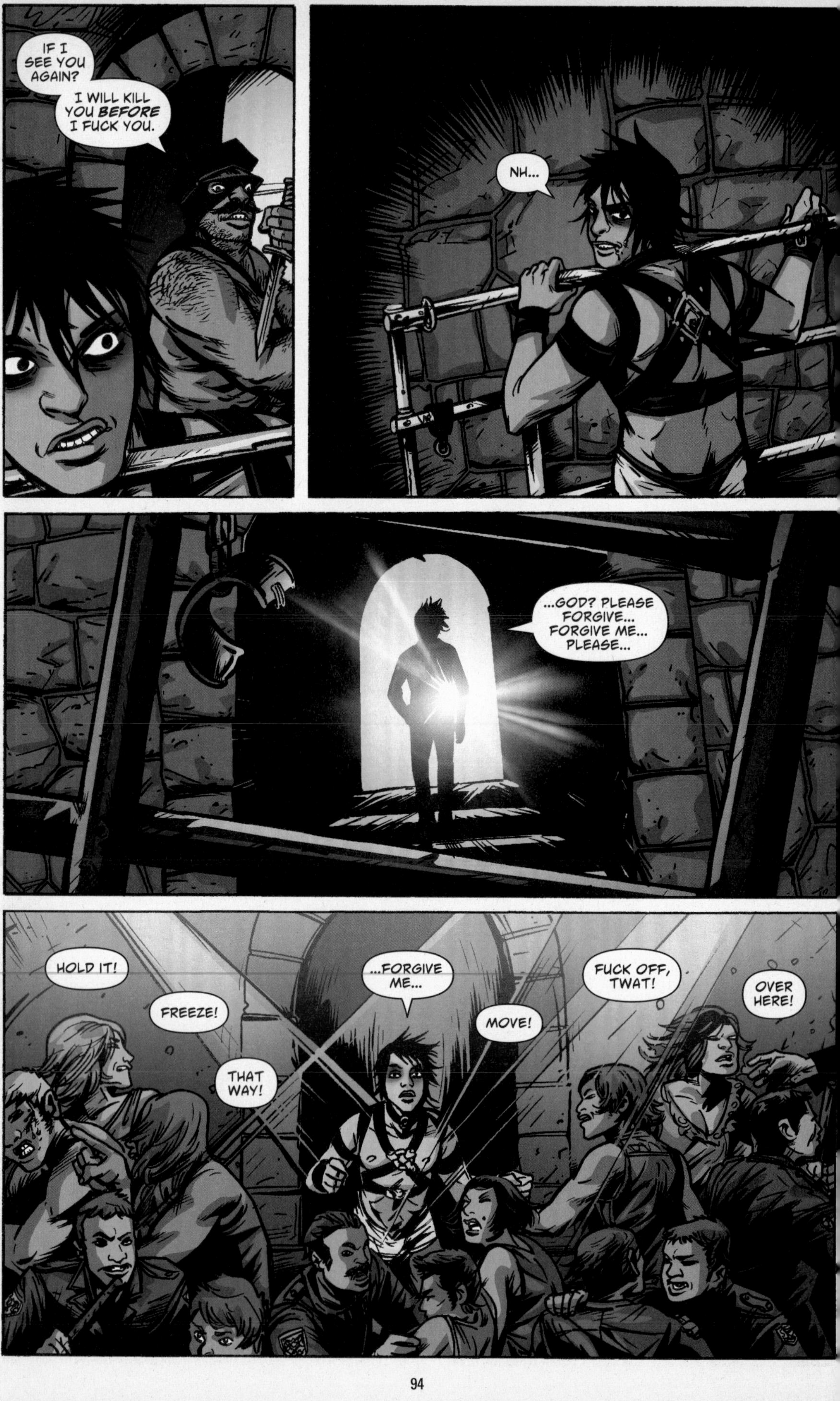
IF I SEE YOU AGAIN?
I WILL KILL YOU BEFORE I FUCK YOU.
NH...
...GOD? PLEASE FORGIVE... FORGIVE ME... PLEASE...
HOLD IT!
FREEZE!
THAT WAY!
...FORGIVE ME...
MOVE!
FUCK OFF, TWAT!
OVER HERE!

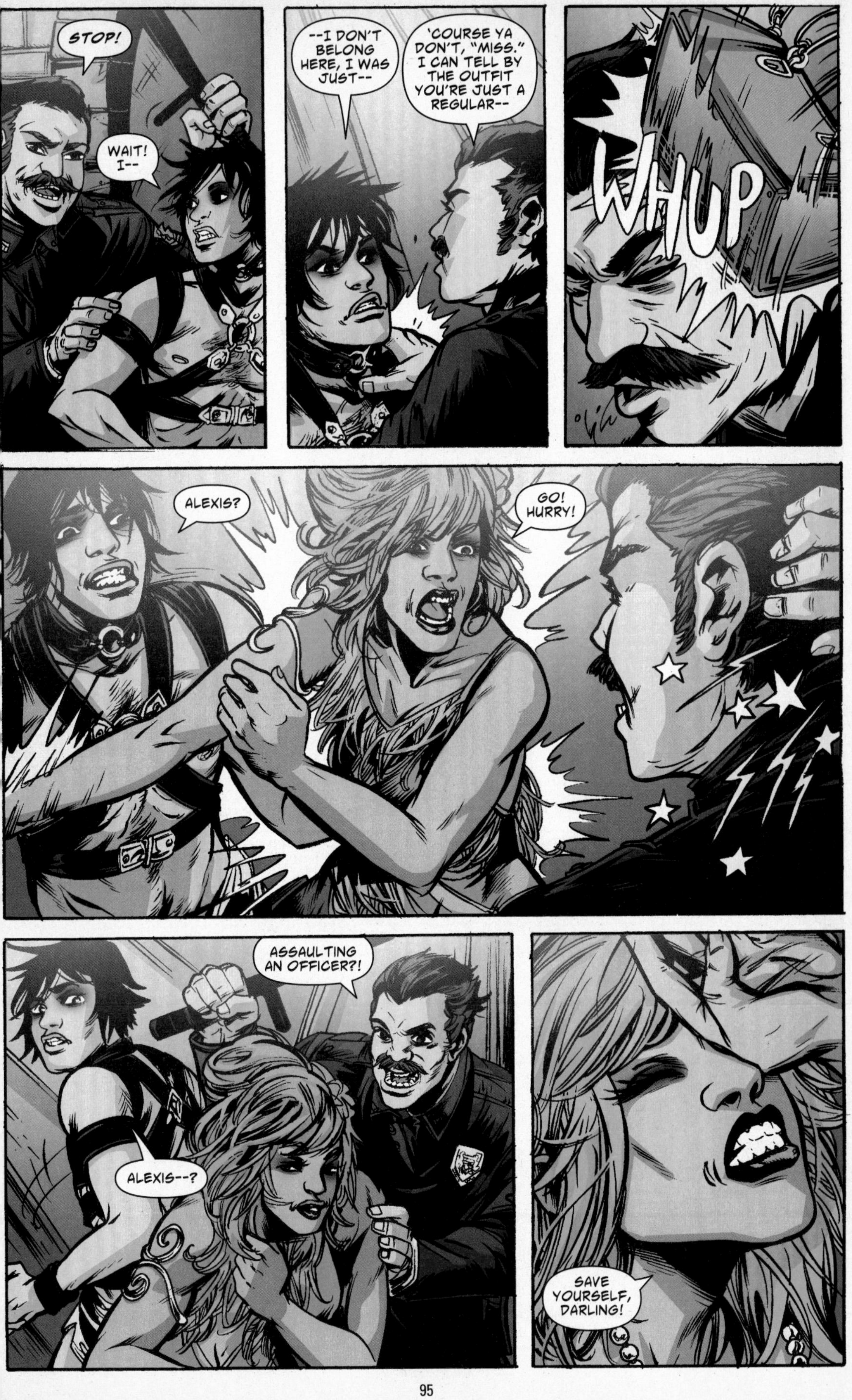
STOP!
WAIT! I--
--I DON'T BELONG HERE, I WAS JUST--
'COURSE YA DON'T, "MISS." I CAN TELL BY THE OUTFIT YOU'RE JUST A REGULAR--
WHUP
ALEXIS?
GO! HURRY!
ASSAULTING AN OFFICER?!
ALEXIS--?
SAVE YOURSELF, DARLING!

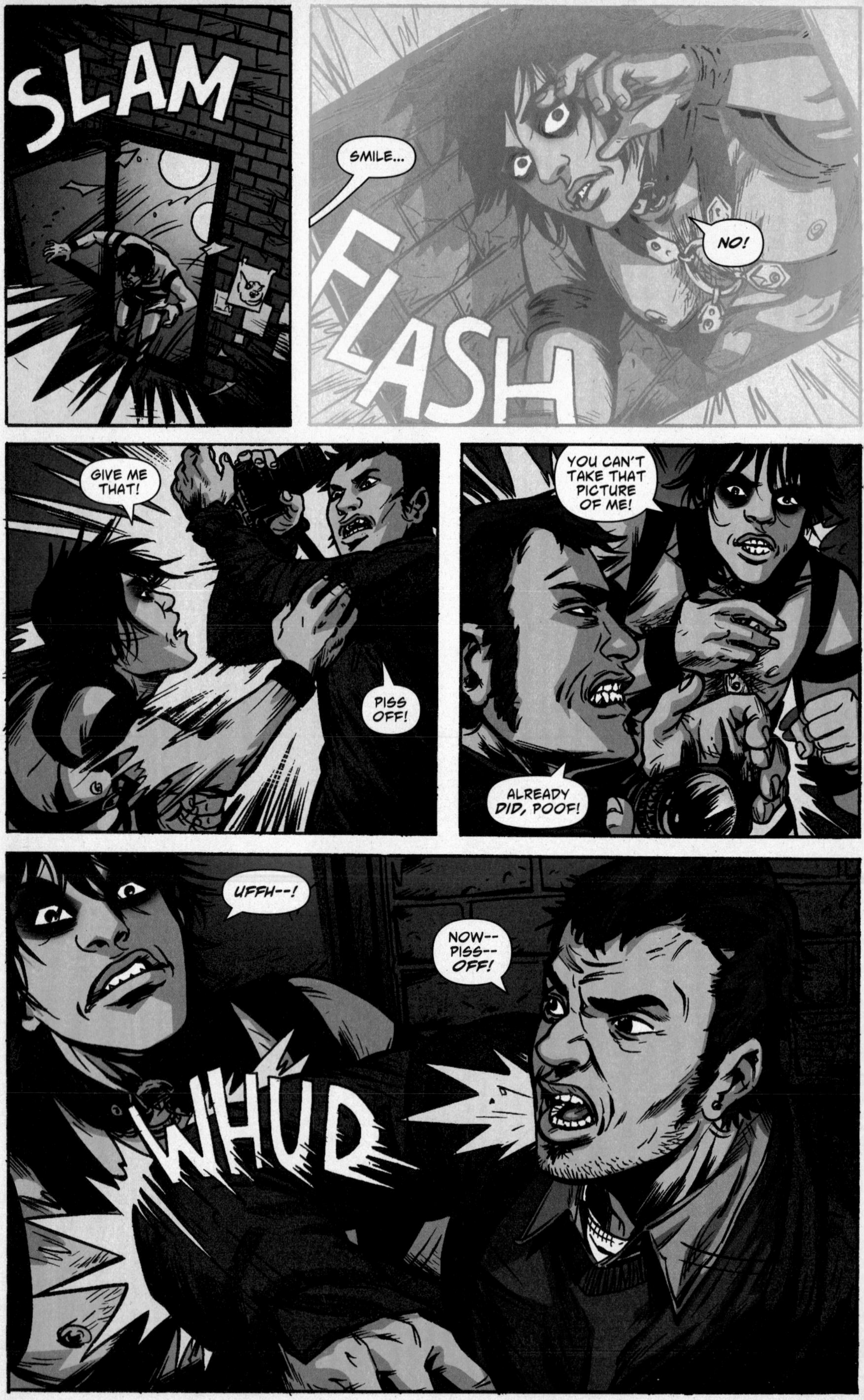
SLAM
SMILE...
NO!
FLASH
GIVE ME THAT!
PISS OFF!
YOU CAN'T TAKE THAT PICTURE OF ME!
ALREADY DID, POOF!
UFFH--!
NOW-- PISS-- OFF!
WHUD

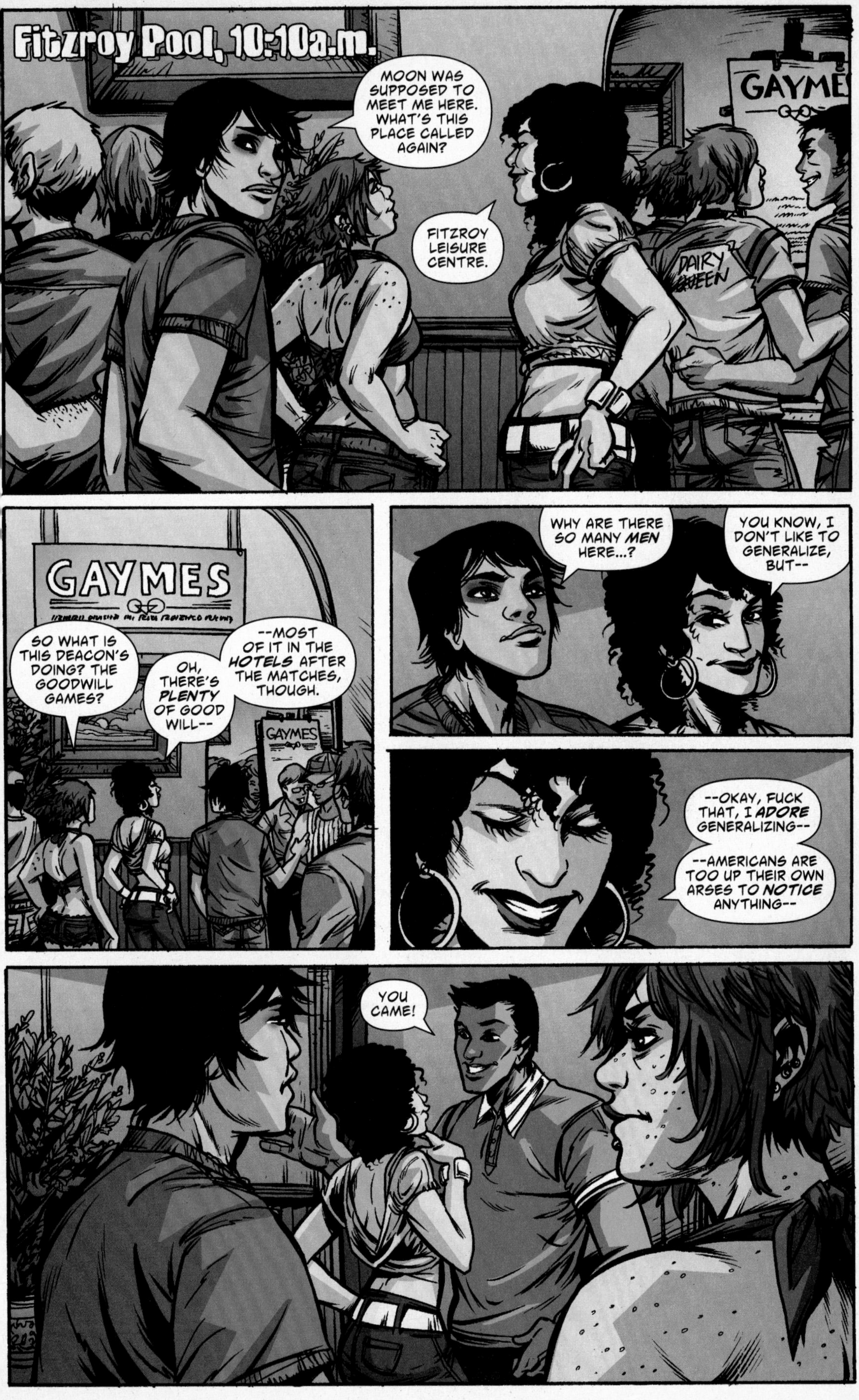
Fitzroy Pool, 10:10a.m.
MOON WAS SUPPOSED TO MEET ME HERE. WHAT'S THIS PLACE CALLED AGAIN?
FITZROY LEISURE CENTRE.
GAYMES
DAIRY QUEEN
GAYMES
SO WHAT IS THIS DEACON'S DOING? THE GOODWILL GAMES?
OH, THERE'S PLENTY OF GOOD WILL--
--MOST OF IT IN THE HOTELS AFTER THE MATCHES, THOUGH.
GAYMES
WHY ARE THERE SO MANY MEN HERE...?
YOU KNOW, I DON'T LIKE TO GENERALIZE, BUT--
--OKAY, FUCK THAT, I ADORE GENERALIZING--
--AMERICANS ARE TOO UP THEIR OWN ARSES TO NOTICE ANYTHING--
YOU CAME!

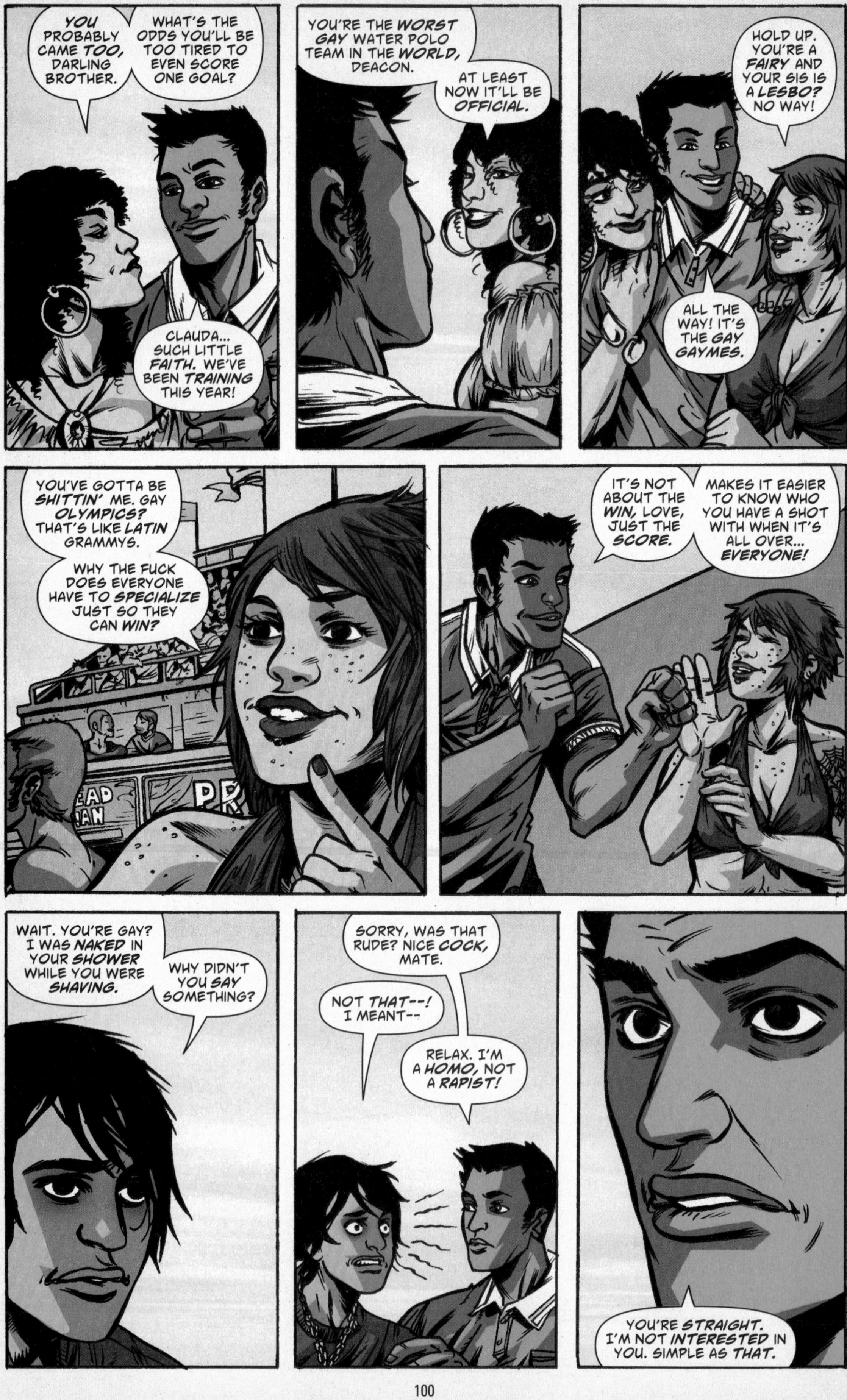
YOU PROBABLY CAME TOO, DARLING BROTHER.
WHAT'S THE ODDS YOU'LL BE TOO TIRED TO EVEN SCORE ONE GOAL?
CLAUDA... SUCH LITTLE FAITH. WE'VE BEEN TRAINING THIS YEAR!
YOU'RE THE WORST GAY WATER POLO TEAM IN THE WORLD, DEACON.
AT LEAST NOW IT'LL BE OFFICIAL.
HOLD UP. YOU'RE A FAIRY AND YOUR SIS IS A LESBO? NO WAY!
ALL THE WAY! IT'S THE GAY GAYMES.
YOU'VE GOTTA BE SHITTIN' ME. GAY OLYMPICS? THAT'S LIKE LATIN GRAMMYS.
WHY THE FUCK DOES EVERYONE HAVE TO SPECIALIZE JUST SO THEY CAN WIN?
IT'S NOT ABOUT THE WIN, LOVE, JUST THE SCORE.
MAKES IT EASIER TO KNOW WHO YOU HAVE A SHOT WITH WHEN IT'S ALL OVER... EVERYONE!
WAIT. YOU'RE GAY? I WAS NAKED IN YOUR SHOWER WHILE YOU WERE SHAVING.
WHY DIDN'T YOU SAY SOMETHING?
SORRY, WAS THAT RUDE? NICE COCK, MATE.
NOT THAT--! I MEANT--
RELAX. I'M A HOMO, NOT A RAPIST!
YOU'RE STRAIGHT. I'M NOT INTERESTED IN YOU. SIMPLE AS THAT.

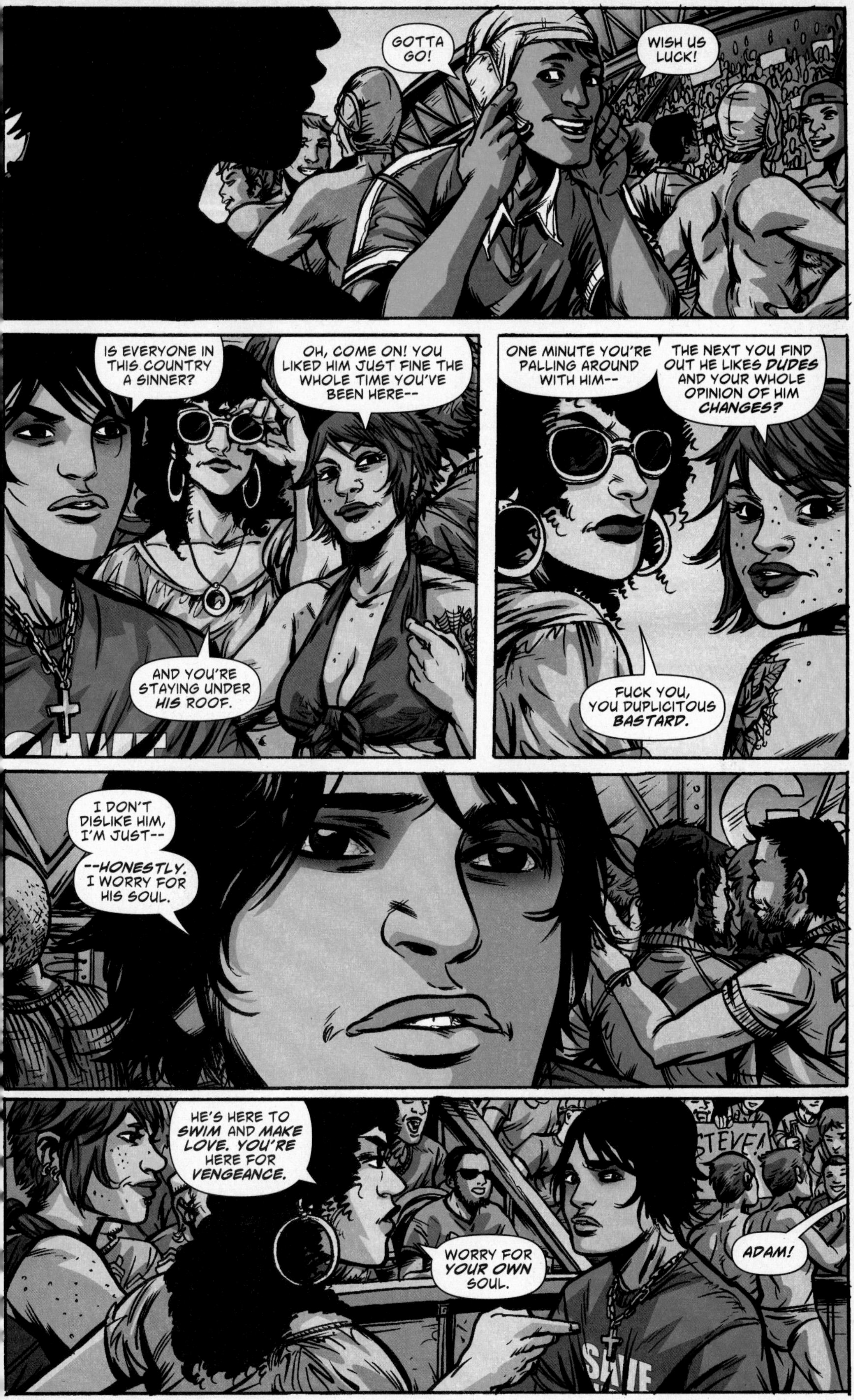
GOTTA GO!
WISH US LUCK!
IS EVERYONE IN THIS COUNTRY A SINNER?
OH, COME ON! YOU LIKED HIM JUST FINE THE WHOLE TIME YOU'VE BEEN HERE--
AND YOU'RE STAYING UNDER HIS ROOF.
ONE MINUTE YOU'RE PALLING AROUND WITH HIM--
THE NEXT YOU FIND OUT HE LIKES DUDES AND YOUR WHOLE OPINION OF HIM CHANGES?
FUCK YOU, YOU DUPLICITOUS BASTARD.
I DON'T DISLIKE HIM, I'M JUST--
--HONESTLY. I WORRY FOR HIS SOUL.
HE'S HERE TO SWIM AND MAKE LOVE. YOU'RE HERE FOR VENGEANCE.
STEVE!
WORRY FOR YOUR OWN SOUL.
ADAM!

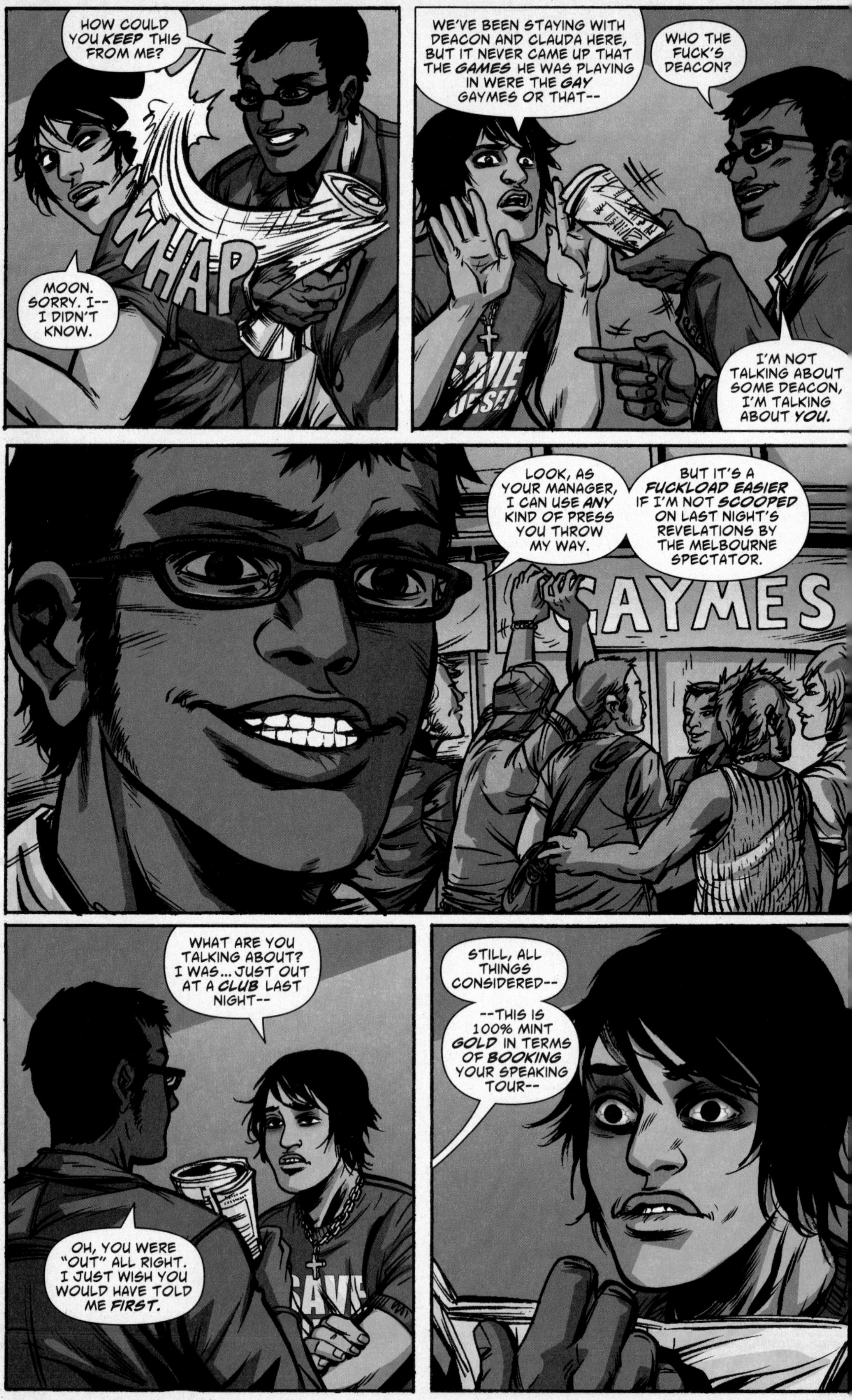
HOW COULD YOU KEEP THIS FROM ME?
WHAP
MOON. SORRY. I-- I DIDN'T KNOW.
WE'VE BEEN STAYING WITH DEACON AND CLAUDA HERE, BUT IT NEVER CAME UP THAT THE GAMES HE WAS PLAYING IN WERE THE GAY GAYMES OR THAT--
WHO THE FUCK'S DEACON?
I'M NOT TALKING ABOUT SOME DEACON, I'M TALKING ABOUT YOU.
LOOK, AS YOUR MANAGER, I CAN USE ANY KIND OF PRESS YOU THROW MY WAY.
BUT IT'S A FUCKLOAD EASIER IF I'M NOT SCOOPED ON LAST NIGHT'S REVELATIONS BY THE MELBOURNE SPECTATOR.
GAYMES
WHAT ARE YOU TALKING ABOUT? I WAS... JUST OUT AT A CLUB LAST NIGHT--
OH, YOU WERE "OUT" ALL RIGHT. I JUST WISH YOU WOULD HAVE TOLD ME FIRST.
STILL, ALL THINGS CONSIDERED--
--THIS IS 100% MINT GOLD IN TERMS OF BOOKING YOUR SPEAKING TOUR--

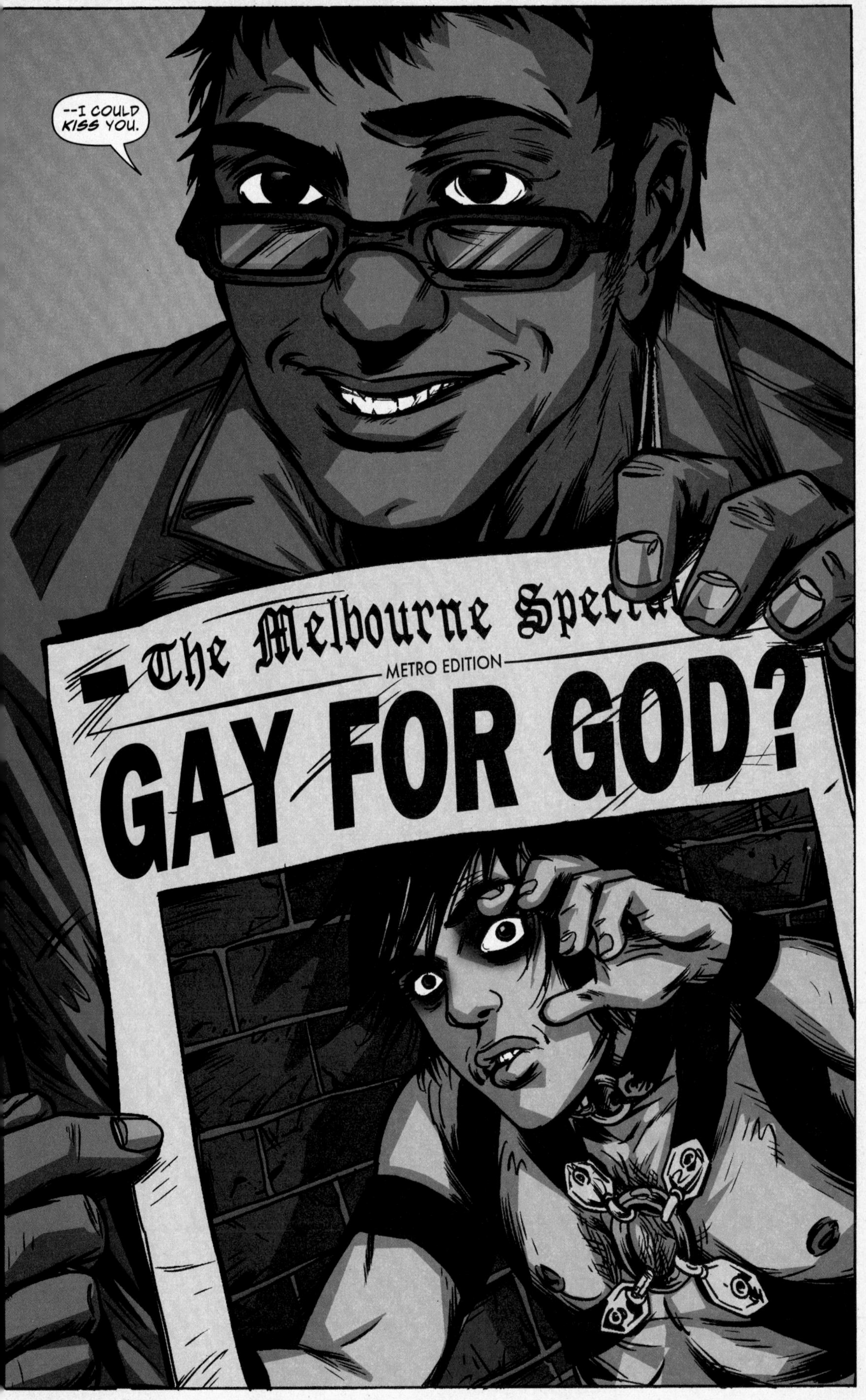
--I COULD KISS YOU.
The Melbourne Special
METRO EDITION
GAY FOR GOD?

CHAPTER FIVE

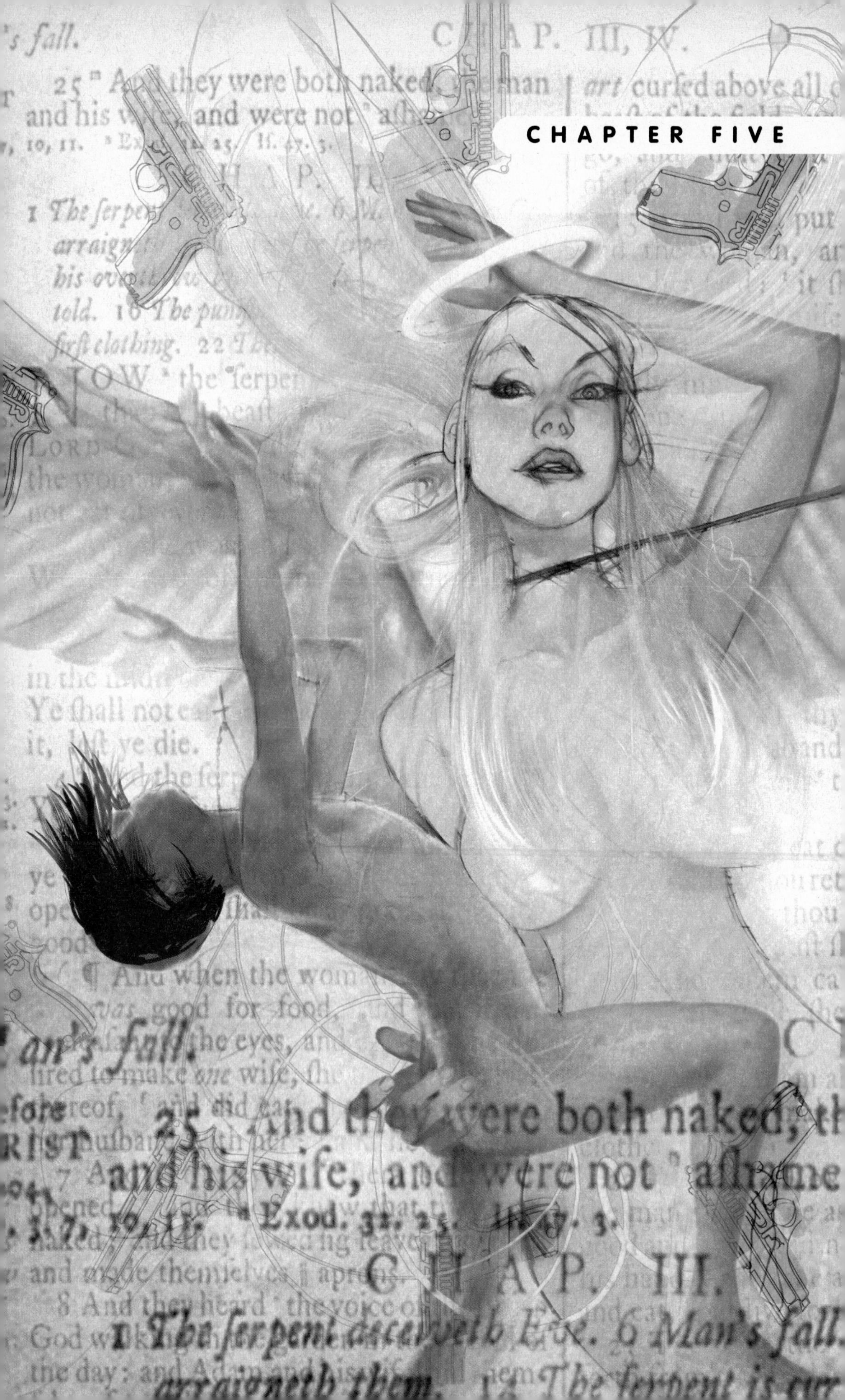

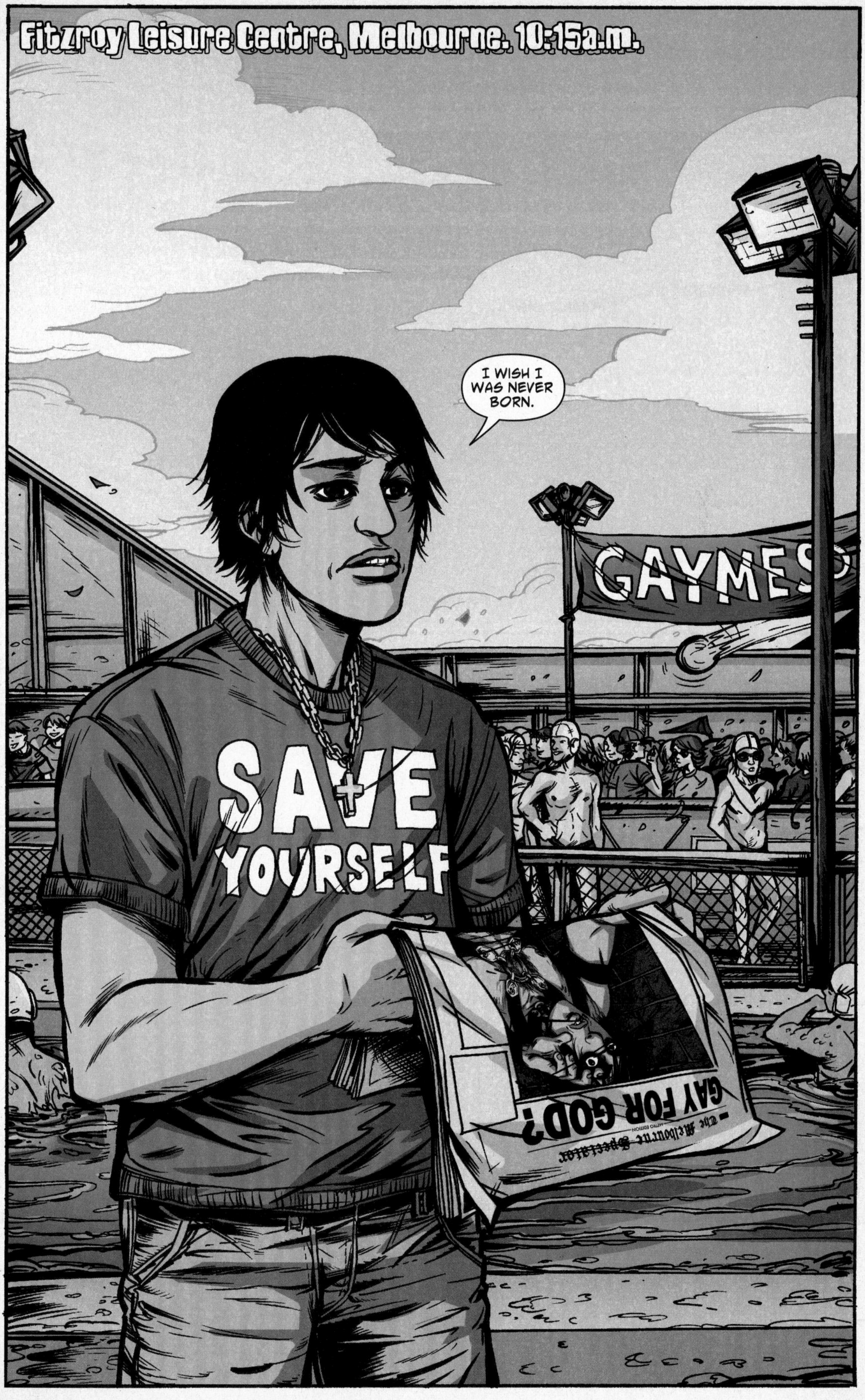
Fitzroy Leisure Centre, Melbourne. 10:15a.m.
I WISH I WAS NEVER BORN.
GAYMES
SAVE YOURSELF
GAY FOR GOD?

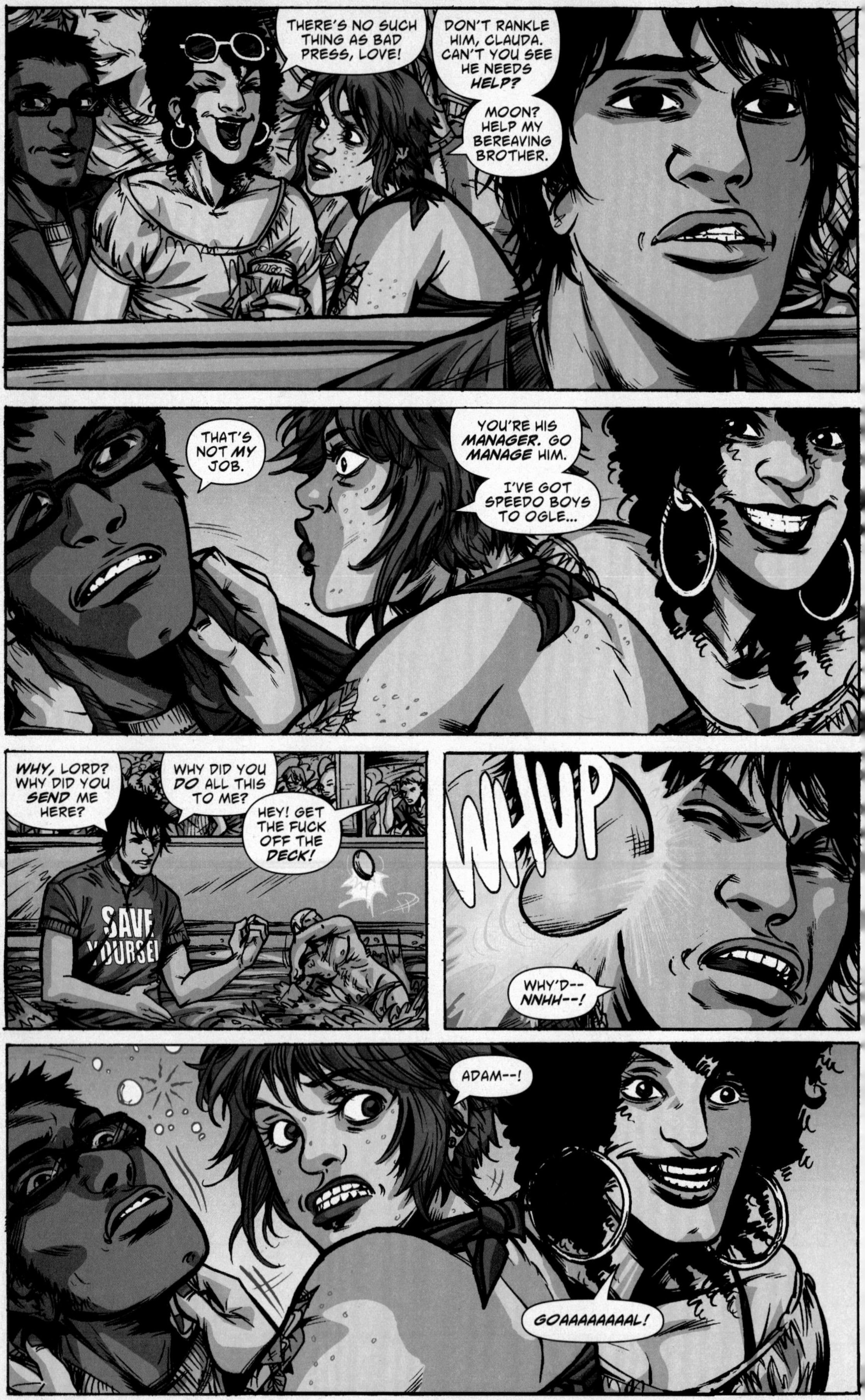

THERE'S NO SUCH THING AS BAD PRESS, LOVE!
DON'T RANKLE HIM, CLAUDA. CAN'T YOU SEE HE NEEDS *HELP?*
MOON? HELP MY BEREAVING BROTHER.
THAT'S NOT *MY* JOB.
YOU'RE HIS *MANAGER.* GO *MANAGE* HIM.
I'VE GOT SPEEDO BOYS TO OGLE...
WHY, LORD? WHY DID YOU *SEND* ME HERE?
WHY DID YOU *DO* ALL THIS TO ME?
HEY! GET THE FUCK OFF THE *DECK!*
SAVE YOURSE
WHUP
WHY'D-- *NNHH--!*
ADAM--!
GOAAAAAAAAL!

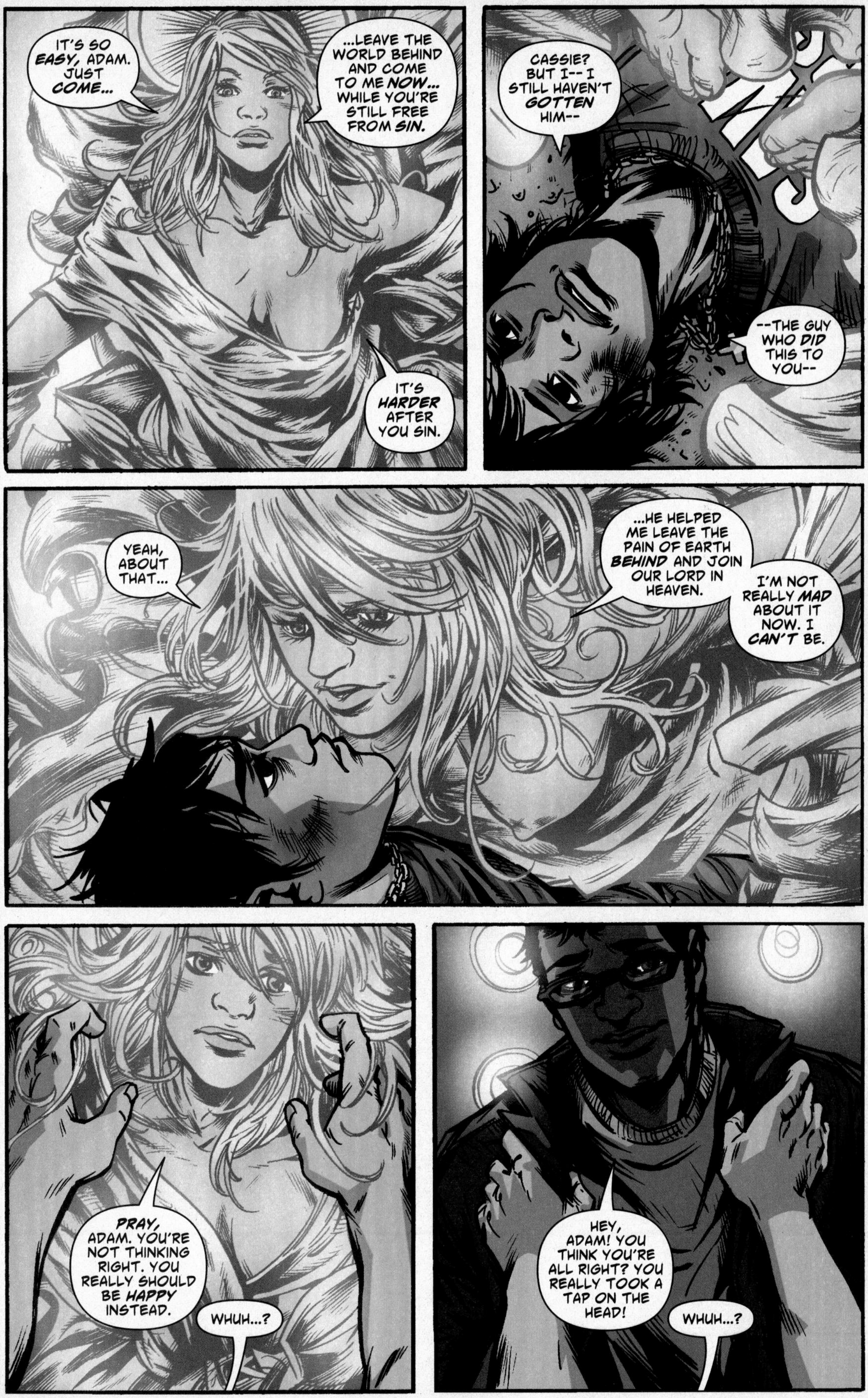
IT'S SO EASY, ADAM. JUST COME...
...LEAVE THE WORLD BEHIND AND COME TO ME NOW... WHILE YOU'RE STILL FREE FROM SIN.
IT'S HARDER AFTER YOU SIN.
CASSIE? BUT I-- I STILL HAVEN'T GOTTEN HIM--
--THE GUY WHO DID THIS TO YOU--
YEAH, ABOUT THAT...
...HE HELPED ME LEAVE THE PAIN OF EARTH BEHIND AND JOIN OUR LORD IN HEAVEN.
I'M NOT REALLY MAD ABOUT IT NOW. I CAN'T BE.
PRAY, ADAM. YOU'RE NOT THINKING RIGHT. YOU REALLY SHOULD BE HAPPY INSTEAD.
WHUH...?
HEY, ADAM! YOU THINK YOU'RE ALL RIGHT? YOU REALLY TOOK A TAP ON THE HEAD!
WHUH...?

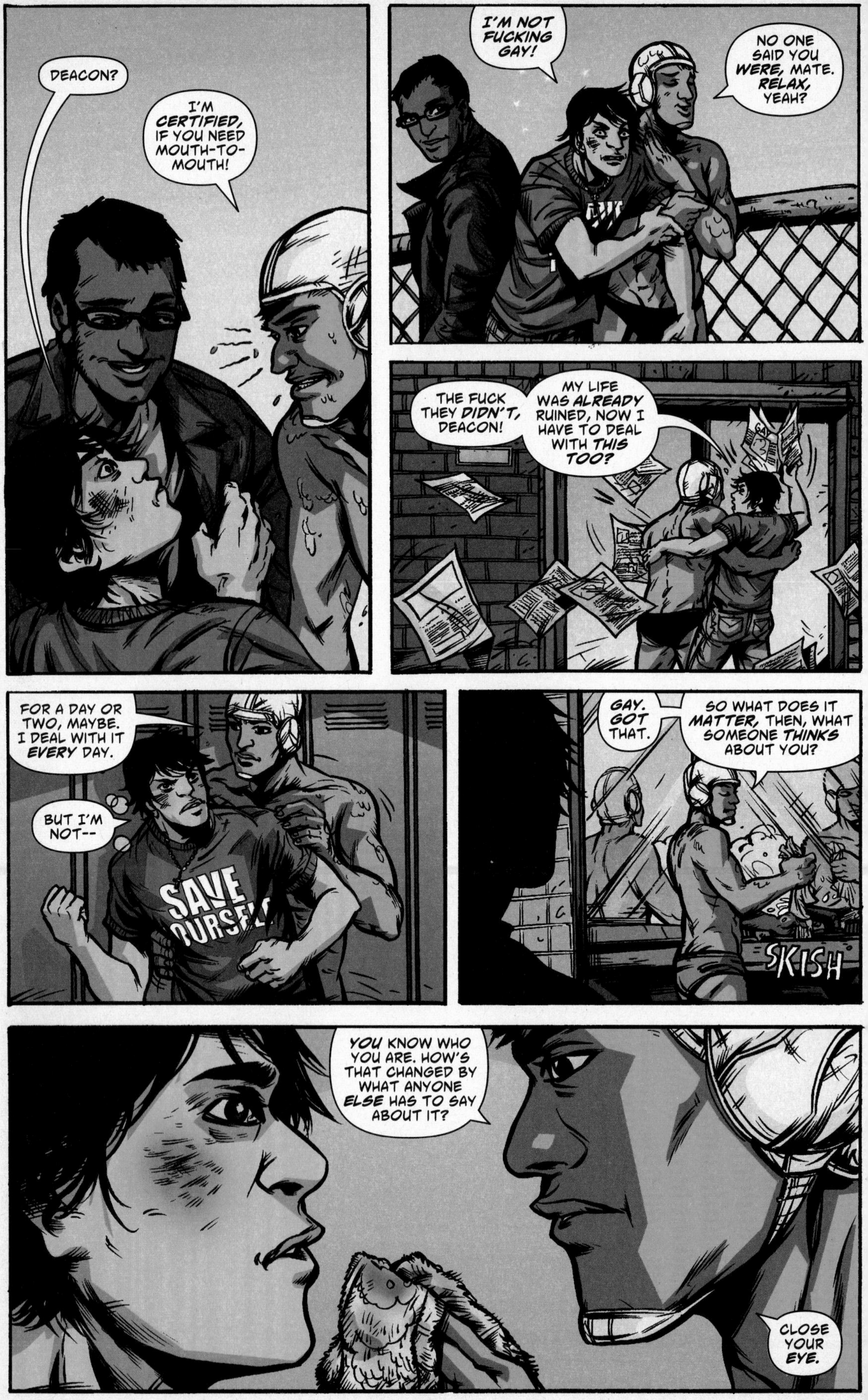
DEACON?
I'M CERTIFIED, IF YOU NEED MOUTH-TO-MOUTH!
I'M NOT FUCKING GAY!
NO ONE SAID YOU WERE, MATE. RELAX, YEAH?
THE FUCK THEY DIDN'T, DEACON!
MY LIFE WAS ALREADY RUINED, NOW I HAVE TO DEAL WITH THIS TOO?
FOR A DAY OR TWO, MAYBE. I DEAL WITH IT EVERY DAY.
BUT I'M NOT--
SAVE
GAY. GOT THAT.
SO WHAT DOES IT MATTER, THEN, WHAT SOMEONE THINKS ABOUT YOU?
SKISH
YOU KNOW WHO YOU ARE. HOW'S THAT CHANGED BY WHAT ANYONE ELSE HAS TO SAY ABOUT IT?
CLOSE YOUR EYE.

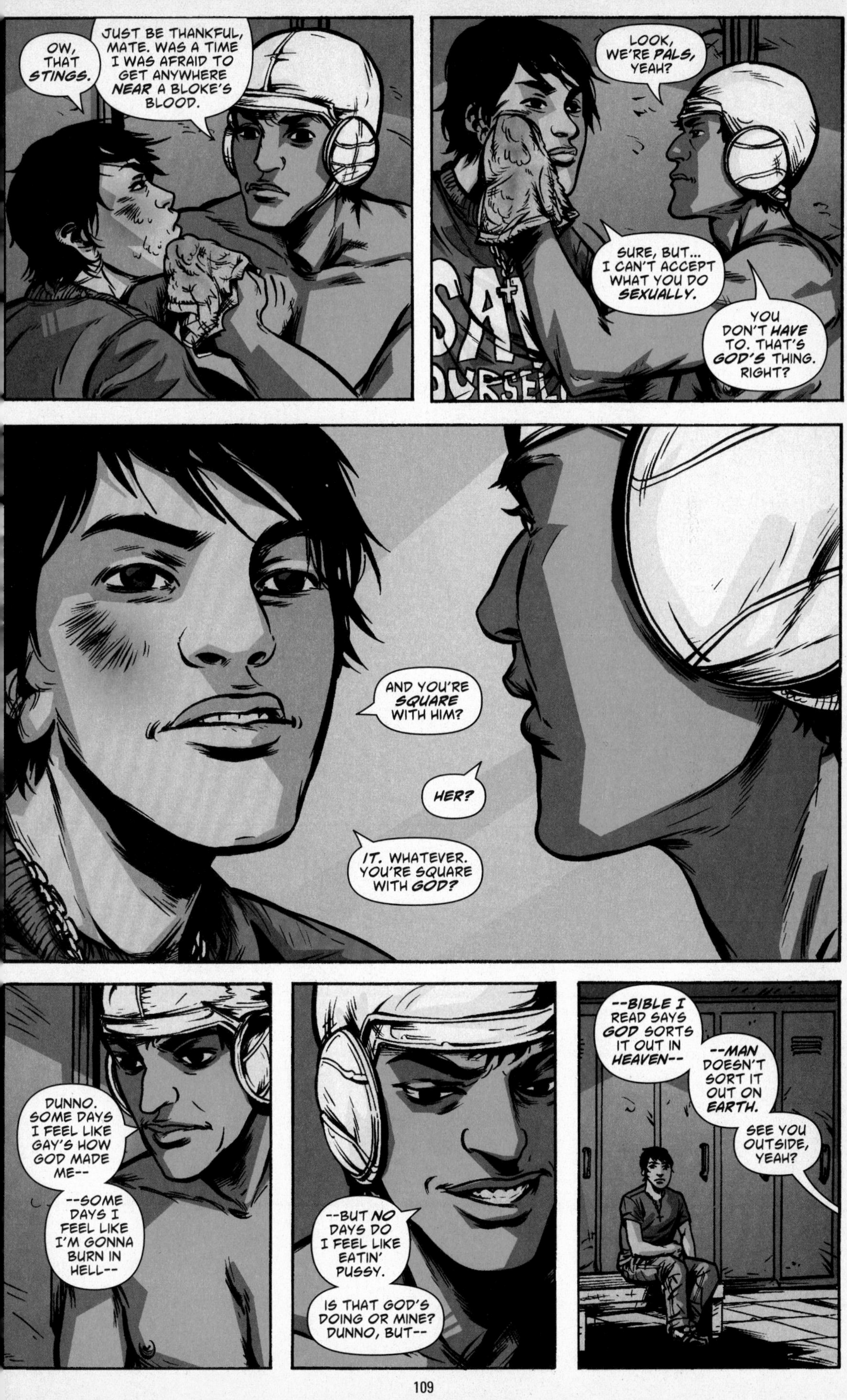
OW, THAT STINGS.
JUST BE THANKFUL, MATE. WAS A TIME I WAS AFRAID TO GET ANYWHERE NEAR A BLOKE'S BLOOD.
LOOK, WE'RE PALS, YEAH?
SURE, BUT... I CAN'T ACCEPT WHAT YOU DO SEXUALLY.
YOU DON'T HAVE TO. THAT'S GOD'S THING. RIGHT?
AND YOU'RE SQUARE WITH HIM?
HER?
IT. WHATEVER. YOU'RE SQUARE WITH GOD?
DUNNO. SOME DAYS I FEEL LIKE GAY'S HOW GOD MADE ME--
--SOME DAYS I FEEL LIKE I'M GONNA BURN IN HELL--
--BUT NO DAYS DO I FEEL LIKE EATIN' PUSSY.
IS THAT GOD'S DOING OR MINE? DUNNO, BUT--
--BIBLE I READ SAYS GOD SORTS IT OUT IN HEAVEN--
--MAN DOESN'T SORT IT OUT ON EARTH.
SEE YOU OUTSIDE, YEAH?

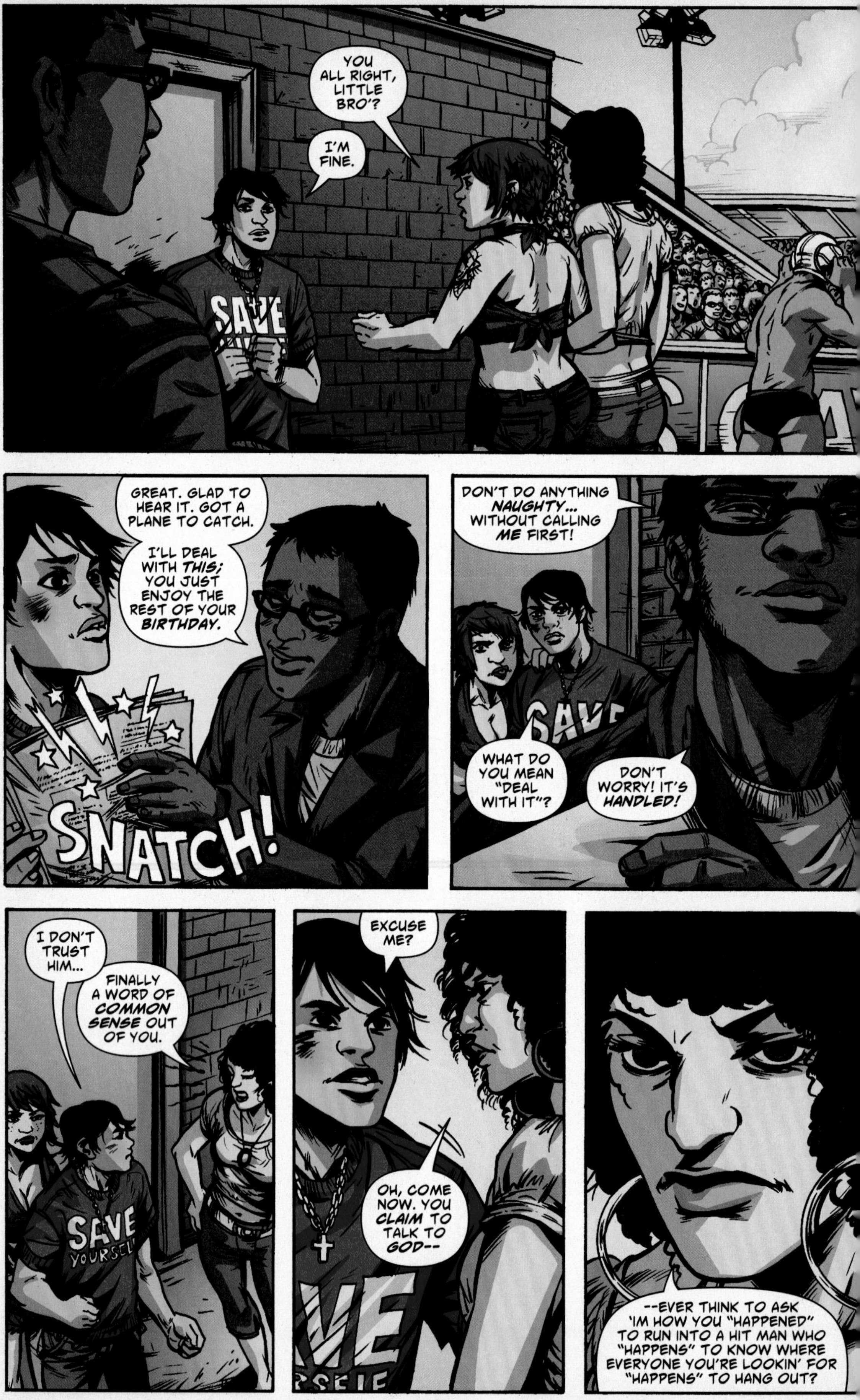

YOU ALL RIGHT, LITTLE BRO'?
I'M FINE.
GREAT. GLAD TO HEAR IT. GOT A PLANE TO CATCH.
I'LL DEAL WITH THIS; YOU JUST ENJOY THE REST OF YOUR BIRTHDAY.
SNATCH!
DON'T DO ANYTHING NAUGHTY... WITHOUT CALLING ME FIRST!
WHAT DO YOU MEAN "DEAL WITH IT"?
DON'T WORRY! IT'S HANDLED!
I DON'T TRUST HIM...
FINALLY A WORD OF COMMON SENSE OUT OF YOU.
EXCUSE ME?
OH, COME NOW. YOU CLAIM TO TALK TO GOD--
--EVER THINK TO ASK 'IM HOW YOU "HAPPENED" TO RUN INTO A HIT MAN WHO "HAPPENS" TO KNOW WHERE EVERYONE YOU'RE LOOKIN' FOR "HAPPENS" TO HANG OUT?

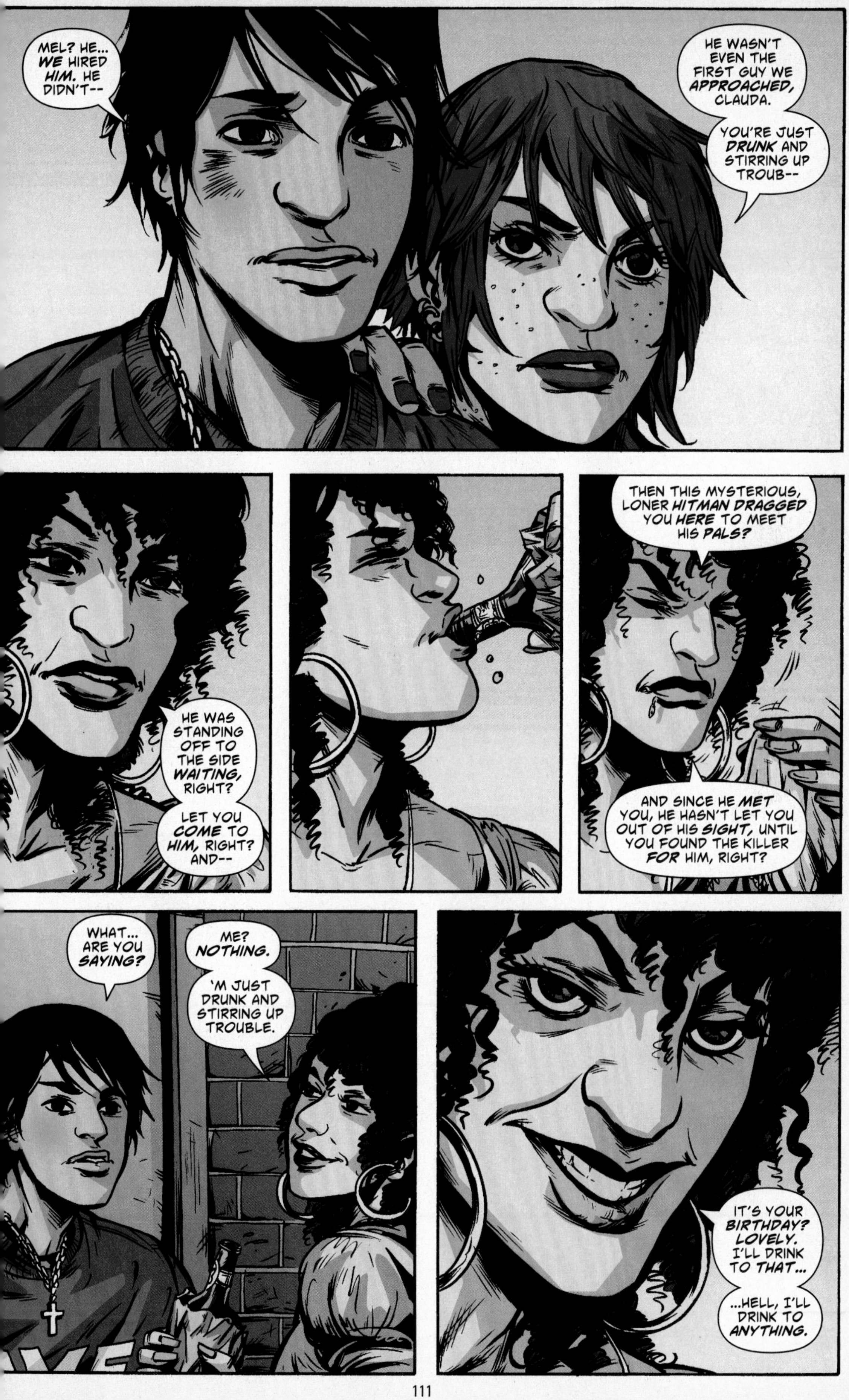
MEL? HE... WE HIRED HIM. HE DIDN'T--
HE WASN'T EVEN THE FIRST GUY WE APPROACHED, CLAUDA.
YOU'RE JUST DRUNK AND STIRRING UP TROUB--
HE WAS STANDING OFF TO THE SIDE WAITING, RIGHT?
LET YOU COME TO HIM, RIGHT? AND--
THEN THIS MYSTERIOUS, LONER HITMAN DRAGGED YOU HERE TO MEET HIS PALS?
AND SINCE HE MET YOU, HE HASN'T LET YOU OUT OF HIS SIGHT, UNTIL YOU FOUND THE KILLER FOR HIM, RIGHT?
WHAT... ARE YOU SAYING?
ME? NOTHING.
'M JUST DRUNK AND STIRRING UP TROUBLE.
IT'S YOUR BIRTHDAY? LOVELY. I'LL DRINK TO THAT...
...HELL, I'LL DRINK TO ANYTHING.

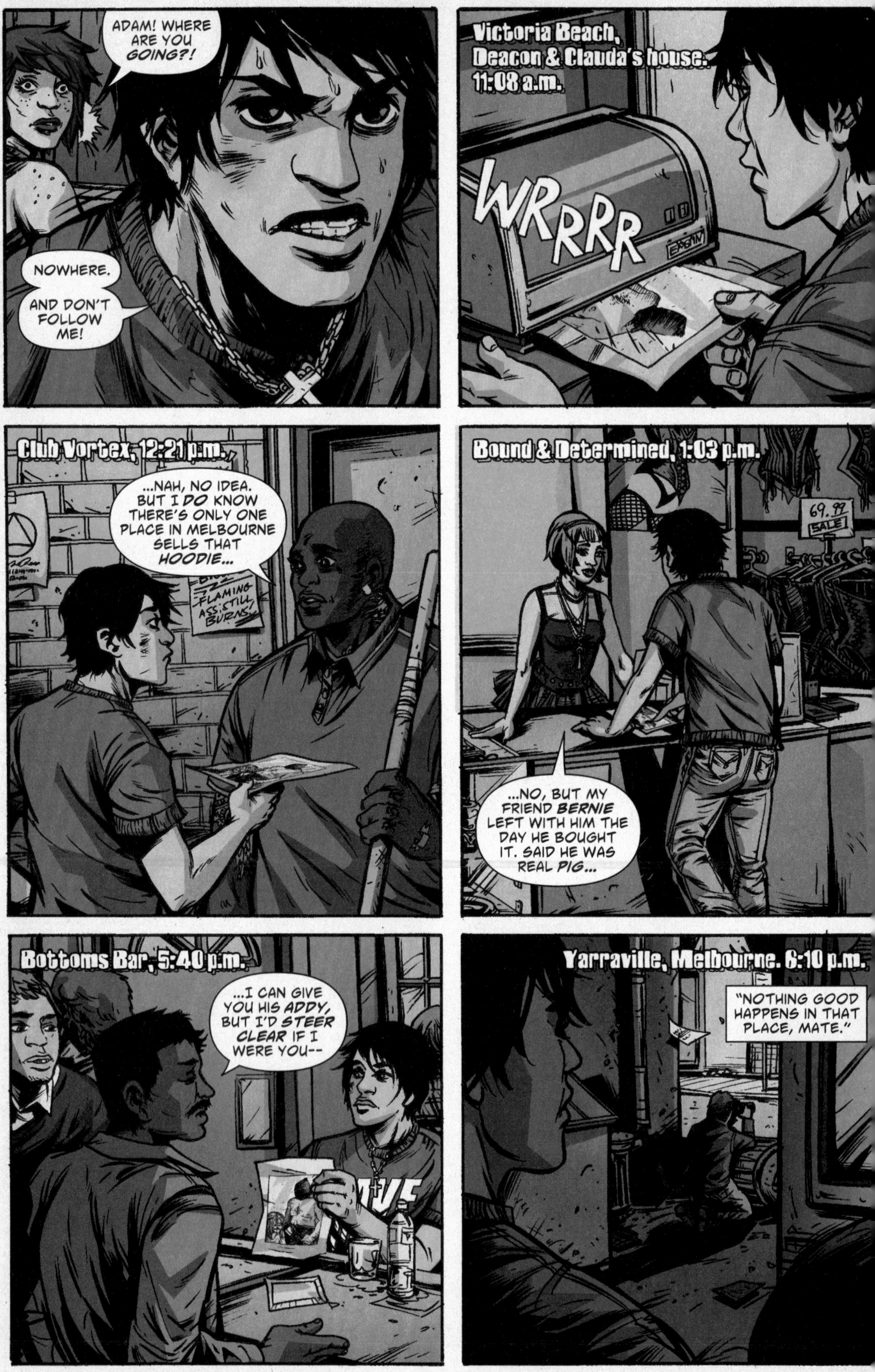
ADAM! WHERE ARE YOU GOING?!
NOWHERE.
AND DON'T FOLLOW ME!
Victoria Beach, Deacon & Clauda's house. 11:08 a.m.
WRRRR
Club Vortex, 12:21 p.m.
...NAH, NO IDEA. BUT I DO KNOW THERE'S ONLY ONE PLACE IN MELBOURNE SELLS THAT HOODIE...
FLAMING ASS: STILL BURNS
Bound & Determined, 1:03 p.m.
69.99
SALE
...NO, BUT MY FRIEND BERNIE LEFT WITH HIM THE DAY HE BOUGHT IT. SAID HE WAS REAL PIG...
Bottoms Bar, 5:40 p.m.
...I CAN GIVE YOU HIS ADDY, BUT I'D STEER CLEAR IF I WERE YOU--
Yarraville, Melbourne. 6:10 p.m.
"NOTHING GOOD HAPPENS IN THAT PLACE, MATE."

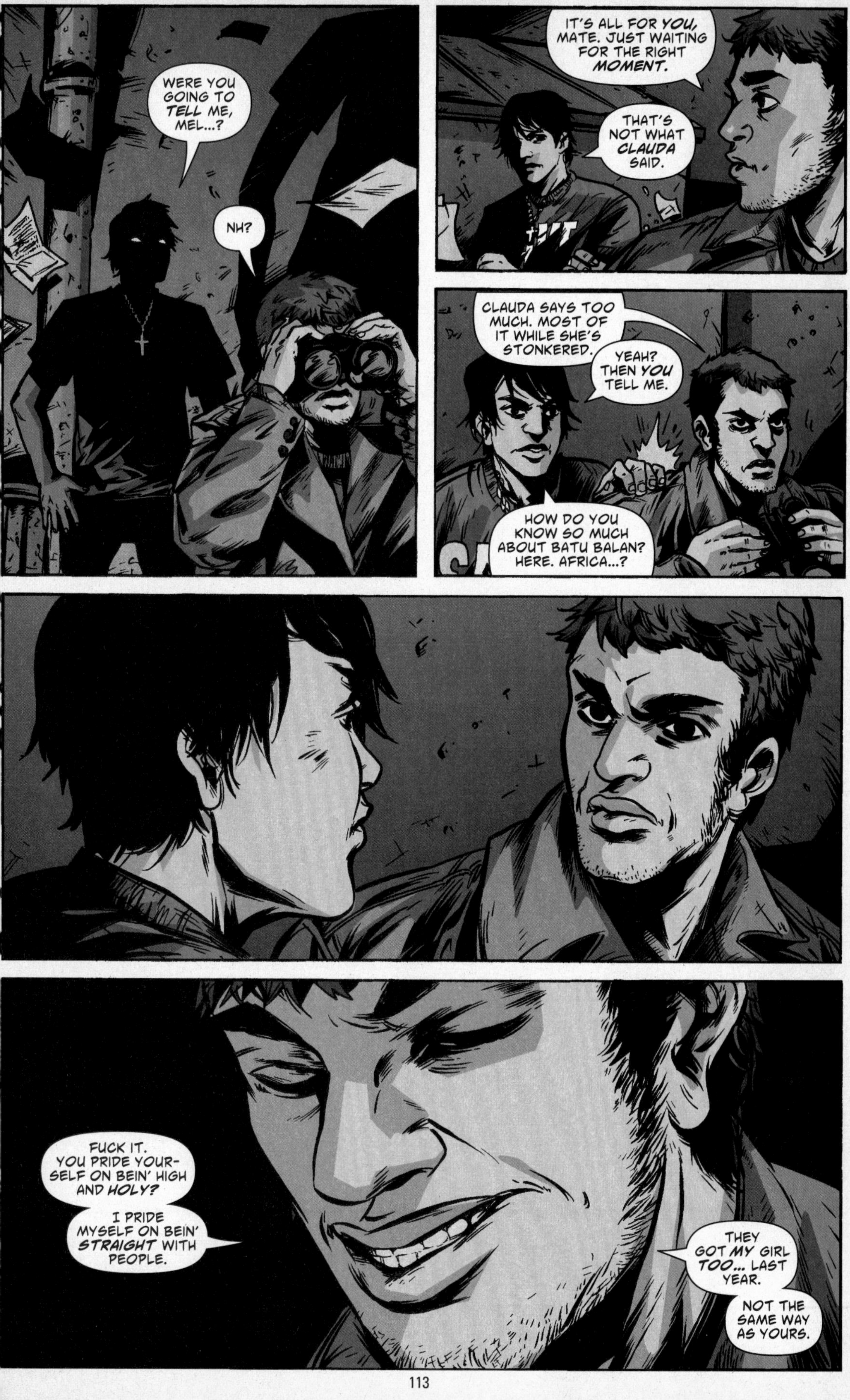
WERE YOU GOING TO TELL ME, MEL...?
NH?
IT'S ALL FOR YOU, MATE. JUST WAITING FOR THE RIGHT MOMENT.
THAT'S NOT WHAT CLAUDA SAID.
CLAUDA SAYS TOO MUCH. MOST OF IT WHILE SHE'S STONKERED.
YEAH? THEN YOU TELL ME.
HOW DO YOU KNOW SO MUCH ABOUT BATU BALAN? HERE. AFRICA...?
FUCK IT. YOU PRIDE YOURSELF ON BEIN' HIGH AND HOLY?
I PRIDE MYSELF ON BEIN' STRAIGHT WITH PEOPLE.
THEY GOT MY GIRL TOO... LAST YEAR.
NOT THE SAME WAY AS YOURS.

THEY DIDN'T MAKE A *POINT* OUT OF HER.

"JUST A SIMPLE LITTLE DEATH. AN 'UNFORTUNATE ACCIDENT' THE COPS TRIED TO SAY.

"BUT A BOMB DON'T GO OFF IN A SYDNEY DISCO BY ACCIDENT.

"SHE WAS DANCING THERE.

"SHRAPNEL MADE A TINY LITTLE HOLE IN HER HEART AND SHE WENT DOWN LIKE AN ANCHOR.

"INSTANT."

BATU BALAN EVENTUALLY TOOK CREDIT.

I TOOK TO MAKIN' THEM PAY OFF THEIR CREDIT.

BUT... HOW DID YOU KNOW? THAT I WAS COMING TO AFRICA? HOW DID WE JUST HAPPEN TO *MEET* YOU?

NO SUCH THING AS CHANCE.

YOU BELIEVE IN GOD'S PLAN?

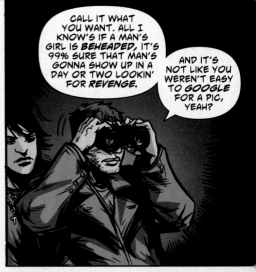

CALL IT WHAT YOU WANT. ALL I KNOW'S IF A MAN'S GIRL IS *BEHEADED*, IT'S 99% SURE THAT MAN'S GONNA SHOW UP IN A DAY OR TWO LOOKIN' FOR *REVENGE*.

AND IT'S NOT LIKE YOU WEREN'T EASY TO *GOOGLE* FOR A PIC, YEAH?

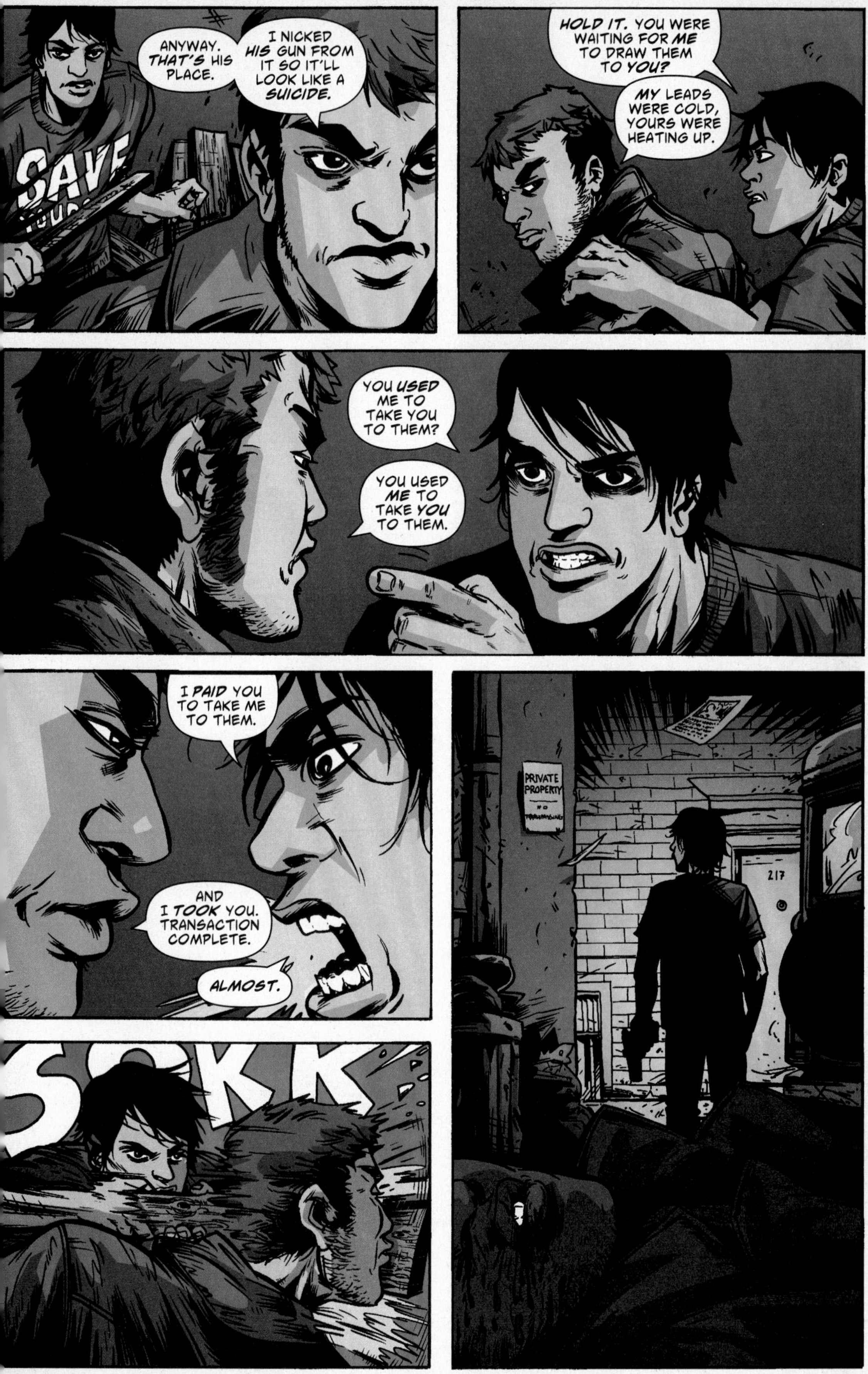

ANYWAY. THAT'S HIS PLACE.
I NICKED HIS GUN FROM IT SO IT'LL LOOK LIKE A SUICIDE.
HOLD IT. YOU WERE WAITING FOR ME TO DRAW THEM TO YOU?
MY LEADS WERE COLD, YOURS WERE HEATING UP.
YOU USED ME TO TAKE YOU TO THEM?
YOU USED ME TO TAKE YOU TO THEM.
I PAID YOU TO TAKE ME TO THEM.
AND I TOOK YOU. TRANSACTION COMPLETE.
ALMOST.
SOKK
PRIVATE PROPERTY
217

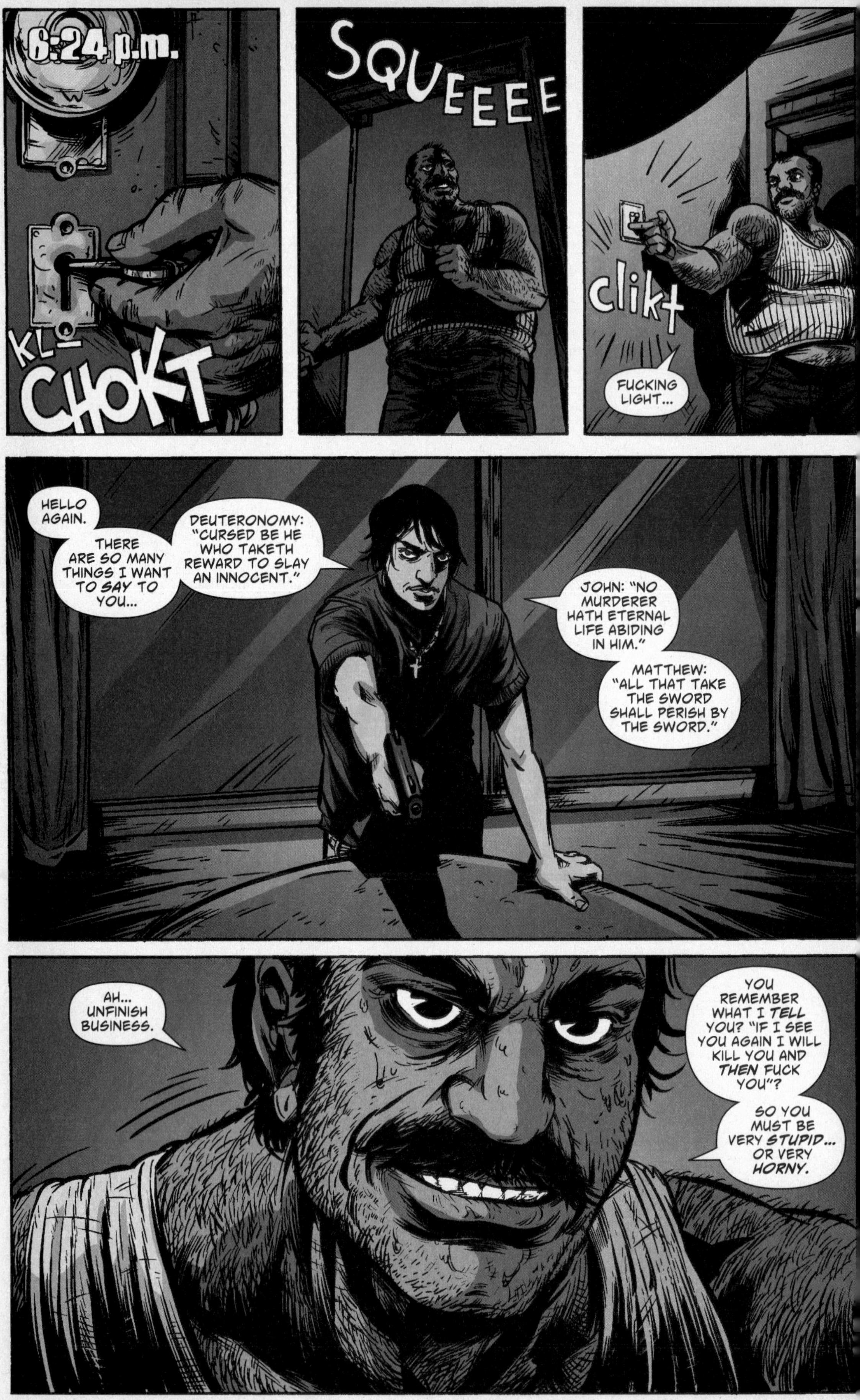
6:24 p.m.
KL-CHOKT
SQUEEEE
CLIKT
FUCKING LIGHT...
HELLO AGAIN.
THERE ARE SO MANY THINGS I WANT TO *SAY* TO YOU...
DEUTERONOMY: "CURSED BE HE WHO TAKETH REWARD TO SLAY AN INNOCENT."
JOHN: "NO MURDERER HATH ETERNAL LIFE ABIDING IN HIM."
MATTHEW: "ALL THAT TAKE THE SWORD SHALL PERISH BY THE SWORD."
AH... UNFINISH BUSINESS.
YOU REMEMBER WHAT I *TELL* YOU? "IF I SEE YOU AGAIN I WILL KILL YOU AND *THEN* FUCK YOU"?
SO YOU MUST BE VERY *STUPID*... OR VERY *HORNY*.

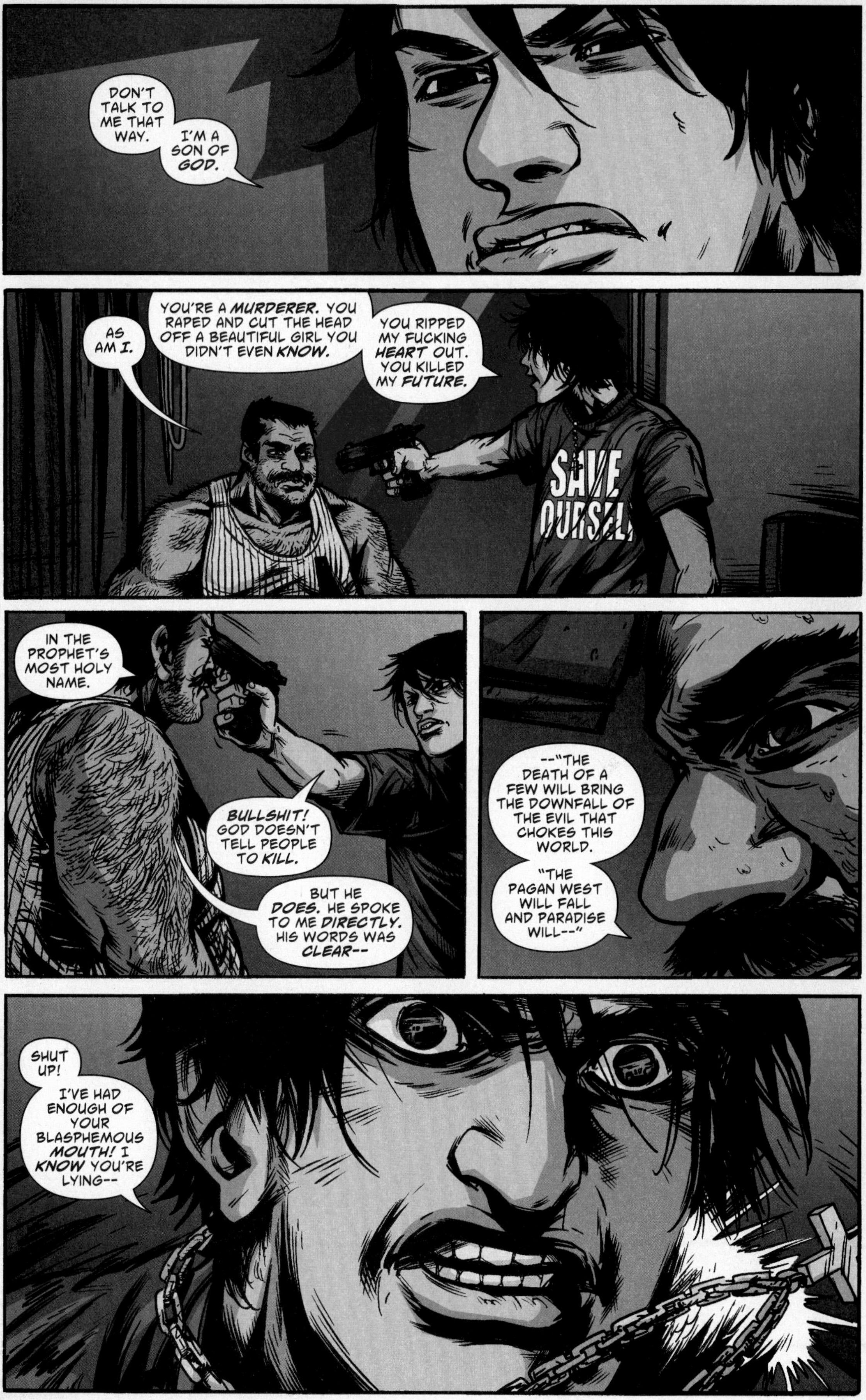
DON'T TALK TO ME THAT WAY.
I'M A SON OF GOD.
AS AM I.
YOU'RE A MURDERER. YOU RAPED AND CUT THE HEAD OFF A BEAUTIFUL GIRL YOU DIDN'T EVEN KNOW.
YOU RIPPED MY FUCKING HEART OUT. YOU KILLED MY FUTURE.
SAVE OURSELF
IN THE PROPHET'S MOST HOLY NAME.
BULLSHIT! GOD DOESN'T TELL PEOPLE TO KILL.
BUT HE DOES. HE SPOKE TO ME DIRECTLY. HIS WORDS WAS CLEAR--
--"THE DEATH OF A FEW WILL BRING THE DOWNFALL OF THE EVIL THAT CHOKES THIS WORLD.
"THE PAGAN WEST WILL FALL AND PARADISE WILL--"
SHUT UP!
I'VE HAD ENOUGH OF YOUR BLASPHEMOUS MOUTH! I KNOW YOU'RE LYING--

IT IS NO QUESTION OF WHAT *YOU* BELIEF.

I MUST FOLLOW THE PROPHET'S WISH. HE TELLS ME, I DO HIS BIDDING.

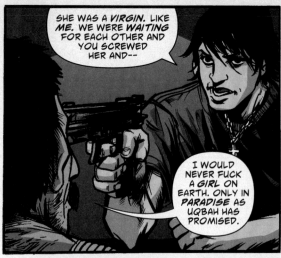

SHE WAS A *VIRGIN.* LIKE *ME.* WE WERE *WAITING* FOR EACH OTHER AND YOU SCREWED HER AND--

I WOULD NEVER FUCK A *GIRL* ON EARTH. ONLY IN *PARADISE* AS UQBAH HAS PROMISED.

THAT'S WHO YOU CALL *GOD?* "*UQBAH*"?

NO. UQBAH IS MAN, VERY *WISE* MAN.

HE IS WHY BATU BALAN EXISTS ON *EARTH* AS IN PARADISE.

GOD TOLD ME CASSIE WAS THE WOMAN I WOULD BE WITH *FOREVER!*

HOW COULD HE TELL *YOU* TO KILL HER?!

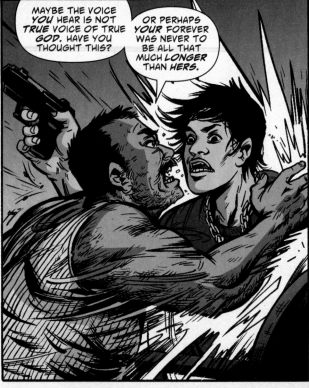

MAYBE THE VOICE *YOU* HEAR IS NOT *TRUE* VOICE OF TRUE *GOD.* HAVE YOU THOUGHT THIS?

OR PERHAPS *YOUR* FOREVER WAS NEVER TO BE ALL THAT MUCH *LONGER* THAN *HERS.*

118

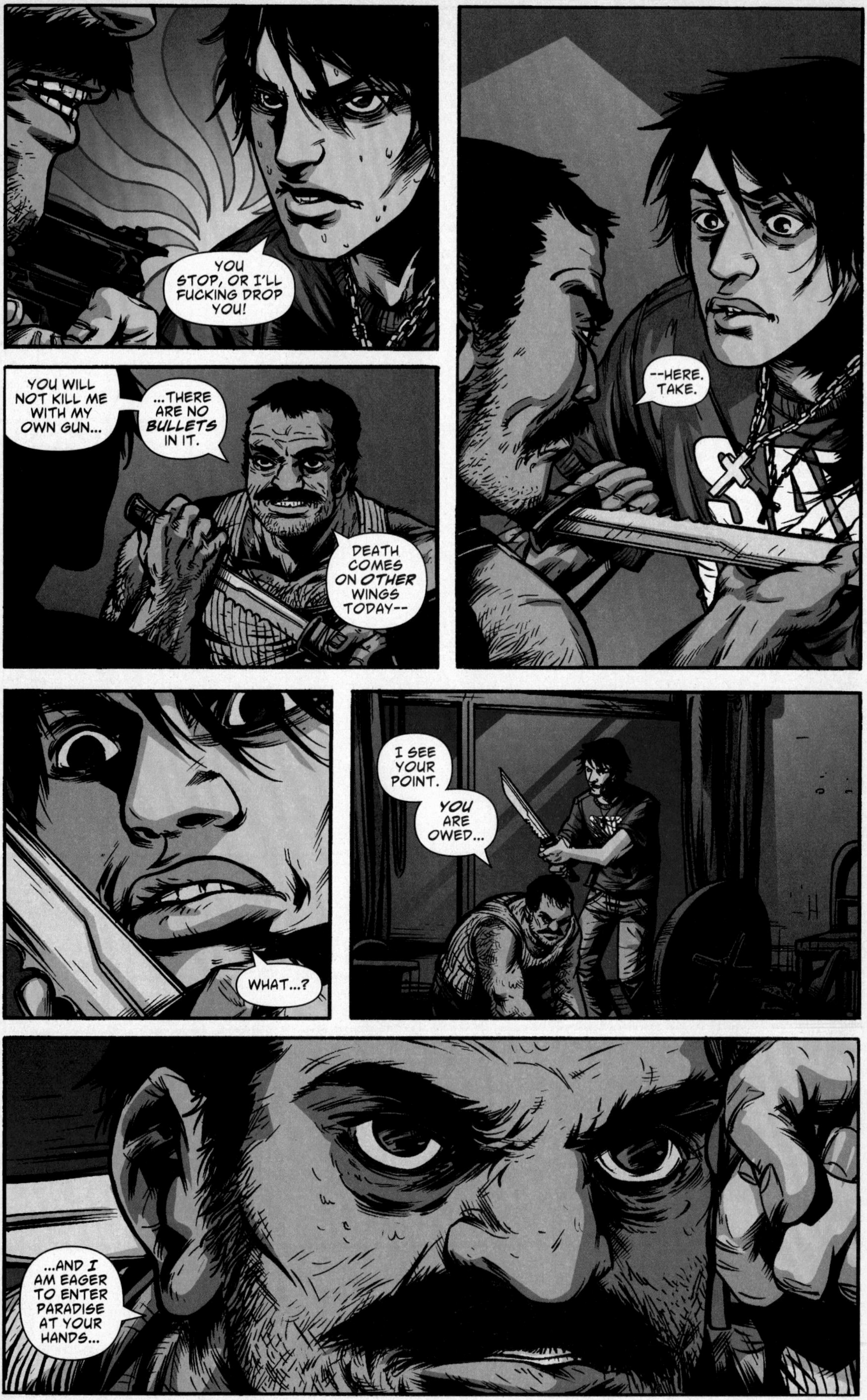
YOU STOP, OR I'LL FUCKING DROP YOU!
--HERE. TAKE.
YOU WILL NOT KILL ME WITH MY OWN GUN...
...THERE ARE NO BULLETS IN IT.
DEATH COMES ON OTHER WINGS TODAY--
WHAT...?
I SEE YOUR POINT.
YOU ARE OWED...
...AND I AM EAGER TO ENTER PARADISE AT YOUR HANDS...

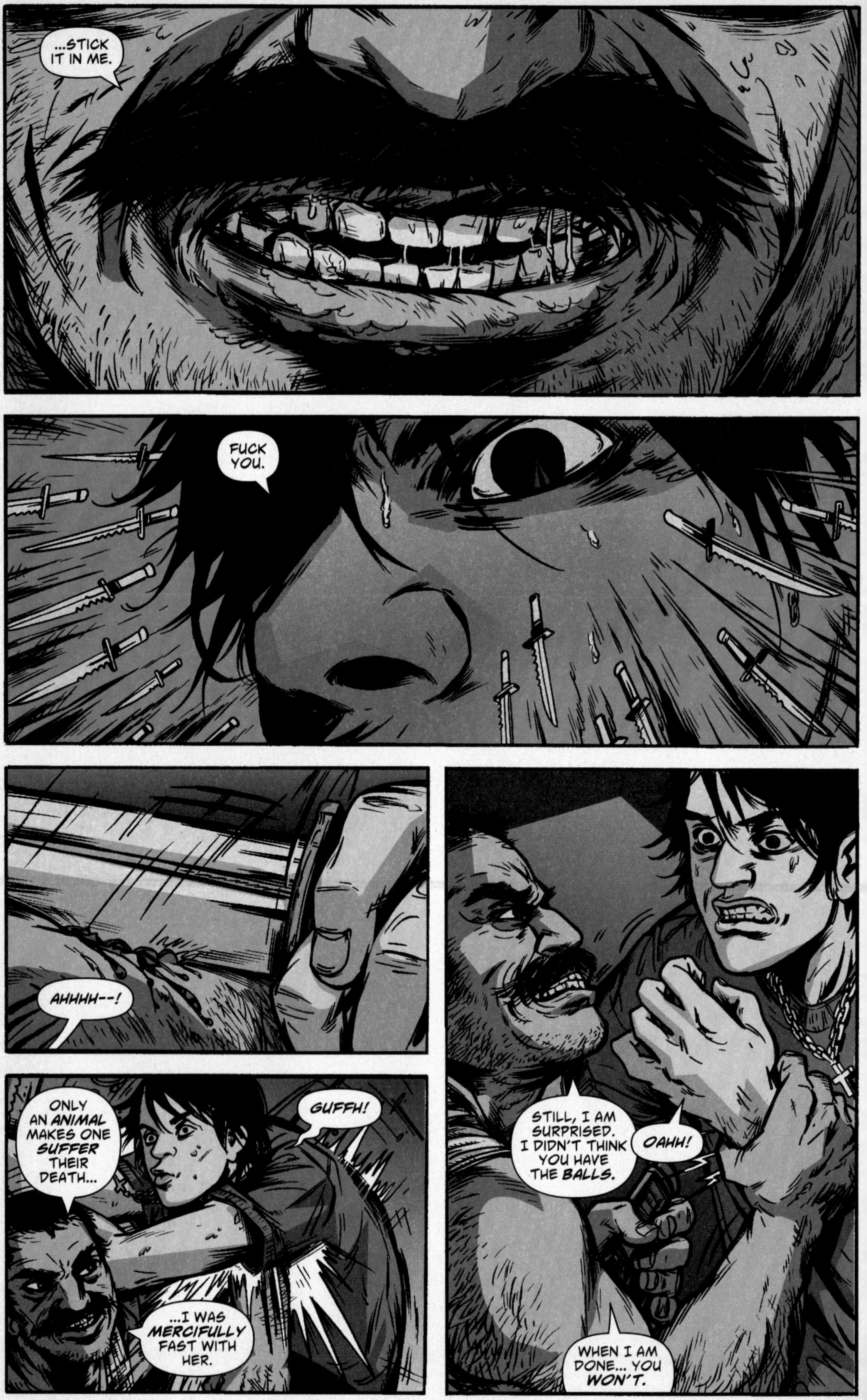
...STICK IT IN ME.
FUCK YOU.
AHHHH--!
ONLY AN ANIMAL MAKES ONE SUFFER THEIR DEATH...
GUFFH!
...I WAS MERCIFULLY FAST WITH HER.
STILL, I AM SURPRISED. I DIDN'T THINK YOU HAVE THE BALLS.
OAHH!
WHEN I AM DONE... YOU WON'T.

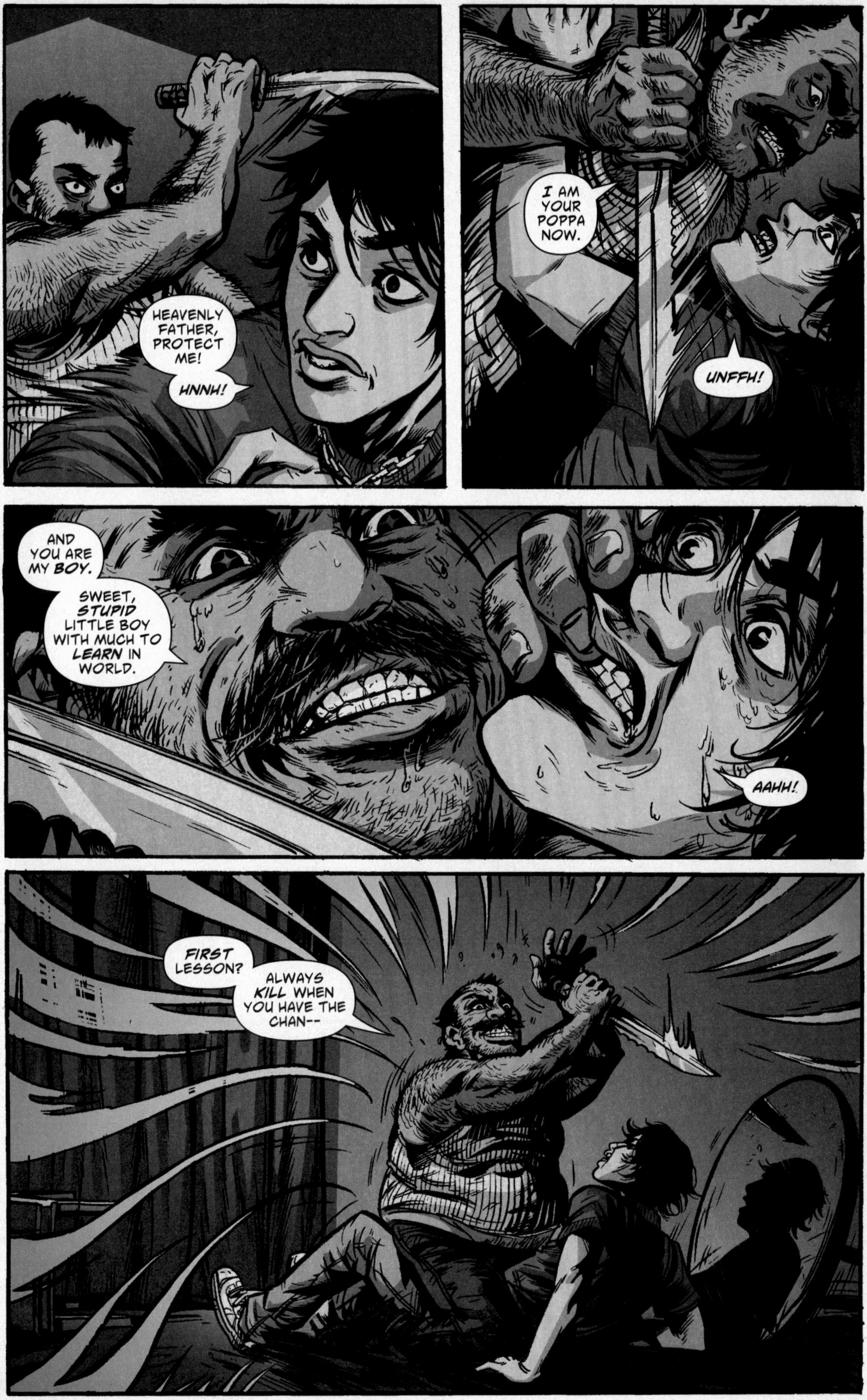
HEAVENLY FATHER, PROTECT ME!
HNNH!
I AM YOUR POPPA NOW.
UNFFH!
AND YOU ARE MY BOY.
SWEET, STUPID LITTLE BOY WITH MUCH TO LEARN IN WORLD.
AAHH!
FIRST LESSON?
ALWAYS KILL WHEN YOU HAVE THE CHAN--

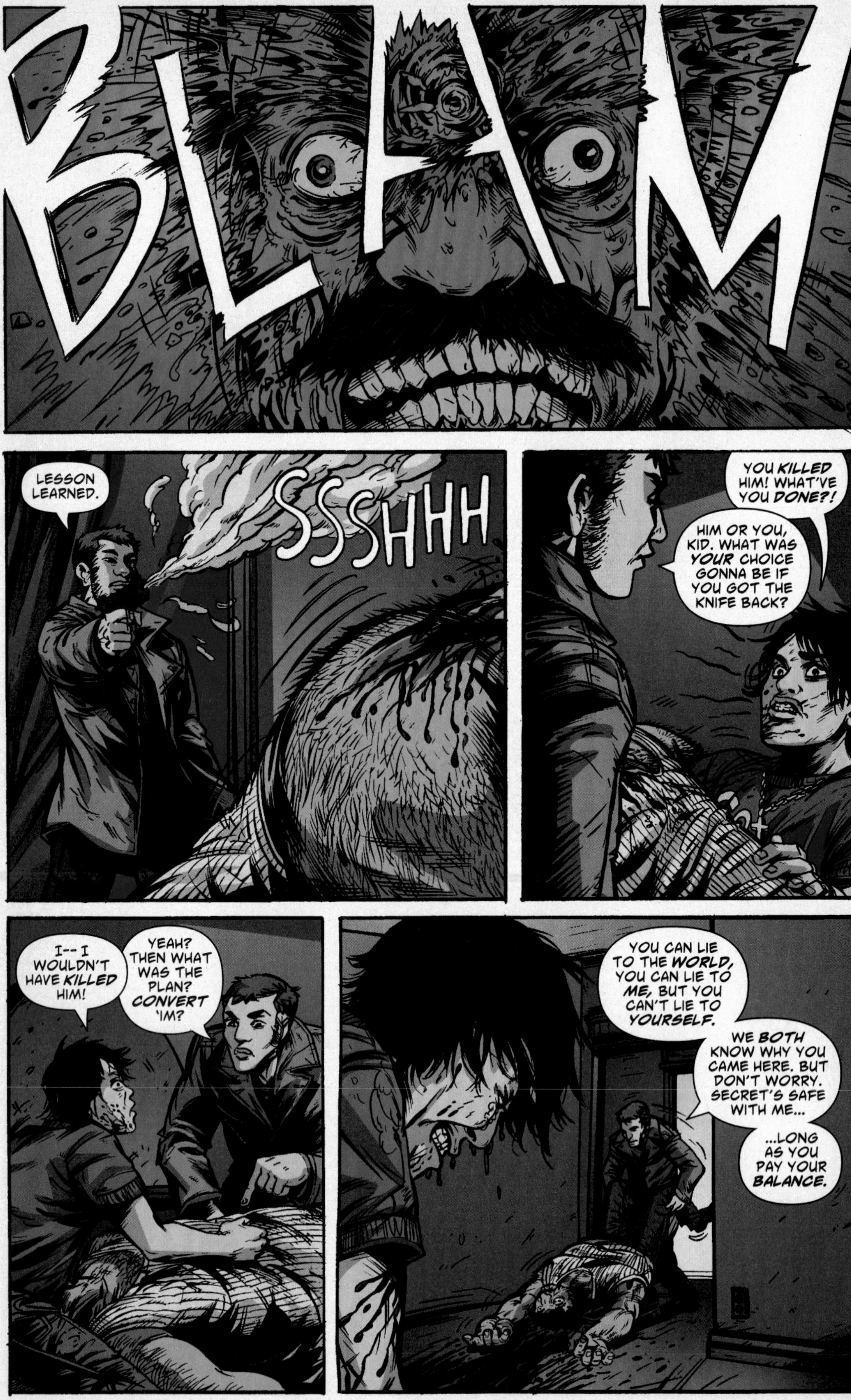
BLAM
LESSON LEARNED.
SSSHHH
YOU KILLED HIM! WHAT'VE YOU DONE?!
HIM OR YOU, KID. WHAT WAS YOUR CHOICE GONNA BE IF YOU GOT THE KNIFE BACK?
I-- I WOULDN'T HAVE KILLED HIM!
YEAH? THEN WHAT WAS THE PLAN? CONVERT 'IM?
YOU CAN LIE TO THE WORLD, YOU CAN LIE TO ME, BUT YOU CAN'T LIE TO YOURSELF.
WE BOTH KNOW WHY YOU CAME HERE. BUT DON'T WORRY. SECRET'S SAFE WITH ME...
...LONG AS YOU PAY YOUR BALANCE.

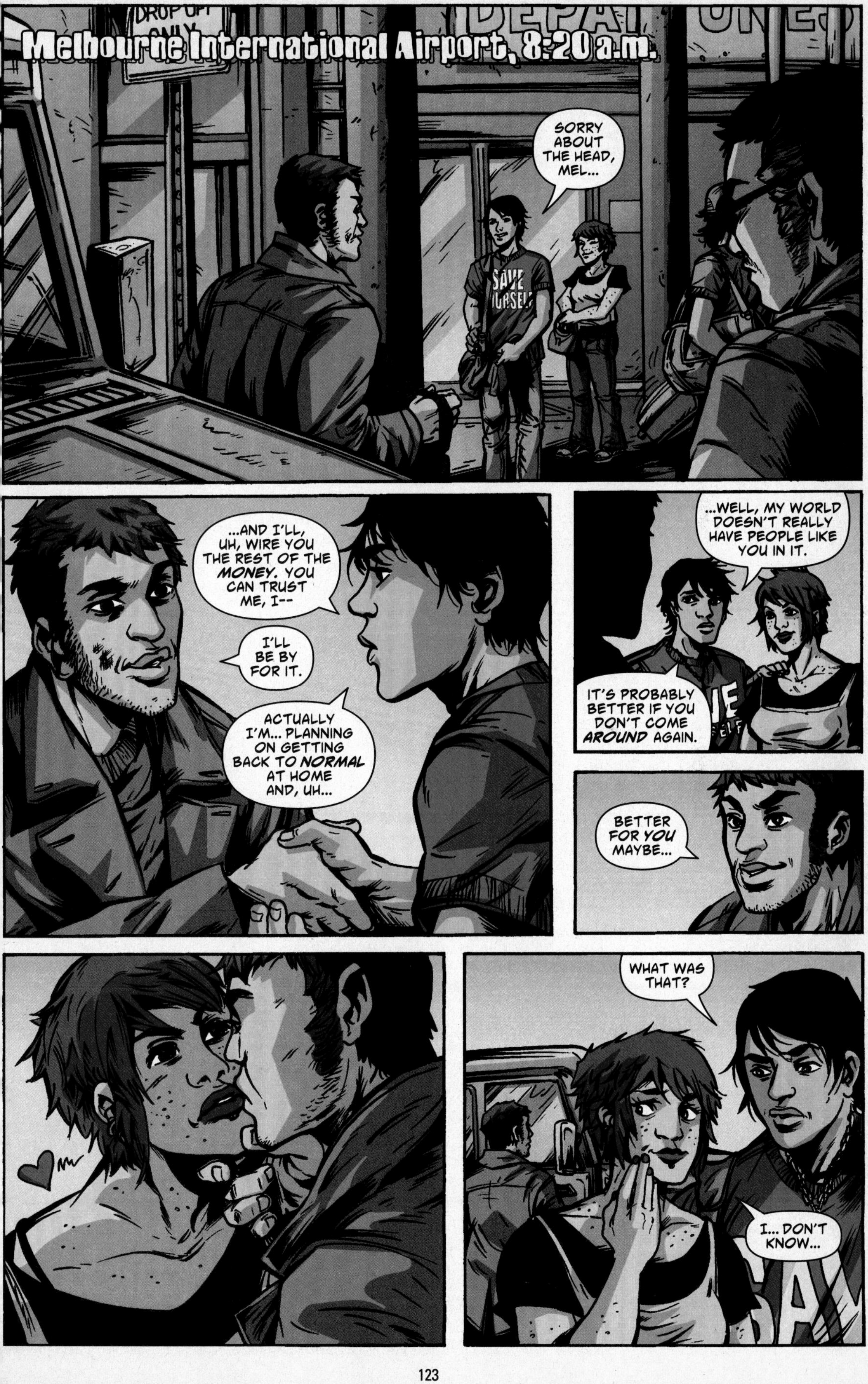
Melbourne International Airport, 8:20 a.m.
SORRY ABOUT THE HEAD, MEL...
...AND I'LL, UH, WIRE YOU THE REST OF THE MONEY. YOU CAN TRUST ME, I--
I'LL BE BY FOR IT.
ACTUALLY I'M... PLANNING ON GETTING BACK TO NORMAL AT HOME AND, UH...
...WELL, MY WORLD DOESN'T REALLY HAVE PEOPLE LIKE YOU IN IT.
IT'S PROBABLY BETTER IF YOU DON'T COME AROUND AGAIN.
BETTER FOR YOU MAYBE...
WHAT WAS THAT?
I... DON'T KNOW...

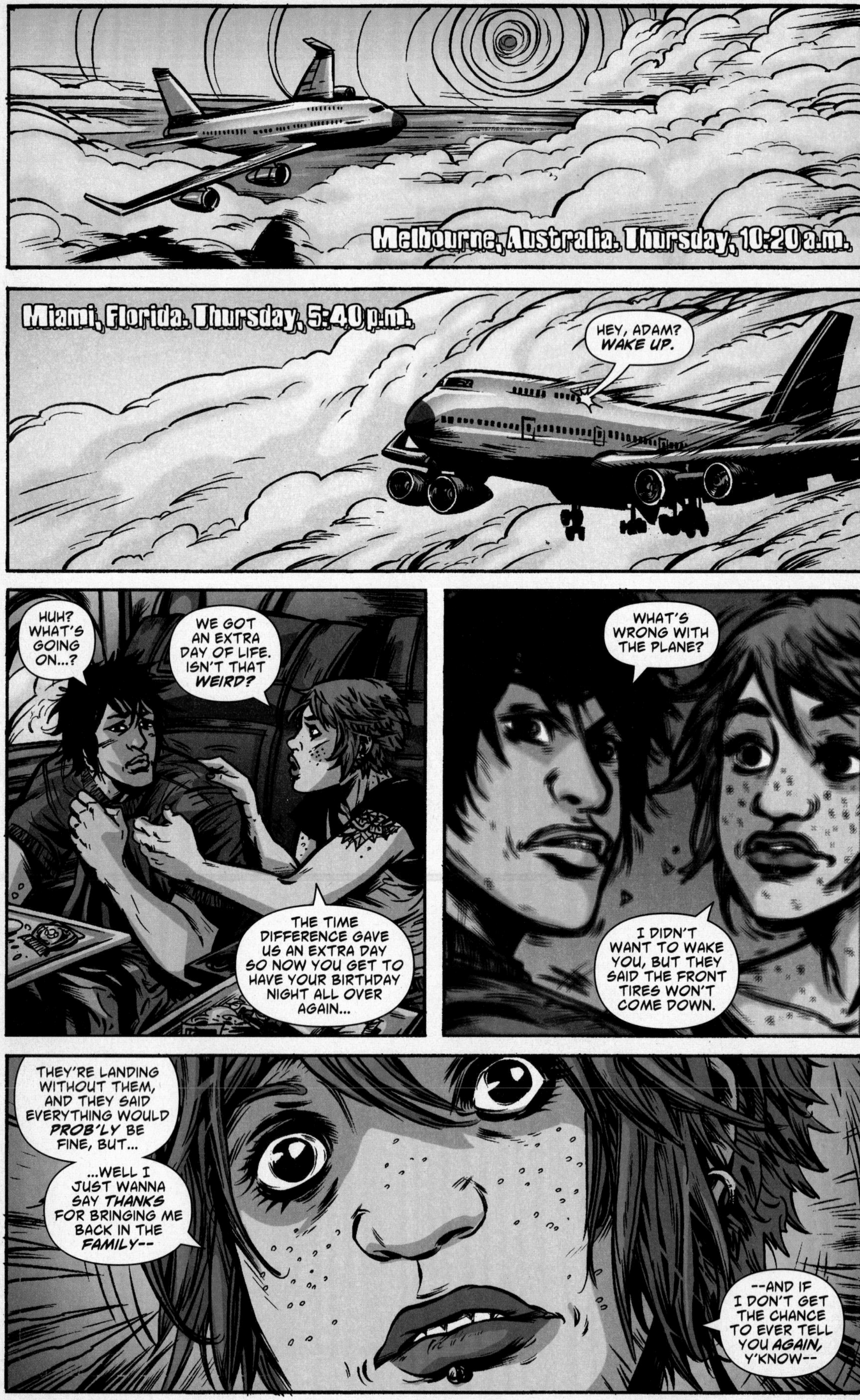
Melbourne, Australia. Thursday, 10:20 a.m.
Miami, Florida. Thursday, 5:40 p.m.
HEY, ADAM? WAKE UP.
HUH? WHAT'S GOING ON...?
WE GOT AN EXTRA DAY OF LIFE. ISN'T THAT WEIRD?
THE TIME DIFFERENCE GAVE US AN EXTRA DAY SO NOW YOU GET TO HAVE YOUR BIRTHDAY NIGHT ALL OVER AGAIN...
WHAT'S WRONG WITH THE PLANE?
I DIDN'T WANT TO WAKE YOU, BUT THEY SAID THE FRONT TIRES WON'T COME DOWN.
THEY'RE LANDING WITHOUT THEM, AND THEY SAID EVERYTHING WOULD PROB'LY BE FINE, BUT...
...WELL I JUST WANNA SAY THANKS FOR BRINGING ME BACK IN THE FAMILY--
--AND IF I DON'T GET THE CHANCE TO EVER TELL YOU AGAIN, Y'KNOW--

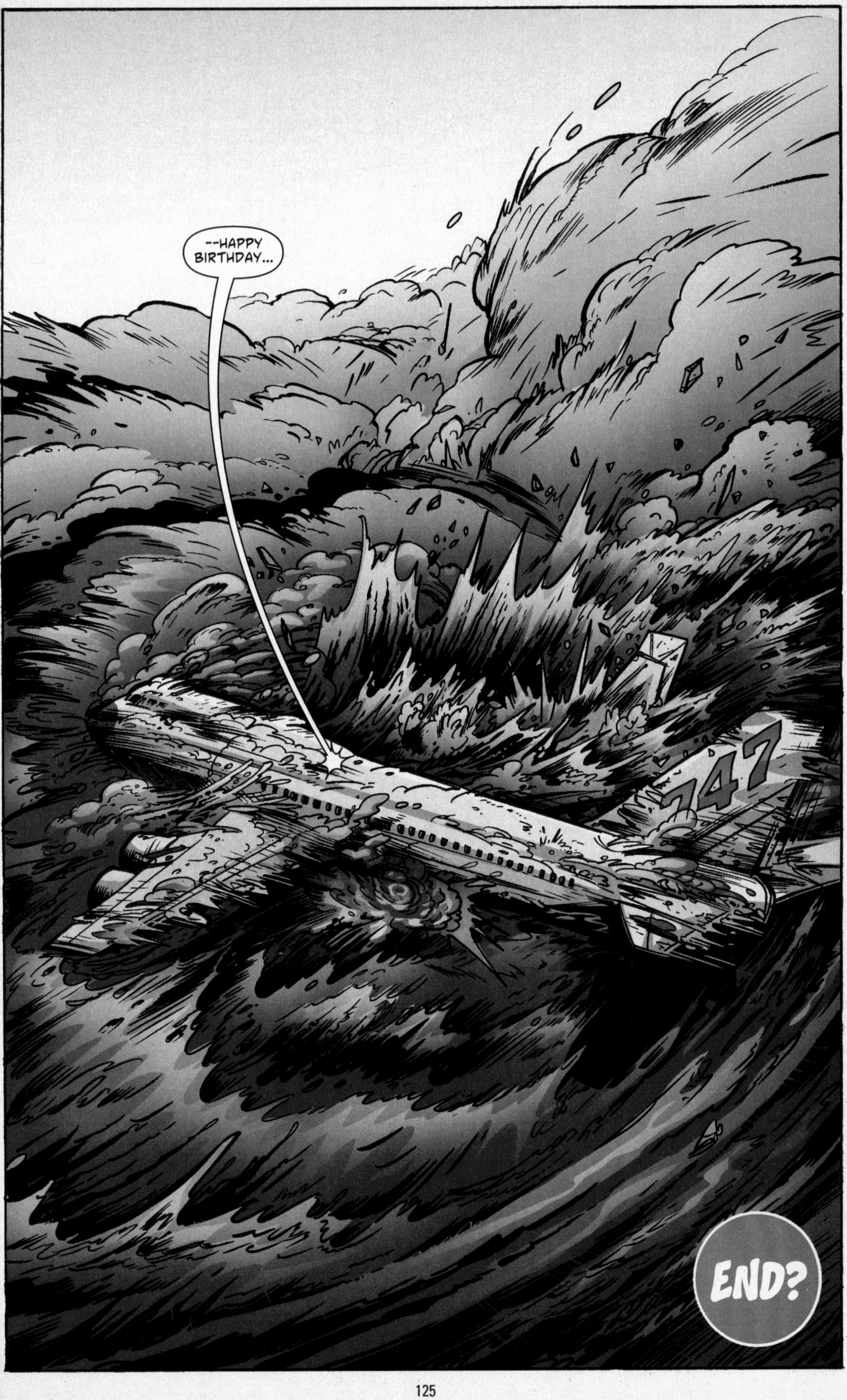
--HAPPY BIRTHDAY...
747
END?

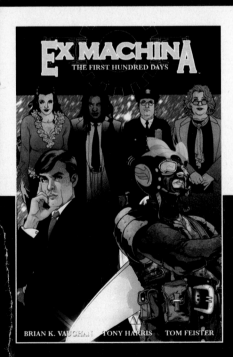

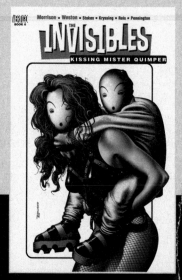